THE STATE OF
BLACK AMERICA 1994

D1533765

Published by **National Urban League, Inc.**

January 1994

THE STATE OF BLACK AMERICA 1994

Editor

Billy J. Tidwell, Ph.D.

Copyright © National Urban League, Inc., 1994

Library of Congress Card Catalog Number 77-647469

ISBN 0-9632071-2-1

Price $24.95

The cover photograph, *"Music—That Lordly Power,"* is the very personal photographic statement portraying the role of music as a binding force in the emotional life of the black family. Its creator: internationally renowned photographer Gordon Parks. It is the seventh limited-edition lithographic print in the *"Great Artists"* series on African Americans commissioned for the National Urban League by the House of Seagram.

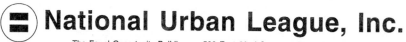

National Urban League, Inc.

The Equal Opportunity Building • 500 East 62nd Street • New York, New York 10021

Founded in 1910, the National Urban League is the premier social service and civil rights organization in America. The League is a nonprofit, community-based organization headquartered in New York City, with 112 affiliates in 34 states and the District of Columbia.

The mission of the National Urban League is to assist African Americans in achieving social and economic equality. The League implements its mission through advocacy, bridge building among the races, program services, and research.

TABLE OF CONTENTS

About the Authors

DR. MARCUS ALEXIS
Board of Trustees Professor of Economics
Professor of Management and Strategy
Northwestern University

Dr. Marcus Alexis is a nationally acclaimed and distinguished economist serving currently as the Board of Trustees Professor of Economics and Professor of Management and Strategy at Northwestern University in Chicago. Before assuming his current post, he was Dean and Professor of Economics at the University of Illinois – Chicago. Other prior positions include Visiting Professorships at the University of California, Swarthmore College, and the University of Minnesota. He has held Professor or Associate Professor positions at the University of Illinois, the University of Rochester, DePaul University, and Macalester College.

Professor Alexis was a Ford Foundation Faculty Study Fellow at Harvard University and the Massachusetts Institute of Technology (MIT). He is the former Acting Chairman and Vice Chairman of the Interstate Commerce Commission. Other national and regional tours of service include his membership on the Federal Reserve Bank of Chicago's board of directors; during that six-year tenure, he was Deputy Chairman (1986-89) and Chairman (1990). Dr. Alexis has chaired the Economic Policy Task Force of the Joint Center for Political and Economic Studies since 1984; he co-chaired the Illinois Commerce Commission Blue Ribbon Task Force on Telecommunications Policy in 1990. He is the former President of the Board of Directors of the Urban League of Rochester. A member of the American Economic Association and the National Economic Association, Dr. Alexis also sits on the Board of Economists for *Black Enterprise* magazine.

A prolific writer, Dr. Alexis is author of seven books, including *Fairness in Employment Testing: Validity Generalization, Minority Issues, and the General Aptitude Test Battery* (Washington, DC: National Academy Press, 1989). He sits on the editorial boards of the *Journal of Black Male Studies; Economic Perspectives; Illinois Issues;* and *Review of Black Political Economy.*

Professor Alexis earned his undergraduate and advanced degrees in economics: his A.B. degree from Brooklyn College; his M.A. degree from Michigan State University; and his Ph.D. degree from the University of Minnesota. He has engaged in postdoctoral studies at Harvard and MIT.

DR. WILLIAM D. BRADFORD

Associate Dean for Academic Affairs
Professor of Finance
Business School
University of Maryland – College Park

Dr. William D. Bradford served as Assistant and then Associate Professor of Finance at Stanford University before coming to the University of Maryland as Professor of Finance in 1980. During his tenure at College Park, he has also chaired the Finance Department.

Dean Bradford has been Visiting Professor at New York University, Ohio State University, Yale University, and the University of California at Los Angeles. He has served as Visiting Scholar at the Federal Home Loan Bank Board and the Board of Governors of the Federal Reserve System.

Dr. Bradford is a member of the Affordable Housing Advisory Council of the Federal Home Loan Mortgage Association.

Professor Bradford has published numerous books and articles on minority business development, entrepreneurship, corporate finance, and financial institutions. His teaching interests include financial institutions, corporate finance, and financial theory.

Dr. Bradford earned his bachelor's degree in economics from Howard University and his M.B.A. and Ph.D. degrees in finance and economics from Ohio State University.

DR. MARY E. DILWORTH

Senior Director, Research
American Association of Colleges for Teacher Education
Director
ERIC Clearinghouse on Teaching and Teacher Education

For the past six years, Dr. Mary E. Dilworth has held the posts of Senior Director of Research at the American Association of Colleges for Teacher Education (AACTE) and Director, ERIC Clearinghouse on Teaching and Teacher Education in Washington, DC. In those dual capacities, she is responsible for the design and implementation of the Association's research agenda, programs, and publications, and for the document development and review of Clearinghouse publication series.

A former Research Fellow at Howard University's Institute for the Study of Educational Policy, Dr. Dilworth was the Coordinator of Education and Training at Howard before moving on to AACTE. She has also been a Senior Program Analyst with the National Institute for Advanced Studies and an

Education Research Analyst for the National Advisory Council on Education Professions Development.

Among Dr. Dilworth's extensive publications are, as editor, *Diversity in Teacher Education: New Expectations* (San Francisco: Jossey-Bass, 1992) and—with Ebo Otuya, Jr., and Peggy Carr—*Academic Achievement of White, Black, and Hispanic Students in Teacher Education Programs* (Washington, DC: AACTE, 1992). She was the executive producer, along with M. Michael-Bandele, of "Accept the Mission: Teach" and "Who's Missing from the Classroom: The Need for Minority Teachers," both AACTE productions.

Dr. Dilworth is affiliated with the American Educational Research Association, the American Association for Higher Education, and the National Alliance of Black School Educators, to name a few. She sits on the boards of the Corwin Press Equity Series, the NAACP Task Force on Teacher Training and Assessment, and the National Center for Research on Teacher Learning. She chairs the board of the Quality Education for Minorities/Teacher Leadership Corps.

Dr. Dilworth is a recipient of the Mary McLeod Bethune Community Service Award from the National Council of Negro Women, Inc. (NCNW) and was most recently honored by Frito-Lay/NCNW as one of the "Black Women Who Make It Happen."

Dr. Dilworth earned her bachelor's and master's degrees from Howard University in elementary education and student personnel administration in higher education, respectively. She earned her Ed.D. degree in higher education administration from The Catholic University.

DR. HARRY EDWARDS
Professor, Department of Sociology
University of California – Berkeley

For nearly quarter of a century, Dr. Harry Edwards has been on the faculty of the Department of Sociology at the University of California – Berkeley, beginning as an Assistant Professor and rising to his current rank of Professor. He also serves as player personnel counselor and staff consultant with the San Francisco 49ers professional football franchise and with the Golden State Warriors of the National Basketball Association.

Professor Edwards has participated in two academic delegations to the People's Republic of China. He has lectured at more than 600 colleges and universities throughout the United States as well as before audiences in Canada, Oslo (Norway), and the former Soviet Union.

Dr. Edwards is a member of the American Sociological Association and the Pacific Sociological Association; the Association of Black Sociologists and the North American Society for the Sociology of Sport; the Society for the Study of Social Problems and the California Association of Black Faculty and Staff. He is also either consulting or advisory editor to a half-dozen professional publications.

Dr. Edwards has authored numerous articles and collaborated on many sports-related projects for television, the feature film industry, and the print media. His four books include *The Revolt of the Black Athlete* (New York: Free Press, 1969); *Sociology of Sport* (Homewood, IL: Dorsey Press, 1973), the first integrated textbook in the sociology of sports discipline, which he helped to pioneer; and his autobiography, *The Struggle That Must Be* (New York: MacMillan, 1980), portions of which are the subject matter of a feature-length film currently under development and due for release in 1996.

Dr. Edwards is an internationally respected expert on issues pertaining to developments at the interface of sports and society. He was the principal organizer and strategist behind the "Olympic Project for Human Rights," an effort to mount boycotts and demonstrations targeting the 1968 U.S. Olympic delegation in protest of racism and discrimination in American sports and society.

The honors and awards of distinction Dr. Edwards has received exceed four dozen, including the President's Distinguished Scholar (Rockhurst College and Youngstown State University) and honorary doctorates from Grinnell College and Columbia College.

Professor Edwards earned all of his degrees in the field of sociology: his B.A. degree from California State University – San Jose; and his M.A. and Ph.D. degrees from Cornell University.

GERALDINE R. HENDERSON
Research Assistant, Marketing Department
Kellogg Graduate School of Management
Assistant Director of Admission
Northwestern University

Geraldine R. Henderson, a marketing/consumer specialist, currently fulfills multiple duties at Northwestern University. She is a Marketing Department Research Assistant in the Kellogg Graduate School of Management as well as the University's Assistant Director of Admission. She is a member of the graduate school's Doctoral Committee and served as a recruiter for doctoral programs at Northwestern. She was also the liaison between the graduate school and the National Black MBA Association.

Before joining Northwestern, as well as during her current time there, Ms. Henderson extensively studied consumer behavior, social and cognitive networks, source credibility, and multicultural marketing. She is the former Brand Assistant – Retail Cheese Division, Kraft General Foods; there, she was responsible for the entire Cheez-Whiz product line. She was employed for seven years with the IBM Corporation, including stints as Account Marketing Representative and Engineering Co-op.

Ms. Henderson chairs the Education Committee of the National Black MBA Association, Chicago chapter. She is a charter member of the Chicago Chapter Alumni Extension and former officer of the National Society of Black Engineers. Active in the community, she is the Coordinator of the IBM Corporation's Adopt-A-School Program at Orr Public High School.

Ms. Henderson has taught or lectured on various aspects of marketing at Northwestern as well as at Purdue University. She was the teaching assistant to Professor Marcus Alexis in an Independent Study to Ghana and Côte d'Ivoire. She refereed, along with Nigel Hopkins and Dawn Iacobucci, "Actor Equivalence in Networks: The Business Ties That Bind," which has been accepted for publication in the *Journal of Business-to-Business Marketing*.

Ms. Henderson is a Northwestern University Scholar and a former University Fellow. Among her other achievements: the Frito-Lay Markie Award for Advertising Strategy; the Center for Leadership Development Business Achievement Award; and the Purdue University Caucus of Black Faculty and Staff Leadership Award (1985, 1986).

Ms. Henderson earned her B.S. degree in electrical engineering from Purdue University and her master's degree in marketing from the Kellogg Graduate School of Management at Northwestern. She is a Ph.D. candidate in marketing (June 1995) at Northwestern.

DR. LENNEAL J. HENDERSON
Distinguished Professor
Government and Public Administration
University of Baltimore

Dr. Lenneal J. Henderson is a fiscal policy expert. In addition to his professorship, he is a Senior Fellow in the William Donald Schaefer Center for Public Policy and a Henry C. Welcome Fellow at the University of Baltimore.

Before assuming his current positions, Dr. Henderson was Head and Professor of Political Science at the University of Tennessee – Knoxville; a senior faculty member at the Federal Executive Institute in Charlottesville, VA; and a professor in the School of Business and Public Administration at Howard University.

Other academic accomplishments include his being a Ford Foundation/ National Research Council Postdoctoral Fellow at the Johns Hopkins School of Advanced International Studies, a Kellogg National Fellow, and a Rockefeller Research Fellow. He received the Distinguished Chair in Teaching at the University of Baltimore for 1992-93.

Professor Henderson has lectured or consulted in Canada, Europe, Japan, Mexico, sub-Saharan Africa, Egypt, Israel, India, Peru, the Caribbean, the former Soviet Union, and the People's Republic of China.

He has published or edited five books and numerous articles in various publications, among them: *The Urban League Review, The Review of Black Political Economy, The Annals, Policy Studies Journal, Howard Law Journal,* and *The Black Scholar.*

Dr. Henderson earned his B.A., M.A., and Ph.D. degrees from the University of California – Berkeley.

DR. SHIRLEY J. JONES
Distinguished Service Professor
School of Social Welfare
State University of New York – Albany

An esteemed practitioner of social policy and community organization, Dr. Shirley J. Jones was Visiting Professor at State University of New York (SUNY) at Albany for four years before assuming the tenured Distinguished Service Professor in 1992. In the decade prior to that, Dr. Jones was Dean of the Graduate School of Social Work, University of Southern Mississippi. She has also held professorships, instructor positions, and lecturer roles in social work at SUNY – Stony Brook, New York, Columbia, Syracuse, and Fairleigh Dickinson universities and at the City College of New York.

A widely published author and reviewer, Dr. Jones refereed "Women as Main Providers of Food—Implications for Social Work" for *The Journal of Intergroup Relations* (1987) and "The Nature of Housing: Implications for the Welfare of the Black Child" for the Association of Black Social Workers (1973). Other scholarly articles include *An Evaluative Report Linking the Public and Private Sectors to Support Rural Facilities* for the Tennessee Valley Authority (1991) and *Sociocultural and Service Issues, Inc., Working with Rural Clients, A Resource Guide* for Human Service Professionals (1991).

Since 1984, Dr. Jones has been a consultant to the U.S. Department of Health and Human Services, Administration for Children, Youth, and Families. Other consulting clients include Jackson State University, the Nelson Rockefeller Institute of Government, and the United Nations Housing, Planning, and Building Center. She has been a much-sought-after participant in national and international conferences focusing on women's, children's, and rural issues.

Dr. Jones is professionally affiliated with the National Association of Social Workers, the National Association of Black Social Workers, the International Council of Social Welfare, and the Council on Social Work Education. She is a Fellow of the American Council on Education's National Women's Incentive Program.

Dr. Jones received the University of Southern Mississippi Award in recognition of the Distinguished Position as first African-American Academic Dean, School of Social Work. She has received prestigious honors from organizations as diverse as the Humane Society—its American Humane Association Award for Distinguished Service, to the U.S. Department of Commerce Bureau of the Census—its Outstanding Leadership in Advancing Public Support for the 1990 Census.

Professor Jones earned her B.S. and M.A. degrees in education from New York University; her M.S.W. degree in social welfare from New York University; and her D.S.W. degree in social welfare from Columbia University.

DR. W. FRANKLYN RICHARDSON
Pastor, Grace Baptist Church
Mount Vernon, New York
General Secretary
National Baptist Convention, U.S.A., Inc.

Dr. W. Franklyn Richardson is a world-renowned preacher who has served as Pastor of historic Grace Baptist Church—the largest black church in Westchester County, NY—since 1975. Each Sunday, he is featured on the Grace Church Radio Ministry, heard throughout New York, New Jersey, and Connecticut. Since 1976, he has been featured on the CBS Christmas Eve special, broadcast nationwide to more than 200 affiliate television stations.

Rev. Richardson is also General Secretary of the National Baptist Convention, U.S.A., Inc., which consists of more than 30,000 churches and eight million black Baptists in America. In 1980, he was selected as a member of the National Baptist Convention Foreign Mission Board's Preaching Team, which preached in seven African countries. Since 1982, he has served as the L.G. Jordan Lecturer for the National Baptist Congress of Christian Education Laymen's Department. He is also a member of the General Council of the Baptist World Alliance.

Dr. Richardson was elected to the governing board of the National Council of Churches in 1983; four months after that election, he was chosen to serve on the Central Committee of the World Council of Churches, which represents more than 400 million Christians from 150 countries. He has crisscrossed America and the world, preaching in Africa, Asia, Australia, Europe, North America, and South America.

Dr. Richardson served for two years as adjunct faculty member to the Certificate Program in Christian Ministry at New York Theological Seminary, where his emphasis was "The Church in Contemporary Society." He edited and wrote the introduction to *Journey Through a Jungle* by the late Dr. Sandy F. Ray. He is author of *The Power of the Pew* (Townsend Press, 1985).

Dr. Richardson is the former: President of the United Black Clergy of Mount Vernon; President of the Black Ministers Coalition Council of Westchester County; Commissioner of Housing for the City of Mount Vernon; and member of the Westchester County Medical Center board of directors. He is Chaplain of the city and county police departments. A member of the National Urban League's Board of Trustees, Dr. Richardson is also a member of the board of directors of the Council of National Black Churches.

While pursuing his undergraduate degree at Virginia Union University in Richmond, Rev. Richardson successfully pastored two different churches in socioeconomically depressed communities, establishing better housing, dental and health clinics, and a pharmacy. His alma mater bestowed upon him an honorary Doctor of Divinity degree in 1985. He is also a graduate of the Yale University School of Divinity. In addition, he has received honorary doctorate degrees from six other U.S. colleges and universities.

DR. JOAN WALLACE-BENJAMIN
President and Chief Executive Officer
Urban League of Eastern Massachusetts

Dr. Joan Wallace-Benjamin joined the Urban League of Eastern Massachusetts as its President and Chief Executive Officer in 1989. In this capacity, she directs the Urban League's efforts to promote racial equality through social, political, and economic programs of service and advocacy.

Prior to joining the Urban League, Dr. Wallace-Benjamin was Director of Operations for the Boys & Girls Clubs of Boston. She has held the positions of Deputy Director of the Head Start program, Boston, MA; Research Analyst with Abt Associates, Cambridge, MA; and Assistant Psychologist at Lena Park Community Development Center, Dorchester, MA.

From 1989 to 1993, Dr. Wallace-Benjamin served as a member of the Massachusetts State Board of Education, holding the post of Vice Chairman in her final year. She is on the boards of the Citywide Education Coalition, Facing History and Ourselves, the Children's Museum, and the Organizing Committee for the Boston Coalition of 100 Black Women; she is also a Dedham Country Day School Trustee. A member of the Boston Chamber of Commerce's Education Committee, she is a former director of the New England Aquarium as well as a board member of Planned Parenthood of

Massachusetts and an incorporator of Leslie College.

In May 1993, Dr. Wallace-Benjamin was bestowed an honorary doctoral degree in public service from the University of Massachusetts – Amherst. A frequent guest speaker at schools, businesses, and organizations, she also received the 1993 Outstanding Young Leaders Award from the Boston Jaycees.

Dr. Wallace-Benjamin earned her bachelor of arts degree in psychology from Wellesley College and her Ph.D. degree from the Florence Heller School for Advanced Studies in Social Welfare, Brandeis University. Her dissertation, "Black Mothers' Attitudes Toward Their Retarded Children," carefully examined the cultural difference in attitudes and expectations between black and white mothers of retarded children.

DR. RONALD WALTERS
Chairman and Professor
Department of Political Science
Howard University

One of the nation's premier political scientists, Dr. Ronald Walters is Professor and Chairman of the Howard University Department of Political Science. He has served on the Council of the American Political Science Association and is the founder of the National Congress of Black Faculty.

In 1984, Dr. Walters was the Deputy Campaign Manager for Issues of the Jesse Jackson Presidential Campaign; in 1988, he was consultant for Platform and Convention Preparation for the Jackson Campaign for President. In the spring semester of 1989, he was a Fellow at the Institute of Politics, Kennedy School of Government, Harvard University. He has also served as Visiting Professor at Princeton University and presented papers at more than 35 professional meetings worldwide.

Dr. Walters is author (with Lucius Barker) of *Jesse Jackson's 1984 Presidential Campaign* (Urbana-Champaign: University of Illinois Press, 1990), and *Black Presidential Politics in America* (Albany: State University of New York Press, 1989). The latter work won the Ralph Bunche Award from the American Political Science Association and the W.E.B. Du Bois Award from the National Alliance of Black Political Scientists.

Dr. Walters is a founding member of TransAfrica, a former Chair of the Board of TransAfrica Forum; former Chair, Committee on Afro-American Societies and Cultures, Social Science Research Council; and member, Overseas Development Council. In June 1991, Dr. Walters was a National Fellow, (Moscow) Center on Inter-Ethnic Conflict, Dartmouth College (counterpart visit with the Soviet delegation).

Professor Walters is a frequent guest on national and local radio and television talk shows, appearing on NBC's "The Today Show," "ABC News Nightwatch," all network and several public television shows, and many Washington, DC-area shows as political analyst. In 1988, he served as Black Entertainment Television (BET) Political Analyst for the presidential campaign; in 1990, he performed the same political election analyst duties for WJLA, the ABC-TV affiliate in the nation's capital.

A prodigious writer, Dr. Walters has published over 85 articles and four research monographs on the subjects of African affairs and American black politics, appearing in *USA Today, The Washington Post, The Los Angeles Times, The Baltimore Sun,* and other national publications.

Professor Walters earned his B.A. degree in history and government from Fisk University and his M.A. and Ph.D. degrees in African Studies and International Relations, respectively, from The American University.

Black America, 1993:
An Overview

John E. Jacob
President and Chief Executive Officer
National Urban League, Inc.

In 1993, the state of Black America was strongly influenced by:
- long-term economic trends that have transformed the economy and our job prospects;
- actions by the new administration in Washington; and
- the African-American community's own efforts toward self-development and self-empowerment.

In this overview, I will briefly discuss these major influences on the state of Black America.

First, the long-term economic trends that are transforming America's economy have the potential to have a positive long-term impact on African Americans, but their short-term impact has been disastrous.

The African-American community can trace many of its economic problems to the shift from manufacturing to services; the expansion of labor-saving technology; the effects of global competition that drives producers to cut payroll costs; and global economic integration, which draws jobs from high-wage countries to low-wage countries.

Those long-term economic trends have created new industries and new opportunities, but they have also helped accelerate the decline of our urban economies and constricted job opportunities for African Americans and other minorities.

These trends must be addressed by the nation, because they have the potential to destroy the delicate fabric of our society. They drive the growing inequality in incomes, the widening gap between the college-educated and those who do not go to college, and the dangerous erosion in job opportunities for people with limited skills.

In recent years, the frustration and anger resulting from the negative effects of some of these trends have contributed to the disturbing breakdowns in family life, to the rise in crime, and to strains in a political system that led to the rise of demagogues and self-styled "populists."

An opportunity to address those increasingly critical issues was missed in 1993 when the debate over the North American Free Trade Agreement (NAFTA) degenerated into a tiresome debate between those who claimed the agreement

1

would create jobs and those who said it would destroy jobs. In fact, it will do both.

Instead of focusing on emotional hot buttons, both sides of the NAFTA debate would have done better to focus on a comprehensive economic thrust that would have accomplished two important goals.

One goal should have been to protect adequately NAFTA's losers. A handful of training programs or compensation payments will not guarantee that today's unemployed textile worker will become tomorrow's computer programmer or entrepreneur. There is a disconcerting indifference to the need to replace many, if not most, of the endangered low-skilled jobs with other low-skilled jobs, and there is a commensurate unfounded optimism about the ability of mature unskilled workers to embark on new careers.

A second goal of a realistic NAFTA debate would have focused more broadly on what it will take to make America competitive, not only with industrial giants like Japan and Germany but also with low-wage countries like Mexico. In other words, NAFTA could have been a springboard to national economic development policies that fully develop all of our human resources, including those of the sorely neglected African-American community.

In 1994, the job issue takes on added significance as major corporations continue to announce plans for massive layoffs and plant closings. And for all the publicity given to white-collar unemployment, blue-collar workers and minorities are most vulnerable to layoffs and are most affected by continued discrimination.

A *Wall Street Journal* study of reports companies file with the Equal Employment Opportunity Commission found that during the recent recession, African Americans were the **only** group to suffer a net job **loss**. At some companies, blacks were laid off at rates double and triple their share of the company's work force. That pattern tells us that many companies are at best indifferent to their social and legal obligations; at worst, it indicates an illegal pattern of discrimination.

Further, *The Journal* article quoted some corporate spokespeople as saying that they were more concerned with aggregate **minority** employment, so they never noticed that blacks were subjected to a disproportionate share of the layoffs. That raises the troubling possibility that corporate diversity programs could become barely disguised "black removal" programs.

The National Urban League has called for government action, but we have also called for corporate America to review immediately and correct all policies and practices that impact negatively on equal opportunities, including ensuring that diversity programs do not result in fewer opportunities for African Americans—the **only** Americans who have historically and persistently been excluded from the workplace.

The seriousness of the economic depression afflicting the African-American community—and minority and working class communities of all races—suggests that job creation must become a top national priority in 1994. The complex interrelationship between the unstoppable realities of long-term economic trends and the short-term need for jobs can be bridged if the administration and the Congress temper their obsession with the budget deficit by serious action to close the job deficit.

The Urban League has urged action on two fronts. One is short-term job creation, focused on the people most vulnerable to layoffs. That can be done by a massive infrastructure rebuilding program that can quickly train and employ today's low-skilled jobless.

The second front is long-term measures in education and training that prepare people to hold the higher-skill jobs that a modern economy needs.

A two-tier jobs policy would train and educate people for the jobs of tomorrow; we still have to find ways for people to work today.

I have, in these pages, expanded on the National Urban League's proposal for a Marshall Plan for America—a coordinated, targeted, accountable investment strategy to develop our nation's physical and human resources to make this nation competitive again. It includes infrastructure rebuilding programs that would train and employ the jobless for skilled and semi-skilled jobs, and human resource programs that prepare the disadvantaged for the jobs being created by a changing economy.

The Marshall Plan for America remains a major pillar of the Urban League's agenda, and a means of moving our nation toward both enhanced economic competitiveness and increased equity. America must make the link between competitiveness and equity; they are co-equal requirements for economic health. We cannot become fully competitive if we neglect our human resources and condemn growing numbers of Americans to poverty and economic marginality. That will lead only to skills shortages and, worse, to social unrest that subverts economic growth.

Equity then, is a key component in assuring national competitiveness, especially when the demographics indicate the economy's increasing reliance on nonwhite minorities and women. Our Marshall Plan for America would attack both the short-term and the long-term problems facing our economy—by creating job opportunities in rebuilding the infrastructure and by preparing disadvantaged children and adults for the high-tech jobs of the future.

More equitable national economic policies are also required to arrest the relentless rise in poverty and in unemployment. In October, the Census Bureau reported that the number of people living in poverty rose in 1992 for the third straight year, to 36.9 million, or 14.7 percent of the population. The poverty rate among African Americans was a staggering 33 percent; for Hispanics, 29.3 percent. One of every four American children was poor. Forty percent of all poor people worked, and almost a fourth of those worked full-time. Even those devastating figures understate the true amount of poverty, since they are based on outdated and unsatisfactory measures of what constitutes poverty-level income.

What should set alarm bells ringing, though, is not the extent of poverty, enormous as it is, but the fact that poverty is in a long-range upward trend that started in the 1970s and accelerated in the 1980s. Breaking that trend will take determined national policies along the lines of our Marshall Plan for America, because even a brisk economic recovery will not reach enough of the poor. The experience of the 1980s definitively proved that a rising tide does not lift all boats; that some sink deeper into the mud. The negative poverty trend line is supported by state cutbacks in assistance to the poor, eroding wages and blue-collar job opportunities, and limited work opportunities for single-parent family heads. So even if the economy picks up in 1994, the most we can expect is that poverty does not increase.

The same holds for unemployment. In the third quarter of 1993, the national unemployment rate was 6.6 percent; for African Americans, it was 12.6 percent. As with the poverty figures, these official unemployment figures are seriously understated. The National Urban League's Hidden Unemployment Index, which uses official government figures to count discouraged workers and involuntary part-time workers, measured total unemployment at 13.1 percent, while putting African-American unemployment at 23.2 percent.

In the past, such figures were associated with recessions, but now they are accepted as inevitable—a sign of social callousness fostered by a general mood of helplessness in the face of the inevitable. But, again, there is nothing inevitable about either poverty or unemployment. The levels of both can be changed with the right mix of government policies and private initiatives. This suggests the nature of the task that lies before the Clinton administration which came to office last January, pledged to restore the economy and to make government an effective force for progress.

There can be little doubt that government does possess the capability to be that force for change, as it commands power and resources unavailable to any other sector. But perhaps government's most important role is to create an environment of opportunity in which people and communities can forge their own destinies. Thus, as the Clinton administration rounds out its first year, it is timely to assess its impact in these terms.

Many in the African-American community have expressed disappointment with the president for various actions. For example, the abandonment of the nomination of Lani Guinier as Director of the Justice Department's Office of Civil Rights after pressure from the right was widely seen as an unfair betrayal of an outstanding person and a politically expedient insult to African Americans. In a similar vein, there was a perception that the administration was too slow to fill key posts relevant to civil rights matters. There was also some dissatisfaction with NAFTA, which was seen as costing minority jobs, and with the failure to develop sweeping job creation and economic development programs.

Part of the disappointment can be traced to the extraordinarily high hopes placed in a new administration whose rhetoric and stated principles represented a major break from prior conservative administrations whose policies for a dozen years were accurately perceived as hostile to black hopes and aspirations. But the disappointment also must be attributed to the severe constraints with which the new administration found itself saddled. Three of these are especially relevant.

First, the structural budget deficit the administration inherited has been a major fiscal straitjacket. While it got Congress to pass a budget plan that will reduce the deficit over the long term, there has been little support for new federal spending.

Second, the president was elected with a plurality of votes—only 43 percent of the total. Thus, he was denied the power that comes from an electoral mandate, a political weakness both reflected and aggravated by a continued failure to win majority approval ratings in the polls.

Third, the president must rely on a largely undisciplined party whose congressional representatives are as likely to vote against him as with him.

Given such constraints, the administration's first-year performance has been rather impressive. Notably, the administration won approval for a budget that includes long-term deficit-reduction initiatives. And even though it failed to secure passage of its modest economic stimulus program, the administration snatched a victory from that defeat that will be felt in virtually every poor household with children and a working parent. The Congress was forced to accept an increased earned income tax credit, which will help move many full-time workers out of poverty, reinforcing the president's oft-stated principle that no one who works should be poor.

Another major accomplishment involves the president's commitment to diversity. The number of African Americans, other minorities, and women appointed to high government positions is unprecedented. The significance of such appointments goes beyond the immediate gratification of having key public service positions finally going to people drawn from outside the club. By making diversity a major objective and backing it up with concrete personnel actions, the president also has sent a clear signal to the private sector that it, too, must make a conscious effort to become more inclusive.

Toward the end of the year, passage of the Brady Bill signaled another momentous achievement. This is now the first administration to win a victory against the concerted efforts of the gun lobby, a victory made all the more significant by coming at a time of heightened public fear of crime. Of course, fighting crime will take major initiatives that get at its root causes—initiatives such as job creation, child development programs, and expanded drug rehabilitation efforts that are not very attractive to a budget-minded Congress and a public opposed to tax increases. Nonetheless, the president's ability to define the Brady Bill as an anti-crime measure and successfully fight for its passage is an important start on the domestic disarmament necessary to reduce the distressingly high level of violence in our society.

Finally, our review of the administration's performance in its first year must include the most serious effort to reform the health care system since Medicaid and Medicare were enacted over a generation ago. Almost every president since Franklin Delano Roosevelt wanted to change a health care system that was serving too few people at too high a cost, but only President Clinton has taken the enormous political risks to put in place a comprehensive health security program for all Americans.

In 1994, the president's health care reform plan will be scrutinized and modified to secure the necessary political support. And the president has said that he will not accept any compromise that weakens the one nonnegotiable feature of his plan, *viz.*, universal coverage for all Americans. But universal coverage is not the only issue that concerns the African-American community. Universal **coverage** must be complemented by universal **access**, and access means more than simply being protected by an insurance plan. It means having doctors, clinics, and hospitals in the neighborhoods where poor people live. It means assuring preventive care for the poor and their children. And it means one health care system serving all, not a two-tier system where the affluent get the best coverage and care, while the poor get the worst. In short, *access means equity*.

The equity issue takes on special significance because the high cost of a reformed health care system is supposed to be funded in part by cuts in Medicaid, the program that now provides medical coverage for some of the poor. Thus, there is a danger that weakening Medicaid or undercutting the finances of hospitals that serve poor neighborhoods could leave the poor worse off than at present. In a lobbying environment in which billions of dollars and the fate of entire industries—pharmaceutical, medical supply, health insurance, etc.—are at stake, we must ensure that the needs of the poor are recognized and provided for in a fair and equitable manner.

In 1994, we can also expect new initiatives in welfare reform, job training, assistance to the homeless, and others of importance to the African-American community. As it develops these programs, the administration can expect a large measure of support and encouragement from the African-American community, so long as the efforts are sensitive to our needs and pursued in consultation with African-American political and civic leadership. In particular, the Congressional Black Caucus, which is more numerous now than ever and whose members occupy key leadership positions in the House of Representatives, must be treated as true partners in the policy-making process.

While we might be hopeful, we should not be overly optimistic about the prospects for major breakthroughs in the coming year. Aside from health security, which appears to be on a track toward legislative action, other initiatives will have to overcome a number of impediments, including congressional reluctance to deal with controversial issues in an election year, the unyielding conservatism of many legislators, continued hostility toward investments that require new taxes, and prevailing spending caps that freeze discretionary spending without allowing inflation adjustments.

However, the Clinton administration should not be dissuaded by such constraints. It should charge ahead with investment programs that clearly are necessary for economic growth and equity, aggressively developing and financing them through cuts in the still massive network of subsidies that benefits politically favored industries and the middle class.

As it moves the investment agenda, the administration must exercise fully the capacity of the White House's "bully pulpit" to educate the public on the damage done by the persisting inequities in our society and the need to eradicate them. Most importantly, the administration must underscore the imperative of overcoming racial discrimination in all of its forms, lest it continue to poison our national life and undermine the common good.

President Clinton seems especially well suited to escalate and sustain the campaign against racial and social injustice. Likewise, through word and deed, he can and should use his high office to create an environment that nurtures community initiatives toward self-development and -empowerment. The latter point is compelling and warrants elaboration.

Self-development efforts have been underway for years in African-American communities and have shown signs of accelerating in the 1990s. The quickening pace may be attributed to a variety of factors—including the devastating effects of the recent recession on black families, the destructive impact of drugs and crime, and the realization that a strengthened community value system is as essential as more progressive public policies in enabling communities and citizens to function effectively in a complex society.

The National Urban League has long been in the forefront of efforts to strengthen black families, curb violence, and assist African-American youth to develop the skills and attitudes they need to survive and thrive in the twenty-first century. Using the tools of community organization and community mobilization, we have determined to be a catalyst for self-development of the African-American community, for we believe that self-development is the firmest strategic foundation for African-American progress.

Faced by the complex problems of today, the League is seeking to regenerate within the African-American community a wholesome vision of the future, the ambition to make it happen, and a categorical rejection of the status quo that thwarts our aspirations. Thus, maintaining high standards and expectations of ourselves; challenging dysfunctional attitudes and entrenched institutional barriers; and restoring hope and positive action from the despair and chaos that presently exist in so many of our neighborhoods are vital prerequisites to securing a brighter future. It is also imperative that we have our communities become more child- and family-centered, which is recognized to be a formidable challenge in a society where traditional values are out of fashion and the jobs that support families are scarce.

Realizing a more prosperous future, then, demands that African Americans be clear about what got us where we are and what can get us to where we need to be—a community mobilized around the concept of self-development to produce healthy, smart, productive twenty-first century citizens. Indeed, we need to stretch ourselves . . . to push the envelope of achievement . . . to explore the outer boundaries of the possible until the desired conditions are achieved.

These observations embody an agenda that the Urban League will vigorously pursue—through advocacy that confronts institutions, services that help children and their families develop, and community mobilization and coalition-building that empower our communities.

Thus, we appreciate African-American self-development in today's context to be a multifaceted enterprise distinguished by clarity of purpose and creative use of collective resources within the African-American community. In this regard, the articles in this volume, addressing the self-development issue from different perspectives, are instructive and timely. Each offers information and insights that are important inputs into discussions of objectives, strategies, and prospects. Each stresses the primacy of initiative-taking by African-American communities themselves on their own behalf.

At the same time, our assessments leave no doubt that successful self-development also requires viable partnerships with government and the business community. The poor and the marginalized in our society simply are not likely to become productive contributors to community or national life if the government and the private sector do not play a substantial supportive role.

Therefore, it is a mistake to assume that the African-American community's more inward-looking thrust toward self-development is isolationist. Such a misapprehension has often earned self-help efforts high marks from those who believe African Americans are responsible for their inferior place in our society and refuse to admit the continuing power of racism as a constraining force in our lives. Thus, destructive myths are perpetuated—such as the myth that attributes the growth of female-headed households to moral laxity or to the welfare system, rather than to the low wages and high unemployment that beset black men and prevent them from earning incomes with which to support families.

To be sure, values are important, and a weakened value system is a factor in the unstable family life, crime, and a host of other problems faced by the black community. That is why a renewed and strengthened value system for our young people is central to self-development efforts. But so, too, are public policies that are supportive of those efforts.

Consequently, the public policy challenge of the 1990s is to find the precise mix of policies that can create an environment in which self-development efforts may flourish. As President Clinton eloquently observed at a black church in Memphis on November 13: "We cannot repair the American community and restore the American family until we provide the structure, the values, the discipline, and the reward that work gives."

The president was acknowledging the fact that talking about values or exhorting people to act right takes place in a vacuum if there isn't a viable alternative to dysfunctional behavior. The crisis of the black family, the violence among our youth, and the disintegration of the sense of community are all largely the result of the job shortage that has left African Americans in a permanent economic depression.

Thus, public policy in the 1990s should focus on the economic revitalization of inner cities and the provision of training and employment opportunities. Such opportunities are essential to the success of self-development efforts that enable people to develop the self-confidence and positive attitudes to seize opportunities. So even as community-based organizations work to regenerate a sense of community and values, government and the private sector must provide the education, training, and jobs that encourage positive values and behaviors.

I want to express my gratitude to the authors who contributed to this edition of *The State of Black America*. Their papers should be rewarding reading for all who are concerned about improving the well-being of both the African-African community and the nation as a whole.

African Americans in the Urban Milieu: Conditions, Trends, and Development Needs

Lenneal J. Henderson, Ph.D.

INTRODUCTION

More than 23 years ago, Harold Cruse wrote that "Black social development of real historical consequence has been an urban development."[1] The migration of African Americans from agrarian and small-town America to urban America in the late nineteenth century and throughout the twentieth century was largely motivated by the adamant expectations of African Americans of greater and better prospects for social justice, employment, education, cultural opportunities and, in short, accelerated social development.[2] African Americans shared these aspirations with immigrants to cities throughout America and throughout the world. However, the city has largely failed to realize these expectations and aspirations. Instead, African Americans look towards the twenty-first century in a besieged, beleaguered, and beguiled urban milieu. They are besieged by perennial disparity in income, net financial worth, housing, education, employment, health care, and quality of life, and by the ever-increasing encroachment of crime, violence, drugs, and anomie among its young. They are beleaguered by the ravages of economic decline reflecting economic erosion in America. And they are beguiled by promises of policymakers at all levels of government to address these severe challenges.[3] The result is the most severe impediments to self-development in the post-World War II era.

Scholars and analysts have chronicled and examined the black urban odyssey for more than 100 years. Du Bois' Atlanta University studies[4] and his monumental *The Philadelphia Negro*[5] provided the first systematic and detailed studies of African-American living conditions, culture, and institutions in a large American city. More than 50 years later, Horace Cayton and St. Clair Drake's *Black Metropolis*[6] revealed both the ravages suffered and adaptations made in the highly structured economic, social, and political environment of Chicago. Ten years later, Kenneth Clark's *Dark Ghetto*[7] offered a compelling portrait of the psychosocial dynamics of black urban life in the convulsive 1960s.

More recently, William Julius Wilson's *The Declining Significance of Race*[8] and *The Truly Disadvantaged*[9] documented the decoupling of the black

11

middle class from the traditional inner city. Even more recently, Harold Rose and Paula McClain's *Race, Place, and Risk: Black Homicide in Urban America*[10] cogently examined the ecology of urban violence at the metropolitan, inner-city, neighborhood, and household levels of black city life. And, most recently, Douglass Massey and Nancy Denton, in *American Apartheid: Segregation and the Making of the Underclass*,[11] thoroughly document the continuing intensification of urban racial segregation as reflected in housing patterns of America's largest cities.

The studies, combined with the shrill and thunderous onslaught of rap lyrics from Ice-T, Ice Cube, other young black lyricists; the depictions of the evolution and risk of black urban life in "New Jack City," "Boys 'n the Hood," "Menace II Society," and other movies; or the stark plays and poems of August Wilson, Maya Angelou, Haki Mahabuti, and Nikki Giovanni portray an urban milieu fraught with risk, uncertainty, fear, and frustration for any class, age, neighborhood, profession, or aspirations in the metropolitan African-American community. Ellis Cose's stirring new book, *The Rage of a Privileged Class*,[12] makes it clear that even middle-class African Americans do not escape urban racism, social stigma, or the adhesive residue of the inner-city terror of African Americans. The struggle to pursue a spiritual, social, economic, and political vision in this milieu; to craft continuously a consciousness linking the dispersed fragments of African Americans across the metropolis; to create durable and portable but effective collective institutions in a media-charged environment daily glorifying individual values, aspirations, and achievements defines the status and prospects of self-development strategies in Black America. This chapter discusses the essential demographic, socioeconomic, and cultural dimensions of the urban struggle. It concludes on a defiant note of hope found thriving in the midst of the worst urban despair. The animus is the legacy of the African-American spiritual heritage born, nourished, and raised in the middle of America's historical struggles with racism.

THE DEMOGRAPHIC DIMENSIONS OF THE AFRICAN-AMERICAN URBAN MILIEU

The demography of urban Black America is changing in structure, scope, and function. The twentieth century has been an increasingly urban century for African Americans, particularly since World War II. As O'Hare indicates, "In 1990, the percentage of blacks living in metropolitan areas stood at 84 percent, compared with 76 percent for whites."[13] The 1990 Census indicates that 31 cities have African-American populations of 100,000 or greater, and 12 have at least 250,000 African Americans. As indicated in Table 1, the African-American population of the top eight cities—New York, Chicago, Detroit, Philadelphia, Los Angeles, Houston, Baltimore, and Washington, DC—would by themselves rank among the 50 largest cities in the country.[14]

12

Table 1
U.S. Cities with Black Populations of 150,000 or Greater, 1990

Black Rank	Overall Rank	City, State	Total Population (in thousands)	Black Population	Percent Black
1	1	New York, NY	7,322.6	2,102.5	29
2	3	Chicago, IL	2,783.7	1,087.7	39
3	7	Detroit, MI	1,028.0	777.9	76
4	5	Philadelphia, PA	1,585.6	631.9	40
5	2	Los Angeles, CA	3,485.4	487.7	14
6	4	Houston, TX	1,630.6	458.0	28
7	13	Baltimore, MD	736.0	435.8	59
8	19	Washington, DC	606.9	399.6	66
9	18	Memphis, TN	610.3	334.7	55
10	25	New Orleans, LA	496.9	307.7	62
11	8	Dallas, TX	1,006.9	297.0	30
12	36	Atlanta, GA	394.0	264.3	67
13	24	Cleveland, OH	505.6	235.4	47
14	17	Milwaukee, WI	628.1	191.3	31
15	34	St. Louis, MO	396.7	188.4	48
16	60	Birmingham, AL	266.0	168.3	63
17	12	Indianapolis, IN	742.0	165.6	22
18	15	Jacksonville, FL	673.0	163.9	24
19	39	Oakland, CA	372.2	163.3	44
20	56	Newark, NJ	275.2	160.9	59

Source: U.S. Bureau of the Census, *Current Population Survey, 1990.*

However, as Rose and McClain argue in their analysis of black urban homicide, the structure of African-American urban demography can be described by *macro* (region, municipality, urban area, community), *meso* (neighborhood), and *micro* (family environment, household) scales.[15] The interlinking of these scales helps to describe the structural dynamics of urban demography. At the macro, or metropolitan-wide, level of analysis,[16] although the majority of both blacks and whites live in metropolitan areas, they tend to live in different communities. Indeed, a key demographic trend in the African-American urban milieu is *the increasingly large and diverse suburbanization of the African-American population.* However, one-half of whites, compared with just over one-quarter of blacks, lived in suburban areas in 1990. As Table 2 indicates, *African-American suburbanization increased from 16 percent in 1970 to 27 percent in 1990.*

Table 2

Total U.S., Black, and White Populations by Metropolitan Residence, 1970-1990

	1970			1980			1990		
	Total	Blacks	Whites	Total	Blacks	Whites	Total	Blacks	Whites
Total number									
(in thousands)	203,212	22,581	177,749	226,546	26,495	188,372	245,992	30,332	206,853
Percent	100.0	100.0	100.0	100.0	100.0	100.0	100.0	100.0	100.0
Metropolitan areas	68.6	74.3	74.3	74.8	81.1	73.3	77.7	83.7	76.4
Central cities	31.4	58.2	58.2	29.9	57.7	24.9	30.5	56.7	26.2
Suburbs	37.2	16.1	16.1	44.8	23.3	48.4	47.2	27.0	50.2
Nonmetropolitan areas	31.4	25.7	25.7	25.2	18.9	26.7	22.3	16.3	23.6

Source: U.S. Bureau of the Census, *Current Population Survey, 1990.*

However, African-American suburbanization often means a change in address, not an upward change in socioeconomic status or lifestyle. Three interrelated dynamics explain this suburban divergence in black and white fortunes. First, at the meso level, many African-American "suburbs" resemble their central-city counterparts more than the stereotype of better suburban living. As suburban communities like East Palo Alto and Marin City, CA; Seat Pleasant, MD; Eatonville, FL; East Orange, NJ; Alton and Centreville, IL; East Cleveland, OH; and many other African-American communities immediately adjacent to central cities will attest, the worst ravages of inner-city life—poverty, severe crime, poor housing, deteriorating infrastructure, declining public schools, declining commercial infrastructure, chronic health conditions, and increasing numbers of young, female-headed households—pervade these communities. Second, beyond the traditional concept of suburb is the emerging concept of *edge city*. Edge cities are large, diverse, information-age cities that have emerged within the last 20 to 30 years as the *standard* form of American urban place. According to Joel Garreau, "We have moved our means of creating wealth, the essence of urbanism—our job—out to where most of us have lived and shopped for two generations. That has led to the rise of Edge City."[17] According to a recent issue of *The Edge City News*, edge cities are defined as job cores that:

(a) Contain most of the commercial office and retail development that occurred during the real estate boom of the 1970s and 1980s;

(b) Have a population base that is dominated by white-collar workers;

(c) Offer a variety of goods and services as well as entertainment and restaurants;

(d) Are perceived as one place, an end destination for mixed use no matter how sprawling they may be; and

(e) Rarely have formal, political government with mayors or city councils.[18]

What clearly distinguishes edge cities from traditional suburbs is *their self-contained social, economic, political, and cultural systems.* Residents of edge cities are more likely to live, work, shop, pray, and locate entertainment *within* the edge-city boundaries. Conversely, traditional suburban dwellers lived in suburbs but worked and patronized cultural institutions in central cities. In edge cities like Tysons Corner, VA; Research Triangle Park, NC; Route 128 in the Boston area; Columbia, MD; and the Dearborn-Fairlane Village area in Michigan, African-American socioeconomic status more closely resembles traditional suburban patterns. The increasing concentration of wealth in these new edge cities benefits their inhabitants and employees, including African Americans. Tables 3 and 4 describe the most and least diverse edge-city areas in America. Many of these most and least racially diverse edge cities abut predominately, or substantially, African-American central cities. The population percentages are derived by dividing the African-American population (most diverse) or the white population (least diverse) into the total metropolitan area population. Consequently, at the macro/metropolitan level, *not only is the separation of central city and suburb evident by the bifurcation of the suburb but also the edge city is an additional trend impacting on the demography and socioeconomic character of urban African Americans.*

Third, given these macro-level trends, meso- and micro-level changes also characterize African-American demography. As O'Hare, Pollard, Mann, and Kent indicate, "Within cities and suburbs, blacks and whites typically live in different neighborhoods, regardless of their income levels or poverty status."[19] This metropolitan and central-city residential segregation reflects a greater concentration of poor and disadvantaged. William Julius Wilson's thesis suggests a decoupling of African-American middle class, lower class, and underclass as lower classes and underclasses remain in central cities and more affluent African Americans (but always less affluent than whites) move to suburbs. What his thesis emphasizes less is the diversity of African Americans in suburbs and edge cities. This diversity is illuminated by examining the meso and micro levels of African-American socioeconomic status.

Table 3
Ten of the Most Diverse Edge Cities
Percentage of Black Population
(with select downtowns for comparisons)

(Atlanta DTN)	86.4%
1. Southfield-Northland Mall area, MI	72.7%
2. Lanham/Landover Area, MD	71.5%
(Detroit DTN)	67.8%
3. Memphis Airport Area, TN	67.4%
4. The Research Triangle Park Area, NC	59.1%
5. Security Boulevard, MD	49.8%
(Oakland DTN)	42.1%
6. Eisenhower Valley, VA	38.8%
7. Crown Center, KS	36.1%
(Washington, DC, DTN)	36.0%
8. Greenspring/I-45, TX	33.5%
9. Silver Spring, MD	29.6%
10. Texas Medical Center—Rice University, TX	28.6%

Note: Attained by dividing the black population in the area by the total population in the area.

Source: *The Edge City News*, 1992.

Table 4
Ten of the Least Diverse Edge Cities
Percentage of White Population

1. Rockside Road/I-77, OH	98.4%
2. Attleboro/Mansfield/Foxboro, MA	97.9%
3. Peabody/Danvers, MA	97.8%
4. Brookfield-Blue Mound Road, WI	97.3%
5. The Penn-Lincoln Parkway—Airport Area, PA	97.2%
6. Minnetonka/Western I-494, MN	97.0%
7. Dearborn—Fairlane Village area, MI	96.6%
8. Scottsdale, AZ	96.4%
9. The Poplar Corridor—East Memphis, TN	96.4%
10. Hauppauge, NY	96.3%

Note: Attained by dividing the white population in the area by the total population in the area.

Source: *The Edge City News*, 1993.

SOCIOECONOMIC TRENDS IN BLACK AMERICA

Ten key trends characterize urban African-American socioeconomic life. (1) *The African-American urban population is a young population.* The median age of blacks was 27.7 years in 1989, nearly five years younger than the median age for all Americans. Within the central city, the median age for blacks is 24.9 years; for other city dwellers, 34.6 years. The younger age structure of the black population creates a momentum for future growth because a larger proportion of blacks than whites are in their childbearing ages. African Americans, particularly in central cities, will continue to grow at a faster rate than whites well into the 21st century, even if fertility, mortality, and migration rates become equal for both groups.[20]

(2) *Fertility rates, particularly in lower-income, central-city, and suburban African-American neighborhoods, will continue to be higher than for most Americans, particularly for female teenagers and young adults.* The total fertility rate was 32 percent higher for blacks than for whites in 1988—2.4 children per black woman compared with 1.8 children per white woman. As Figure 1 indicates, in 1988, 64 percent of black babies were born out of wedlock, compared with 18 percent of white babies. In the same year, unmarried white teenagers ages 15 to 17 bore 17 births per 1,000 girls, while unmarried black teenagers bore 74 births per 1,000.[21] Thus, the micro level of urban black households experiences severe strain. The traditional nuclear family is an endangered species. Younger parents with less life experience, education, or employment are raising larger proportions of urban African-American children. At the meso, or neighborhood, level, the church, fraternal organizations, schools, health care organizations, commercial infrastructure, cultural organizations, and other essential institutions erode and stumble as a result of these significant changes in socioeconomic status.

(3) *Mortality and health continue to challenge urban African Americans.* Not only is the life expectancy of an African American six to eight years less than for other Americans (69.2 years versus 77.9 years), but also African Americans, particularly African-American males, are more likely to die from acquired immune deficiency syndrome (AIDS) or, between the ages of 15 and 29, to be victims of homicides.[22] Table 5 describes the ratio of black to white death rates in 1988. These ratios are projected to become worse through the year 2000, particularly in large central cities.

(4) *African-American families in cities continue to experience restructuring and stress.* O'Hare argues that, "While the vast majority of the 10 million African-American households are family households (that is, the household members are related by birth, marriage, or adoptions), only about half the families were headed by a married couple in 1990, down from 68 percent in 1970 and 56 percent in 1980."[23] These trends profoundly affect all members of the urban African-American community: men, women, youth, the elderly and, *most dramatically, children.* The proportion of African-American chil-

17

dren living with two parents declined from 58 percent in 1970 to 38 percent in 1990.[24] By the year 2000, the proportion of African-American children living with both parents will decline to 24 percent.

Figure 1
Babies Born Out-Of-Wedlock, By Race
1970, 1980, and 1988

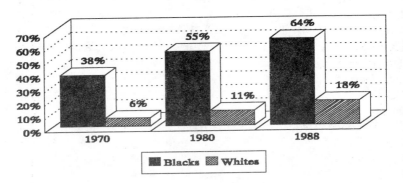

Source: National Center for Health Statistics, *Monthly Vital Statistics, Report 39*, No. 4., Supplement (1990), Table 18, and *Vital Statistics of the United States 1987* (Washington, DC: GPO, 1989), Table 1-31.

(5) *Urban public schools continue to experience the double trauma of declining academic performance, particularly among African-American children, and declining financial, professional, and moral support.* Declining academic performance among African-American children is particularly evident in many of the nation's largest schools where they are the vast majority of the students: roughly 90 percent in Atlanta, Detroit, and Washington, DC. These challenges have reached the inner-ring suburbs, those suburbs adjacent to central cities, and threaten to pervade the metropolis.

Table 5
Ratio of Black-to-White Death Rates for the
15 Major Causes of Death, 1988

CAUSE OF DEATH	BOTH SEXES	BLACK-TO-WHITE RATIO MALES	FEMALES
Heart disease	1.4	1.3	1.6
Cancer	1.3	1.4	1.2
Stroke	1.9	1.9	1.8
Accidents	1.3	1.4	1.2
Chronic lung disease	0.8	0.9	0.7
Pneumonia, flu	1.4	1.6	1.3
Diabetes	2.4	2.1	2.6
Suicide	0.6	0.6	0.5
Cirrhosis, liver disease	1.7	1.7	1.9
Kidney diseases	2.8	2.6	3.1
Atherosclerosis	1.1	1.2	1.1
Homicide	6.4	7.6	4.5
Septicemia	2.6	2.7	2.6
Conditions of newborns	2.7	3.1	3.2
AIDS	3.4	3.2	8.9

Source: National Center for Health Statistics, *Monthly Vital Statistics, Report 39*, No. 7, Supplement (1990); and unpublished data.

(6) *Economic disparity between urban America and urban Black America is becoming more pronounced whether in central cities, suburbs, or edge cities.* African-American employment prospects have declined in central cities, increased slightly in suburbs, and increased substantially for the few African Americans living and working in edge cities. William Julius Wilson cites the decline in stable, higher-paying, blue-collar employment in the industrial cities throughout America.[25] Others identify the changing structure of metropolitan employment characterized by more rapid professional and white-collar employment growth in suburbs and edge cities and declining employment in central cities. In his book, *Cities Without Suburbs*, David Rusk argues that there is a distinction between the growth patterns of *elastic* and *inelastic cities*. Elastic cities grow from within and are sufficiently flexible to transcend official boundaries. Inelastic cities experience declining demographic, economic, employment, and tax growth. Suburbs gain what the central cities lose.[26] These trends are manifested in the stark disparities in income, wealth, and poverty between African Americans and other Americans and among urban African Americans. The rise of young, African-American, female-headed households, the burgeoning employment

in edge cities, and the lower incomes of African Americans who obtain college educations and professional training contribute collectively to economic trends in urban status among African Americans. Beyond differences in the incomes of urban African Americans, O'Hare has also identified critical differences, particularly in urban areas between African-American and overall American *net worth*. As Table 6 indicates, African Americans' net worth, the ratio of household assets to liabilities, is nearly 10 times less than for all Americans.[27]

Table 6
Black and White Households by Net Worth, 1988

Net Worth (in dollars)	Blacks (percent of total)	Whites (percent of total)
Zero or negative	29.1	8.7
1 to 4,999	22.8	13.9
5,000 to 9,999	8.1	5.9
10,000 to 24,999	11.6	11.5
25,000 to 49,999	12.9	13.1
50,000 to 99,999	10.3	17.7
100,000 to 249,999	4.4	19.3
250,000 to 499,999	0.7	6.7
500,000 or more	0.1	3.2
Median net worth	$ 4,169	$43,279
Total households (in thousands)	10,278	79,169

Source: Bureau of the Census, *Current Population Reports*, P-70, No. 2: (Washington, DC: U.S. Government Printing Office, 1990).

(7) *Residential segregation and poorer housing continue to define the spatial and locational choices of most urban African Americans.* Given the historic role of cities as points of entry for American nonwhites; given the historical patterns of racial segregation of these nonwhites, particularly in industrial cities; given discriminatory real estate practices and current patterns of inner-city disinvestment; and given the role of increasingly intense inner-city poverty in impeding the financial capacity of central-city residents to buy in suburbs, sociologists Massey and Kanaiaupuni combine these structural explanations for both the rise in central-city poverty and racial segregation with the contributions of public housing policies. They argue that, since low-income housing projects use poverty as a criterion for entry, they build concentrated poverty structurally into any neighborhood that contains them.[28] However, beyond public housing, patterns of residential

segregation are evident in owner-occupied and rental housing in both inner-city and suburban African-American households.[29]

(8) *Environmental degradation is an increasingly alarming artifact of urban life for African Americans.* Although environmental issues are most often associated with endangered species of flora and fauna, the combination of exposure to increasing levels of lead poisoning, asbestos, and radon; exposure to the disproportionate citing of noxious facilities such as sewer treatment plants, garbage dumps, landfills, incinerators, hazardous waste disposal sites, lead smelters, and other risky technologies;[30] the location of large urban African-American communities in areas designated as "nonattainment" for air pollution by the 1992 Clean Air Act amendments; and the exposure of African Americans to the severe health consequences of disproportionate exposure to water pollution, collectively create a deadly environment of risk in urban Black America far in excess of risks experienced by any animal species. Bullard categorized these problems with environmental justice into procedural, geographical, and social inequities.[31]

(9) *The urban African-American political dynamic is increasingly characterized by both continuing increases in the number and distribution of African-American elected officials at all levels of urban government and the tyranny of jurisdictional boundary between city and suburb.* According to the Joint Center for Political and Economic Studies, there are currently more than 8,000 African-American elected officials. More than 90 percent of these elected officials serve cities of varying sizes. Although there is an increasing number of African-American elected officials serving both cities with nonblack majorities like Seattle, WA; Minneapolis, MN; and Rochester, NY; and suburban areas like Howard County, MD; Shelby County, TN; and Broward County, FL, most African-American urban elected officials serve large and small cities with impoverished African-American populations. Three interrelated challenges face these elected officials: (a) the continued erosion of African-American political representation in central cities as the population of these cities declines. Combined with the increasing representation of suburban areas in Congress and state legislatures, central-city black elected officials face severe challenges in their advocacy of the central city. Following the reappointment of congressional and legislative districts in Maryland, the two African-American members of Congress—Reps. Kweisi Mfume (D-MD) and Albert R. Wynn (D-MD)—now represent a split city-county congressional district and a suburban congressional district with a large and diverse African-American population, respectively; (b) the impact of poverty on the political behavior and opinions of African Americans presents a severe impediment to African-American political mobilization among the young and, particularly, among "the underclass." Cohen and Dawson indicate that social scientists "have neglected the one area that could lead to the empowerment and involvement of poor individuals in struggles to

change their status, namely, politics (as distinguished from policy formation)"[32]; and (c) African-American elected officials must balance central-city, suburban, and edge-city visions. Business, industry, new housing, and public and private infrastructural investment must proceed on a metro-regional basis. Consequently, African Americans must engineer self-development on a macro, metro, and micro (community) basis. As Neal Peirce indicates in his new book, *Citistates*, cities and suburbs must make a deal for their mutual survival. Neither can survive alone.[33]

(10) *Urban Black America has a profound and continuing stake in a fledgling national urban policy. Recent attempts by the Clinton administration to promote "empowerment zones," economic stimulus, and greater investment in infrastructure, particularly in the nation's metropolitan areas, have met with both congressional opposition and intense lobbying by interest groups not as interested in central-city development.* The basic impact of these proposed policies is not only economic but also human: they represent an investment in the human infrastructure of central cities. The development of the urban African-American community is a joint venture of both public policy and the determined mobilization of African-American households and institutions.

LIGHT IN DEEP DARKNESS: SELF-DEVELOPMENT INITIATIVES IN BLACK AMERICA

The mere description of these 10 trends wraps a cloak of apparent deep darkness around urban Black America. Destruction, decay, and atrophy seem intractable. But, beneath these trends persist thousands of initiatives promoting the survival and development of households, neighborhoods, cities, and metropolitan African-American communities. Despite sharp and devastating declines in federal assistance to cities in the last 12 years,[34] many of these initiatives mobilize citizen resources: churches, corporations, foundations, and nonprofit institutions; they adamantly confront a range of complex and ominous challenges including violent crime, housing shortages and deterioration, environmental justice, education, employment development, business and commercial development, and the development of physical infrastructures. This light flows from a dynamic, restless, stirring, spiritual reservoir deep within those who care not only within the African-American community and about African Americans but also, ultimately, themselves. Examples of self-development in urban Black America illustrate this light in deep darkness. In Oakland, CA, Safe Streets Now! is an innovative, low-cost, and effective program that empowers neighborhood residents with a safe, fast, and efficient step-by-step program to eliminate drug houses in their neighborhoods and to prevent them from reforming. Its primary purpose is to provide citizens with direct action tools to eliminate neighborhood nuisance house by house, street by street, and neighborhood by neighborhood. Under

22

e guidance of a community organizer, neighbors take control of drug afficking by pursuing legal action against property owners who rent to drug ealers. Since 1989, Safe Streets Now! has trained over 3,500 citizens to lose over 250 drug houses. More than $700,000 in judgments in small laims courts have been won for neighborhood residents. In 1992 alone, Safe treets Now! provided 33 Oakland Safe Streets Now! Community Workhops and consultation to 385 volunteers that have closed down 67 drug ouses.[35]

A huge, dynamic, and multifaceted initiative in community development is ccurring in the Sandtown-Winchester community on the west side of Baltiore, MD, a 20-block area that is home to 12,500 of the city's poorest esidents. This initiative is the result of a dynamic and diverse coalition, icluding Mayor Kurt Schmoke and his administration; the Enterprise Founation, founded by urban developer James Rouse; and the Community Buildig In Partnership, Inc. (CBP). A massive development of some 300 new omes has been launched, diverse and intensive social services support ystems have been developed to sustain neighborhood transformation, and ommunity self-development is the prevailing norm animating much of the iccess of this nationally recognized project.[36]

Shaker Heights, OH, a relatively affluent suburban community adjacent to leveland, is pursuing a "prointegrative" housing policy aimed at a "stable itegrative process" (SIP). SIP seeks to promote racially diverse suburban eighborhoods by providing legal, financial, technical, and social support to oth black and white families seeking housing in suburban Shaker Heights. he city has established the Community Services Department to implement ie SIP. DeMarco and Galster describe the services provided by the Commuity Services Department:

> The housing services that are offered are supplemental to traditional housing market services and are implemented in ways that enhance housing choices for minority and nonminority households and encourage housing decisions in favor of integration. Hence, Anglo homeseekers are assisted in the purchase and rental of housing in those areas of the city and school district in which they are underrepresented in the resident population or in the current demand for housing as related to the Anglo population of Cuyahoga County and Shaker Heights. Similarly, assistance is given to black households for moves into areas in which blacks are underrepresented in the current population or in current demand.[37]

In Pittsburgh, PA, Crawford Square is a new housing development located the predominantly and historically African-American neighborhood known "The Hill." To date, more than 140 rental units have been built, and ngle-family detached homes are under construction. Upon completion, the entire complex will include more than 500 rental and for-sale units available at both market rates and reduced rates for low- to moderate-income families in the African-American community. The 18.5-acre site is the result of effective coordination and management by a coalition including the Hill Project Area Committee (PAC), the Urban Redevelopment Authority of Pittsburgh (URA), and the Hill Community Development Corporation (CDC). The project also emphasizes the development and utilization of African-American entrepreneurs as an empowerment tool.[38]

Many initiatives in urban environmental justice are flourishing in urban Black America. The first National Environmental Summit for People of Color convened in Washington, DC, in October 1991, under the leadership of the Commission on Racial Justice, the Environmental Equity Task Force, and urban environmental analysts and activists like Carl Anthony, Robert Bullard and Charles Lee. During and since that summit, many urban environmental projects, programs, and coalitions proceeded in the midst of the worst urban conditions. In Maryland, a unique coalition has emerged between the Baltimore Urban League under the leadership of Roger Lyons and the 80,000 member Chesapeake Bay Foundation under the leadership of Will Baker. With the support of the Morris Goldseker Foundation, this inner-city environmental partnership will pursue environmental education, environmental employment development, urban revitalization through more balanced metropolitan growth strategies, and toxic waste reduction in Baltimore City. In addition, the work of African-American architect and planner Carl Anthony and his Earth Island Institute in San Francisco focuses on effective and balanced approaches to the development of energy-efficient and environmentally sound urban transportation alternatives. Add to these examples hundreds of urban forestry, greenway, and water relief efforts and public policy initiatives to reduce urban air pollution; clearly the battle to reclaim and to restore the ecology of urban African-American communities is escalating.

A sparkling example of the combination of the development of consciousness about the *history* of the African-American urban community through historic preservation and the *cultivation of a local self-development ethos* is the development of old but historically significant geographic areas and structures in African-American neighborhoods and central business districts. According to Nelson and Talley, there are two generic kinds of historic districts: (1) those that are listed in the National Register of Historic Places pursuant to the National Historic Preservation Act of 1966, and (2) districts created or regulated by local governments pursuant to state enabling legislation.[39] Historic preservation not only promotes consciousness of the historic significance and evolution of urban neighborhoods and commercial areas but also increases commerce, raises property values, and promotes *investment in the contemporary city*. History and current function coalesce in a mutually reinforcing partnership.

Two examples of historic preservation as contemporary self-development define this opportunity for self-development in urban black America: the Sweet Auburn Historic District in Atlanta and the Orchard Street Church Development in Baltimore. In the early 1890s, the Auburn Street area in Atlanta became a focal point for black business development. It became to blacks what downtown Atlanta had become for whites. Black and white downtown districts functioned virtually side by side. Many of the original buildings were destroyed in a huge fire in 1917 but were replaced by larger and grander buildings. By the 1920s, Auburn Avenue became known as the wealthiest black street in America, thus earning its nickname, "Sweet Auburn."[40] Beginning with the late 1950s, Sweet Auburn experienced rapid decline; little building renovation or new development occurred. Then, in 1977, part of Auburn Avenue west of the downtown expressway was designated the Sweet Auburn Historic District. The area between the District and the Martin Luther King, Jr., National Historic Landmark was named a historic conservation district under Georgia law. Slowly, combined with local community organizations, the historic preservation designation is facilitating both a commercial renewal and a tenacious self-development spirit in this vital black community.

In Baltimore, the Urban League affiliate acquired the property rights to the abandoned, 19th-century Orchard Street Church at the intersection of two historic African-American neighborhoods. The League not only successfully advocated historic designation for the church but also renovated the building as its metropolitan headquarters. *Architectural Digest* and other magazines identify Orchard Street as a brilliant example of historic preservation, community consciousness, current function, and self-development potential. The church has enabled the local Urban League to realize its aspiration to locate itself constructively within those African-American communities for whom it works and advocates.

TOWARDS A CONCEPT OF URBAN SELF-DEVELOPMENT

These examples illustrate the essential and recurring elements of urban self-development in the state of urban Black America. These elements are inextricably intertwined and characterize most current urban initiatives.

(1) *Collective community resolve.* From deep within the spirit of those pursuing the social, economic, political, and cultural development of the African-American community is a collective resolve undaunted by the encroachments and setbacks of crime, reduced government support, or institutional atrophy. No effort succeeds without this faith and tenacity.

(2) *Pervasive transformation.* No concept of self-development ultimately succeeds by benefiting only a fleeting segment of its community. Development initiatives should involve Du Bois' "talented tenth," the vital majority of the community, *and the underclass.* The engendering of class divisions or

conflicts within the African-American community will retard and defeat development of the community's capacity to renew and sustain itself and to transact strategically with other communities and institutions.

(3) *Dynamic coalitions.* As the current trade status of the United States indicates, no successful nation can thrive without diplomacy, trade, and alliance. Urban Black America requires strategic coalitions to promote self-development. Those coalitions proceed on mutual self-interest and on the maintenance of community vision—even in the most intense bargaining with communities and institutions outside of the African-American community. Coalitions proceed on the recognition of their vital interdependency.[41]

(4) *Developmental entrepreneurship.* Much rhetoric about black business pervades public policy and dialogue in the African-American community. However, urban African-American entrepreneurship is ultimately useless without making more than money in the community. Constructive employment, quality services, physical infrastructural development, environmental consciousness, youth development, historic preservation, and institutional development must also animate business as communities are empowered by urban entrepreneurs.[42]

(5) *Constructive, creative, and consistent use of public policy.* The National Urban League's Marshall Plan consistently calls for an annual investment of $50 billion to revitalize and develop urban communities. That is an investment not just in Black America but also, ultimately and finally, in America itself. Public policy now invests nearly $77 billion annually in public assistance, public housing, law enforcement, and correctional facilities. This investment is anti-self-development in Black America. The Marshall Plan pursues a public policy aimed at human and physical infrastructural development that is self-sustaining and results in an urban multiplier effect. Most importantly, the engines of self-renewal, spiritual dynamism, and growth are switched on in the architecture of the plan. No development, whether self- or otherwise, can proceed without such engines.

MY CITY

I drive slowly through intersections of my city.
Buildings tire. Their skins are wrinkled.
They sing historic songs to deaf ears.
They sing in hoarse voice.
I stop at permanent red lights
to find billboards and funeral parlor ads,
"golden arches" and liquor bottles
strewn on the broken floors of my city.
I back up and back into other cities
whose drivers are greeted by trees and flowers
and whose streets boast of home.
Occasionally, I drive through red lights
to find on small, unnoticed streets and alleys,
lights, lights, lights!
Humble lights shining in small, clean homes.
Lights dim only to those walking by.
Lights illuminating new intersections
and passing on more candles
for those, like me, who drive,
who drive in search of passengers
in my city!

© 1994 Lenneal J. Henderson, Jr.

The author expresses gratitude to Diane Aull, Tonya Meredith, and Charles Wilson of the University of Baltimore for their assistance in the preparation of this paper.

ENDNOTES

[1]Harold Cruse, "Black and White: Outlines of the Next Stage," *The Black World*, Vol. 20, No. 5, March 1971, p. 7.

[2]See Ruth Hoogland DeHoog, David Lowery, and William E. Lyons, "Metropolitan Fragmentation and Suburban Ghettos: Some Empirical Observations on Institutional Racism," *The Journal of Urban Affairs*, Vol. 13, No. 4, 1991, pp. 479-494.

[3]Joe Darden, Harriet Orcutt Duleep, and George Galster, "Civil Rights in Metropolitan America," *The Journal of Urban Affairs*, Vol. 14, Nos. 3 and 4, 1992, pp. 469-496.

[4]For a description of the Atlanta University studies, see Francis L. Broderick, *W.E.B. Du Bois: The Biography of a Negro Leader* (Stanford, CA: Stanford University Press, 1958).

[5]W.E.B. Du Bois, *The Philadelphia Negro: A Social Study* (Milwood, NY: Krause-Thomson Organization Limited, 1973, reissued from the 1899 study).

[6]Horace Cayton and St. Clair Drake, *Black Metropolis: A Study of Negro Life in a Northern City* (New York: Harcourt Brace, 1945).

[7]Kenneth Clark, *Dark Ghetto* (New York: Harper and Row, 1965).

[8]William Julius Wilson, *The Declining Significance of Race* (Chicago: The University of Chicago Press, 1978).

[9]William Julius Wilson, *The Truly Disadvantaged: The Inner City, The Underclass, and Public Policy* (Chicago: The University of Chicago Press, 1987).

[10]Harold Rose and Paula D. McClain, *Race, Place, and Risk: Black Homicide in Urban America* (Albany, NY: State University of New York Press, 1990).

[11]Douglass Massey and Nancy Denton, *American Apartheid: Segregation and the Making of the Underclass* (Cambridge: Harvard University Press, 1993).

[12]Ellis Cose, *The Rage of a Privileged Class* (New York: HarperCollins, Inc., 1993).

[13]William O'Hare, Kelvin M. Pollard, Taynia L. Mann, and Mary M. Kent, "African Americans in the 1990s," *Population Bulletin*, Vol. 46, No. 1 (Washington, DC: Population Reference Bureau, Inc., July 1991), p. 8.

[14]*Ibid.*

[15]Rose and McClain, *op. cit.*, pp. 7-8.

[16]Howard F. Andrews, "The Ecology of Risk and the Geography of Intervention: From Research to Practice for the Health and Well-Being of Urban Children," *The Annals of the Association of American Geographers*, Vol. 75, September 1985, pp. 370-382.

[17]Joel Garreau, *Edge City: Life on the New Frontier* (New York: Doubleday, 1988), p. 4.

[18]"What is an Edge City," *The Edge City News*, Vol. 1, No. 7, 1993, p. 1.

[19]O'Hare et al., *op. cit.*, p. 9.

[20]*Ibid.*, p. 11.

[21]*Ibid.*, pp. 11-12.

[22]National Center for Health Statistics, *Health: United States 1990* (Hyattsville, MD: Public Health Service, 1991); and Harvey V. Fineberg, "The Social Dimensions of AIDS," *Scientific American* 259, October 1988, pp. 41-48.

[23]O'Hare et al., *op. cit.*, p. 19.

[24]*Ibid.*

[25]Wilson, *The Declining Significance of Race*, pp. 12-43.

[26]David Rusk, *Cities Without Suburbs* (Washington, DC: Woodrow Wilson International Center for Scholars, 1993).

[27]William O'Hare, *Black Wealth in the United States* (Washington, DC: The Joint Center for Political Studies, 1988).

[28]Douglass S. Massey and Shawn M. Kanaiaupuni, "Public Housing and the Concentration of Poverty," *Social Science Quarterly*, Vol. 74, No. 1, March 1993, p. 110.

[29]See, for example, Dennis E. Gale, *Washington, DC: Inner-City Revitalization and Minority Suburbanization* (Philadelphia: Temple University Press, 1987).

[30]Robert Bullard, "Race and Environmental Justice in the United States," *The Yale Journal of International Law*, Vol. 18, No. 1, Winter 1993, p. 319.

[31]Robert Bullard, "Waste and Racism: A Stacked Deck?," *Forum for Applied Research and Public Policy*, 1993, p. 29. See also Robert Bullard, *Dumping in Dixie: Race, Class, and Environmental Quality* (Boulder, CO: Westview Press, 1990).

[32]Cathy J. Cohen and Michael C. Dawson, "Neighborhood Poverty and African-American Politics," *American Political Science Review*, Vol. 87, No. 2, June 1993, p. 286.

[33]Neal Peirce, *Citistates* (Washington, DC: Seven Locks Press, 1993).

[34]Demetrious Caralley, "Washington Abandons the Cities," *Political Science Quarterly*, Fall 1992, pp. 1-30.

[35]Application of the City of Oakland, CA, to the National Civic League All-American City Competition, April 1993, p. 3.

[36]Lenneal J. Henderson, "Baltimore: Managing the Civics of a Turnaround Community," *National Civic Review*, Vol. 82, No. 4, Fall 1993, pp. 4-12.

[37]Donald L. DeMarco and George C. Galster, "Prointegrative Policy: Theory and Practice," *The Journal of Urban Affairs*, Vol. 15, No. 2, 1993, pp. 141-160.

[38]Application of the City of Pittsburgh, PA, to the National Civic League All-American City Competition, February 1993.

[39]Arthur C. Nelson and Janice Talley, "Revitalizing Minority Commercial Areas Through Commercial Historic District Designation: A Case Study of Atlanta, Georgia," *The Journal of Urban Affairs*, Vol. 13, No. 2, 1991, p. 222.

[40]*Ibid.*, pp. 224-225.

[41]Lenneal J. Henderson, "Looking at the Birds: Economics and the African-American Challenge," *The Good News Herald*, Vol. 8, No. 5, March 1993.

[42]On the concept of empowerment, see Lenneal J. Henderson, "Empowerment Through Enterprise: African-American Business Development," in Billy J. Tidwell, ed., *The State of Black America 1993* (Washington, DC: National Urban League, Inc., 1993), pp. 91-108.

Dollars for Deeds:
Prospects and Prescriptions for African-American Financial Institutions

William D. Bradford, Ph.D.

INTRODUCTION

African-American financial institutions are highly visible members of the U.S. business sector. Financial institutions (banks, savings and loan associations, insurance companies) are important simply as businesses which employ people and earn income for both owners and employees. But the importance of black-owned financial institutions is magnified in that they form depositories for savings and that their investment decisions can affect the amount and mix of capital formation among black families and within black communities. If African Americans are to become involved substantively in determining their direction and amount of participation in the U.S. economy, then the creation and viability of black-owned financial institutions are important.

This study will examine the outlook and general operating issues for banks, savings and loans, and insurance companies owned by African Americans. In many respects, these firms are bellwethers for the general black business community.

An overview of the study is as follows. At the start of 1993, there were 77 black-owned banks, S&Ls, and insurance companies in total, and they held $4.06 billion in assets. These represent 0.5 percent of the number and 0.06 percent of the assets of all banks, S&Ls, and insurance companies in the United States. In the 20-year period ending in 1993, individually and collectively, black banks, S&Ls, and insurance companies lost ground with regard to the number of firms and the proportion of industry assets held. Of course, the 1973-93 period (especially the latter half) was a significant challenge to all financial institutions, with record post-Depression failures in both the commercial banking and S&L industries. As a group, the black financial institutions have survived, but not without casualties. In addition, the next five years will be crucial in predicting the long-term viability of these firms, as the changes in the competitive conditions in the financial markets become more pervasive and permanent.

It is likely that the black banks and S&Ls have already absorbed most of the negative impact of the transition in the financial markets over the last 20 years, so that the survival of these firms is not at question. But the problem is the appropriate set of strategies which they must undertake to regain and exceed their earlier significance in the financial markets. Most firms will need to specialize in certain types of loans, deposits, and other financial services in order to take advantage of market niches. The management problem is to identify the market opportunities which they can exploit, given the local characteristics of their communities. A small proportion of black banks and S&Ls can become almost full-service operations and can take advantage of the growing number of blacks who have developed expertise in banking and finance.

The black insurance companies have an even more difficult road ahead. Many of them are offering services which lack mainstream competitiveness and a clientele which does not have sufficient resources to enable them to grow. The captive market which they serve has enabled many black insurance companies to survive thus far, but the long-term viability of exclusively serving this market is highly suspect. This is slow death, albeit a manageable one. On the other hand, it has been difficult for black insurance companies to enter successfully the mainstream insurance market because of a lack of the capital and management talent required. Several black insurance companies have shifted into other industries altogether. For some black insurers, this is the best option. How this problem is resolved will be a significant model of how black-owned businesses adapt to change.

The overriding issue for all black financial institutions is being able to identify market opportunities and the appropriate venture partners to take advantage of those opportunities. In the past, the basis of their growth has been their black customers. They must regain the support of these customers but also be able to compete to some extent in the mainstream market. For banks and S&Ls, this may mean locating branches in downtown and ethnically diverse communities, such that both blacks and nonminority customers can be served. This also means identifying the appropriate set of services to offer. For black insurance companies, it means identifying products and services which are applicable to any person who has the income to support a policy or financial service which the firm might offer. The formation of joint ownership groups such as holding companies with other black or nonminority companies appears to hold promise for all minority financial institutions. Finally, the survival of black financial institutions will be enhanced by mergers and acquisitions among these firms to increase their size such that economies of scale and expertise can be utilized.

The rest of this paper is organized as follows. "Black Financial Institutions: Background" provides an overview of the economic characteristics of black financial institutions, based upon the numerous studies which have investigated these firms. "Black Banks and Savings and Loan Associations:

Current Issues" discusses black banks and S&Ls. They are in a period of transition, and the next few years will tell much of the story about their ultimate survival. "Black Insurance Companies" presents the state of affairs of these firms, whose clientele and products threaten their ultimate survival. The final section contains the conclusions.

BLACK FINANCIAL INSTITUTIONS: BACKGROUND

Economic theory describes the major role of financial institutions as gathering many relatively small deposits of households and other economic units and combining them to support capital formation through lending for business and housing capital investment. The service which black financial institutions can provide may be magnified by the much discussed inability of many black families and communities to obtain financing from majority financial institutions for business capital investment and for housing investment. The concept of pooling the savings of black community residents and using the savings to finance the development of the community may be sound in theory, but what does the empirical evidence indicate about its practical implementation?

Black banks were analyzed quite frequently in the 1970s. The studies by Brimmer[1] and Irons[2] on black-owned banks reached contradictory conclusions. Brimmer interpreted his data as indicating that black banks as a group are financially weak and slow- or no-growth firms. Based upon his findings, he concluded that black banks could not contribute significantly to black economic development. Irons (who used the same basic data as Brimmer) viewed black banks as similar to new banks. Thus, the weak financial condition of black banks was comparable to typical new banks and would be eliminated over time as the banks grew and developed experience and expertise. He reached more positive conclusions than Brimmer on both the current financial condition of black banks and their potential for impacting black economic development. In retrospect (the period observed in these studies went only through 1969), black banks have performed somewhere between the pessimistic predictions of Brimmer and the optimistic predictions of Irons but perhaps closer to those of Brimmer.

The studies of Brimmer and Irons formed the analytical basis for most of the subsequent research on black banks. In their important studies of the comparative performance of minority-owned banks and the start-up experience of minority banks, Boorman[3] and Boorman and Kwast[4] remedied many of the methodological shortcomings of Brimmer and Irons. Subsequent studies by Bradford,[5] Bates,[6] Bates and Bradford,[7] Black,[8] Doctors et al.,[9] Duker and Morton,[10] Summers and Tucker,[11] Kwast,[12] Gardner,[13] Clair,[14] Wright,[15] Cole et al.,[16] and Kwast and Black[17] have provided additional analyses in selected aspects of the financial attributes of black banks in the 1970s and 1980s.

With regard to black S&Ls, a series of studies by Bradford and his co-authors remains the dominant work on black S&Ls.[18] His studies analyzed black S&Ls through the mid-1970s, except for a study on black and other minority S&Ls in California through 1979.[19] King[20] updated one of Bradford's earlier studies through 1979 and came to conclusions similar to those of Bradford.

Unlike black banks and S&Ls, black insurance companies have not been examined by economic scholars. There are two possible reasons for this. First, it is generally felt that insurance companies are a slower growth sector of the financial services industry than banks or S&Ls (the reasons for which will be discussed below), and their investment patterns have less impact on the economy. Second (and perhaps of more relevance), data on banks and S&Ls are much easier to obtain than data on insurance companies. Insurance companies have no federal agency overseeing their operations, as do banks and S&Ls. Thus, the consistency and availability of data on insurance companies are far less than for commercial banks and S&Ls.

Nevertheless, the numerous studies on black banks and S&Ls do allow us to develop a perspective in examining the current state of black financial institutions. These studies have generally concluded that black financial institutions, relative to comparable firms (i.e., same class size, age, general location—MSA or county, same type—federal or state chartered): (1) have lower average deposit account sizes, (2) have lower average loan sizes, (3) experience a higher proportion of loan default or bad debts, (4) have higher operating expenses, (5) have lower capital accounts with which to cushion loan losses and support growth, and (6) have lower overall financial viability. These findings have been attributed to lower per capita income and less stable employment characteristics of the communities which the black financial institutions serve.

Although it has also been found that black banks and S&Ls pay lower average interest on deposits and obtain higher loan yields, these positive attributes have not been able to offset the negative attributes above in affecting their financial viability. Also, differences in financial viability have been found between mature black financial institutions created before the 1950s and those created after the 1950s, the latter being generally more viable. Given this background, the next section will update the general performance of the black financial institutions.

BLACK BANKS AND SAVINGS AND LOAN ASSOCIATIONS: CURRENT ISSUES

Background

Black commercial banks and S&Ls are currently involved in a significant transition. Between the early 1980s and 1993, deregulation, the entry of nonbanks into traditional banking services, wide fluctuations in interest rates, and a recession and slow recovery during the late 1980s and early 1990s have challenged the financial viability of both banks and S&Ls. It is helpful to summarize the regulatory changes which form the backdrop for the current environment of banks and S&Ls. The regulatory environment of banks and S&Ls was profoundly changed in the early 1980s by two laws: the Depository Institutions Deregulation and Monetary Control Act of 1980 (DIDMCA) and the Garn-St. Germain Depository Institutions Act of 1982 (1982 Act). These acts have been well-chronicled, being preceded by the Hunt Commission and the Fine Study, which recommended major structural changes in the banking and savings and loan industries.

The DIDMCA was passed in a period in which banks and S&Ls were experiencing high interest rates and greater competition for savers' dollars from money market mutual funds and other nonbank financial institutions. It aimed to strengthen depository institutions' positions by permitting somewhat greater flexibility on both the asset and liability sides of their balance sheets. The DIDMCA provides for all S&Ls and banks to offer NOW accounts; for S&Ls to invest in credit card activities, consumer loans, commercial paper, and corporate debt securities. The act also allows S&Ls to offer trust services; to make first or second mortgage loans without regard to size or geographic restrictions; to operate remote service units; and to offer adjustable rate mortgages. The act imposes uniform reserve requirements on transactions accounts for all depository institutions, including banks and S&Ls. A critically important feature of the DIDMCA provides for the phase-out of limitations on the maximum rates of interest that may be paid on deposits at banks and S&Ls.

It was clear then that the DIDMCA, although it significantly changed the environment of both banks and S&Ls, was an operating panacea for neither. It was felt that it would take several years for the new asset powers to impact significantly the S&Ls, which subsequently posted record losses in 1981 and 1982.

Legislation often derives from Congress's perception of a crisis. Such is a description of the process leading to the Garn-St. Germain Act of 1982. It is primarily a rescue operation for S&Ls and savings banks, but it also enlarges the options for commercial banks. The 1982 Act authorized the money market deposit account and the Super NOW account for banks and S&Ls;

allowed S&Ls to accept business deposits and NOW accounts from federal, state, and local governments; removed (effective the start of 1984) any existing interest rate differential between the interest rate which banks and S&Ls can pay for deposits; authorized S&Ls to make overdraft loans; and expanded the ability of S&Ls to make commercial loans and consumer loans and to invest in state and local government obligations.

Despite the 1982 Act, S&Ls continued to fail in record numbers between 1982 and 1989. The Financial Institutions Reform, Recovery, and Enforcement Act of 1989 (FIRREA) was an S&L bailout bill aimed at promoting a safe and stable system of affordable housing finance. It reorganized the S&L regulation, supervision, and deposit insurance. It also permitted commercial banks to buy healthy S&Ls and placed the full faith and credit of the U.S. government behind federal deposit insurance.

A more recent law is the Federal Deposit Insurance Corporation Improvement Act of 1991, or FDICIA, which concerns mainly commercial banks. Through more stringent provisions, this law requires federal regulators to tighten their surveillance on banks and to close down more quickly weak banks. It requires that regulatory accounting principles be no less stringent than generally accepted accounting principles and requires new reporting, legal, and auditing costs for banks. This law is Congress's attempt to keep banks from staging the same loss to the FDIC that the $160 billion savings and loan failures have to the federal government. Under the law, the FDIC is required to close down promptly any bank whose tangible equity capital falls below 2 percent of its assets. The FDIC is also directed to build its insurance fund to 1.25 percent of insured deposits. The FDIC has set up a plan to reach the required ratio in 15 years, but even with this gradual schedule, deposit insurance paid by banks increased by 10 percent between 1991 and 1992.

Institutional Characteristics

Depository institutions provide intermediation services by borrowing from one economic unit at an interest rate and lending at a higher interest rate the borrowed funds to another economic unit. The "spread," which is the difference between the average yield on lending and the average cost of borrowing, must be sufficient to cover operating costs (personnel, advertising, rent, etc.) and net a profit to the firm. There are three risks inherent in this business. The first is the traditional and recognized risk of the borrower defaulting on the loan. Coping with this risk has remained the responsibility of management, although the current problems facing commercial banks of potential and actual default are testing this responsibility.

The second risk arises from the possibility that depositors may unexpectedly withdraw their deposits and the institution may not have enough liquid assets to meet the demand; this is liquidity risk. Central banks in general have long served as lenders of last resort to commercial banks and S&Ls to limit their exposure to this risk.

The third risk relates to interest rates rising unexpectedly. In a world where financial institutions pay market interest rates for their deposits, rapidly rising interest rates raise the cost of funds faster than the yield on assets because assets have a longer maturity than deposits.

The first risk was more dominant in bank insolvencies such as Continental and Penn Square, whereas the third risk was dominant in S&L difficulties such as Financial Corporation of America and Financial Federation; but both banks and S&Ls experience all of these risks. The future of banks and S&Ls can thus be related to their ability to manage these risks while earning a profit.

Black Banks

The status of black banks will be discussed first. Table 1 provides background and current data on black banks. At year-end 1992, the assets of the 36 existing black banks totaled $2.11 billion. In the 19-year period ending December 31, 1992, the assets of black banks grew by 220 percent, which translates into an average annual growth rate of 6.3 percent. The number of black banks decreased by 1, from 37 to 36. In the same period, assets of all commercial banks increased by 353 percent, an average annual growth rate of 8.3 percent. The number of commercial banks in the United States declined from 14,161 to 11,461, or 19 percent. If these rates of change continue for black banks from 1992 to the year 2000, then the number of black banks will remain at 36, and they will have assets of $3.23 billion on January 1, 2000.

Table 1
Overview of Black Commercial Banks

	1973	1980	1983	1989	1991	1992
Black Banks						
Number	37	48	47	37	38	36
Assets ($billion)	0.66	1.26	1.55	1.88	2.01	2.11
All Commercial Banks						
Number	14,161	14,435	14,460	12,705	12,163	11,461
Assets ($billion)	806.4	1,702.8	2,113.1	3,245.8	3,545.4	3,652.7
Black Banks						
% Number	0.26	0.32	0.31	0.29	0.31	0.31
% Assets	0.08	0.07	0.07	0.05	0.06	0.06

Annual Compound Rate of Change, 1973-92

Black Banks
    Number   -0.1%
    Assets   +6.3%
All Commercial Banks
    Number   -1.1%
    Assets   +8.3%

Projected for January 1, 2000, Based Upon 1973-92 Experience

Black Banks
    Number   36
    (-0.1% annual change)
    Assets $3.23 billion
    (+6.3% annual change)

Sources: *Black Enterprise*, Federal Reserve *Bulletin*, various issues, 1973-
    1993.

With regard to the most recent performance, in 1992 the largest black bank surpassed $200 million in assets for the first time, and the total assets of all black banks increased by $100 million to $2.11 billion. Two black banks changed to nonminority control through merger or sale of majority ownership. One new black-owned bank opened: United Bank of Philadelphia is the first black bank to open in Philadelphia in 40 years. Overall, in 1992 the number of black banks declined by 5.3 percent, and their assets increased by 4.8 percent. For the industry, the number of banks decreased by 5.8 percent, and the total assets increased by 3.0 percent. Thus, with regard to change in number and growth in assets in the most current year, black banks as a group compare favorably to the entire U.S. commercial banking industry. The surviving black banks have weathered the new environment thus far, and many have taken advantage of the more liberal attitude of regulators (especially regulators of national banks) toward the activities of banks.

However, the outlook for black banks overall is not a pleasant one. These banks remain a small and fragile part of the industry. At year-end 1992, black banks were only 0.31 percent of the number and held only 0.06 percent of the total assets of all commercial banks. In fact, black banks held a lower proportion of the industry assets at year-end 1992 than at year-end 1973. Thus, on a relative basis, they have lost ground with regard to their position in the industry. At year-end 1992, the average black bank held only $59 million in assets, while the average for the industry was $319 million. The largest black bank, Seaway National Bank of Chicago—with assets of $202 million at year-end 1992—is a small bank by industry standards.

Another significant point is that the average black bank has a lower net worth per dollar of assets to cushion losses than comparable nonminority banks. This has been a traditional problem with black banks, and it is based upon their lower overall profitability relative to assets. Finally, Table 2 provides some data on survival rates of black banks over the 20-year period ending at the start of 1993. Sixty-five percent, or approximately two out of three black banks in existence in 1973, have disappeared (been acquired or ceased operations) by year-end 1992. Although data on the entire commercial banking industry are not available, this disappearance rate is thought to be much higher than that of the industry as a whole.

Table 2
Survival Analysis of Black Commercial Banks

Which still exist in:

Those existing in:		1978		1980		1983		1989		1993	
		No.	%	No.	%	No.	%	No.	%	No.	%
1973	37	34	92	30	81	27	73	20	54	13	35
1978	49			44	90	39	80	27	55	16	33
1981	46					40	87	27	59	16	35
1982	44					43	98	29	66	16	36

Sources: *Black Enterprise,* various issues, 1973-1993.

Table 2 also shows that the 10-year survival rate of the 1982 group of black banks, 36 percent, appears to be forecasting an even higher 20-year disappearance rate than the 1973 group. That is, the 10-year survival rate of the 1982 group, 36 percent, is lower than the 10-year survival rate of the 1973 group, 73 percent. It is felt that the cause of the lower 10-year survival rates for the 1981 and 1982 groups is the economic and financial turmoil experienced between 1982 and 1992. Only to the extent that these transitional impacts are less between 1993 and 2000 will we expect the survival rate for black banks to improve from the dismal 10-year period ending in 1993.

Consistent with the passage of the four acts mentioned above, black banks have competed for funds not only with S&Ls but also with nonbanking institutions, who have decided that the activities of depository institutions are profitable. Companies such as Prudential-Bache have bought banks and sold off their commercial lending activities, thereby setting up interstate depository institutions that fall outside the legal definition—and thus regulatory restrictions—of a bank.

The combination of the foregoing results in black banks being susceptible to a further shakeout. However, it is felt that the majority of the 36 black banks existing at year-end 1992 will survive until the year 2000, and that those surviving plus the new banks most likely to open will result in black banks numbering between 40 and 45. As a group, the traditional black banks—those which serve exclusively the low- and moderate-income blacks in the inner city—are at the greatest risk. They should concentrate on offering loan, deposit, and other services which are narrower than mainstream large banks but are suited to the financial needs of their communities. Even those black banks that have locations in the peripheral areas and thus serve both black and nonminority customers should attempt to restrict their products and services to fit certain market niches such as small business loans. In so doing, they can take advantage of economies of scale and reduce the number of hats which management must wear in order for the banks to be profitable. The risk here is that potential customers may be lost because of the narrower range of services and products offered by the banks.

Finally, for the larger black banks, competing in the full-service banking arena (or close to it) will be appropriate, as they take advantage of the new technologies available and the growing pool of black talent in the banking and financial institutions sector. Black-owned banks will find that strategic combinations of services connected to other financial and nonfinancial firms are the key to growth and profitability. For example, a traditional black bank can offer additional services by renting space in its branches to sellers of such financial products as insurance, stocks, and tax shelters.

Black S&Ls

The future of black S&Ls is similar to that of black banks.

Table 3
Overview of Black S&Ls

	1973	1980	1983	1989	1991	1992
Black S&Ls						
Number	43	42	36	24	18	18
Assets ($billion)	0.45	0.95	1.16	1.33	1.16	1.23
All S&Ls						
Number	4,177	4,042	3,391	2,878	2,096	1,894
Assets ($billion)	272.4	629.8	771.7	1,249.0	875.8	808.2
Black S&Ls						
% Number	1.02	1.04	1.06	0.83	0.86	0.95
% Assets	0.17	0.15	0.15	0.11	0.13	0.15

Annual Compound Rate of Change, 1973-92

Black S&Ls
- Number   -4.5%
- Assets   +5.4%

All S&Ls
- Number   -4.0%
- Assets   +5.8%

Projected for January 1, 2000

Black S&Ls
- Number   13
  (-4.5% annual change)
- Assets $1.78 billion
  (+5.4% annual change)

Sources: *Black Enterprise*, Federal Reserve *Bulletin*, various issues, 1973-1993.

Table 3 provides background and current data on black S&Ls. At year-end 1992, the assets of the 18 existing black S&Ls totaled $1.23 billion. In the 19-year period ending December 31, 1992, the assets of black S&Ls grew by 173 percent, which translates into an average annual growth rate of 5.4 percent. The number of black S&Ls decreased by 25, from 43 to 18, a 58 percent decline. In the same period, assets of all S&Ls increased by 196 percent, an average annual growth rate of 5.8 percent. The number of S&Ls in the United States declined from 4,177 to 1,894, a 55 percent decrease. If these rates of change continue for black S&Ls from 1992 to the year 2000, then there will be 13 black S&Ls, with assets of $1.78 billion on January 1, 2000.

With regard to the most recent performance, the two largest black financial institutions in the United States are savings and loan associations. At the start of 1993, Carver Federal Savings Bank of New York and Independence Federal Savings Bank of Washington, DC, held assets of $321 million and $239 million, respectively. No new black S&Ls opened, but none was closed. Overall, in 1992 the number of black S&Ls remained the same, and their assets increased by 5.9 percent. For the industry, the number of S&Ls decreased by 9.6 percent, and the total assets decreased by 7.7 percent. Thus, with regard to change in number and growth in assets in the most recent year, black S&Ls as a group compare favorably to the entire U.S. S&L industry. The surviving black S&Ls have weathered the new environment thus far, and in the cases of Carver Federal and Independence Federal, the new environment has not inhibited their growth.

The black S&Ls, at year-end 1992, were 0.95 percent of the number and held 0.15 percent of the assets of all S&Ls. These are better than the proportions for black banks but are still reflective of the small and fragile participation rates of blacks in the financial sector. Black S&Ls were a lower proportion in number and held a lower proportion of the industry assets at year-end 1992 than at year-end 1973. Thus, they have lost ground with regard to their position in the industry. At year-end 1992, the average black S&L held only $68 million in assets. While this is higher than the average for black banks, the average for the S&L industry is $426 million. On the other hand, as mentioned earlier, the two largest black S&Ls have grown substantially and are larger than any of the black banks.

Table 4
Survival Analysis of Black S&Ls

Which still exist in:

Those existing in:	existing	1978 No.	1978 %	1980 No.	1980 %	1983 No.	1983 %	1989 No.	1989 %	1993 No.	1993 %
1973	43	37	86	36	84	33	77	23	53	16	37
1978	40			39	98	34	85	24	60	16	40
1981	40					35	88	24	60	16	40
1982	37					35	95	24	65	16	43

Sources: *Black Enterprise*, various issues, 1973-1993.

Table 4 provides survival rates for the black S&Ls. These firms have survival rates which are about equal to those of black banks, when we look at the 20-year survival rate of those existing in 1973. The black S&Ls are likely surviving at a rate which is close to the average for S&Ls. The S&L industry, as shown in Table 3, has substantially declined in number over the last 20 years. Most of the decline occurred between 1983 and 1992 because of the recession and collapse of the real estate market in many major geographical areas. Black S&Ls have declined in number only slightly faster than the S&L industry, as shown in Table 3.

Much of the previous discussion concerning the potential and problems of black commercial banks can be said about black S&Ls. In essence, there is no one strategy which will serve as a panacea for success for these firms. The competitive environment of S&Ls has become more complicated, and more solutions to this new environment are available: interest rate futures to hedge interest rates, expanded asset powers, more liberalized branching powers, and the ability to pay higher rates to obtain more deposits. But with the greater problems and possible solutions, the greater demand for managerial talent exists. On balance, the black S&Ls which have survived 1982-93 intact should be able to meet the significant challenges which will undoubtedly be faced over the next decade. But it is likely that very few black S&Ls will be formed over the next 10 years. It is likely that the black S&Ls will number 15 to 20 by the year 2000.

BLACK INSURANCE COMPANIES

Background

The transition occurring in the banking and S&L industry is reflected somewhat in the insurance industry. But it is felt that the threat for survival of black insurance companies is even greater than that of the black banks and S&Ls. The threat is less a function of the economy (although economic conditions are important for these firms) but more so the nature of the insurance industry and how it is changing. The traditional formula of success for life insurance companies—selling whole life policies, which combines insurance with a low-interest-rate savings plan through the career agent—has slowly eroded. The cost inefficiency of this strategy and intensifying competition from other forms of savings have eroded the life insurance industry's position in the financial markets. Another way to look at this is to note that since 1970, the assets of life insurance companies have increased at an average annual rate slower than that of all financial industries as a whole.

Of course, the life insurance industry has attempted to respond to competitors for savings. In the 1970s, with whole life in disrepute for low interest rates paid on the savings portion of the insurance contract, new kinds of policies offering higher and variable returns were created and promoted by some insurance companies. This trend still exists. For example, universal life lets policyholders vary the amount of insurance protection and the size and timing of premium payments. The premium is unbundled, enabling buyers to see how much goes for the death benefit and how much to cash value. Moreover, the premiums are placed in separate accounts and invested in securities yielding far more than the old bonds in the company's general account. Variable life also features an unbundled premium and separate account investing; in its case, in a wider range of assets. However, unlike universal, the premium payments for variable life are fixed. Other products, such as single premium whole life, have been offered.

In addition, some insurance companies are acquiring financial services firms, increasing their offerings of comprehensive financial counseling, brokerage services, pension management, mortgages, centralized cash management, and related services. Currently 60 percent of U.S. life insurance companies provide financial counseling and mutual or money market funds. In addition to increased competition from within the field, the life insurance industry is threatened by competition from the banking and finance sector, which is currently lobbying for deregulation, allowing it to participate in insurance activities.

Competitive companies in the insurance industry must invest to retrain continually their sales forces and to upgrade their computer systems to cope with the new products being offered by other financial firms and insurance companies. For example, to sell variable life, an agent must be licensed by the National Association of Securities Dealers and must operate under the supervision of a registered broker-dealer. Group life insurance, once very profitable, has become marginally profitable as more insurance companies compete for this business and potential business clients develop self-insurance programs.

In the life/health insurance field, the increase in the number of older Americans is bringing about new developments in long-term health care, including home care plans, retirement home cooperatives, and government/insurance company partnerships. AIDS is introducing many new and difficult questions. Rising health care costs are inducing companies to expand their management programs and health maintenance organization (HMO) facilities. The industry has also been affected by rising costs of health care technology (CAT scans, X-rays, etc.), medical procedures (e.g., heart transplants), and medicines. In addition, many states are requiring companies to include alcohol and drug treatment in their coverage, further increasing insurance premiums.

In the property/casualty (PC) field, price competition, underwriting losses, increased government regulation, and rising litigation costs have trimmed the profits of many companies. The adoption of Proposition 103 by California voters, which mandates lower insurance rates, has had repercussions throughout the industry. There are many new products being introduced in the PC market, including sky-jacking insurance, satellite insurance, insurance to protect clients against the failure of securities brokers, and various types of corporate insurance. In addition, many PC companies are expanding into international markets, which are growing faster than the domestic market. This is due in part to less competition and less government regulation abroad.

Implications and Issues for Black Insurance Companies

Given this background on the industry, black insurance companies are reflective of the industry itself, but with an added characteristic of having more low- and moderate-income blacks as clients compared to other firms in the industry. Many black insurance companies tend to sell more industrial insurance than any other type of insurance. Industrial insurance is similar to whole life, but the premium is collected door-to-door by the insurance company on a weekly basis. Black insurance companies, in recent years, have been plagued by several occurrences: continued unemployment in their traditional lower- and moderate-income markets; the push by mainstream insurance to get the business of black middle- and upper-income customers; the heavy reliance on whole life insurance policies; and the outmoded operating techniques of some of the companies.

Table 5
Overview of Black Insurance Companies

	1973	1980	1983	1989	1991	1992
Black Insurance Companies						
Number	41	38	38	30	27	23
Assets ($billion)	0.52	0.70	0.77	0.80	0.74	0.72
All Life Insurance Companies						
Number	1,766	1,958	2,117	2,770	2,065	2,005
Assets ($billion)	252.1	479.2	663.0	1,300.0	1,551.2	1,664.5
Black Insurance Companies						
% Number	2.32	1.94	1.79	1.08	1.31	1.15
% Assets	0.21	0.15	0.12	0.06	0.05	0.04

Annual Compound Rate of Change, 1973-92

Black Insurance Companies
Number   -3.0%
Assets   +1.7%

All Life Insurance Companies
Number   +0.7%
Assets   +10.4%

Projected for January 1, 2000

Black Insurance Companies
Number   19
(+3.0% annual change)
Assets $1.16 billion
(-1.7% annual change)

Sources: *Black Enterprise*, Federal Reserve *Bulletin*, various issues, 1973-1993.

Table 5 provides an overview of the growth of black insurance companies over the 1973-92 period. At year-end 1992, black life insurance companies were 1.2 percent of the number and held 0.04 percent of the assets of all life insurance companies in the United States. Both percentages have declined since 1973. In 1992, two black-owned insurance companies were closed and two others reorganized as companies doing a different type of business. Thus, the number of black insurance companies declined from 27 to 23, or 14.8 percent. The assets of black insurance companies declined by 2.2 percent, from $736 million to $720 million from year-end 1991 to year-end 1992. Net income declined for black insurance companies as a group from 1991 to 1992. For the life insurance industry as a whole, assets increased by

7.3 percent, to $1.7 trillion, and the number declined by 2.9 percent, to 2,005. Thus, the black insurance companies as a group performed less favorably than the industry as a whole in 1992. Black insurers serve primarily their traditional market of moderate-income families while mainstream insurers are augmenting their product lines and attempting to reach more affluent clientele.

By targeting low- to moderate-income blacks, black insurance agents have neglected potentially more profitable clients among more financially sound black families. Many black insurance companies do not offer the variety of insurance options that the mainstream companies offer. The proportion of the premium income dollar of black insurance companies coming from industrial insurance has declined over the last decade, but it is being replaced by whole life insurance, which the industry is moving away from because of the low yields offered on the savings portion of the policy. Black insurers have also been slow to market noninsurance financial instruments that many insurers are using to attract new business, as previously mentioned.

The reason that black insurance companies specialize in low- to moderate-income blacks is because this is at least partially a "captive" market. Most major insurance companies have minimum whole life policies of $20,000, whose premiums do not enable low- and moderate-income blacks to purchase them. Some black insurers feel that they can survive if they cater to this market. This captive market enabled the black insurance companies to attain a survival rate which is higher than those of black banks and S&Ls between 1973 and 1983 as shown in tables 2, 4, and 6. But between 1983 and 1993, the survival rate for black insurance companies reflected the ongoing shakeout among these firms.

Table 6
Survival Analysis of Black Insurance Companies

Which still exist in:

Those existing in:		1978 No. %	1980 No. %	1983 No. %	1989 No. %	1993 No. %
1973	41	38 93	36 88	34 83	28 68	16 39
1978	39		37 95	35 90	28 72	17 44
1981	38			35 92	29 76	19 50
1982	38			36 95	29 76	19 50

Sources: *Black Enterprise*, various issues, 1973-1993.

The policy of concentrating on the lower-income black market has not been a growth-oriented one for black insurance companies as a group, although some have been successful. Black insurance companies must answer some difficult questions. One is whether it is desirable to continue servicing primarily the low-end market. The growth and viability of these firms have been negatively impacted by serving this market. But their clientele would have little or no insurance available if not provided by the black insurers. If it is decided that the viability of the firm requires serving a different market, the questions become what to market, to whom to market, and how to market it. The insurance industry itself is experiencing significant competition from other financial and nonfinancial firms.

The black insurance companies are plagued by increased competition in the middle- and upper-income level black population by nonminority insurance companies. In addition, the expense of technological change and bad press following high profile insolvencies of black insurance companies are problems for these firms in attracting new business. Finally, there is a 12 to 14 percent unemployment rate among blacks, which results in policy cancellations. These firms have been less profitable than the industry as a whole, but some have survived. These companies may avoid further shakeout by staying in a sheltered market. This is slow death, but perhaps a manageable one.

On the other hand, expanding into pension fund management and insuring debt obligations of business firms and local governments appear to be of growing potential for the insurance industry. In addition, the formation of joint ownership groups such as holding companies with other black companies appears to hold promise, especially given that underwriting life insurance is of growing interest to bankers and that affiliation of a life insurance company and a savings bank or S&L is now permitted under federal and most state laws. Finally, the survival of black insurance companies will be enhanced by mergers and acquisitions among these firms to increase size to a critical mass such that economies of scale and expertise can be developed in more specialized areas.

CONCLUSION

Financial deregulation, widely ranging interest rates, a stagnating economy, and greater competition among the financial industries have resulted in black financial institutions' slower relative growth than nonminority financial firms. Of course, the 1973-92 period (especially the latter half) was a significant challenge to all financial institutions, with record post-Depression failures in both the S&L and commercial banking industries. As a group, the black commercial banks and S&Ls have survived, but not without casualties. In addition, the next five years will be crucial in predicting the long-term viability of these firms, as the changes in the competitive environment in the financial markets become more pervasive and permanent.

The black insurance companies have an even more difficult road ahead. Many of them are offering services which lack mainstream competitiveness and a clientele which does not have sufficient resources to enable them to grow. The captive market which they serve has enabled many black insurers to survive thus far, but the long-term viability of exclusively serving this market is highly suspect. On the other hand, it has been difficult for black insurance companies to enter successfully the mainstream insurance market because of a lack of the capital and management talent required. How this problem is resolved will be a significant model of how black-owned businesses adapt to change.

ENDNOTES

[1] A. Brimmer, "The Black Banks: An Assessment of Performance and Prospects," *Journal of Finance* (May 1971); A. Brimmer, "Recent Developments in Black Banking," *Review of Black Political Economy* (Fall 1972).

[2] E. Irons, "Black Banking: Problems and Prospects," *Journal of Finance* (May 1971).

[3] J. Boorman, "The Recent Loan Loss Experience of New Minority-Owned Commercial Banks," Working Paper No. 74-6, Federal Deposit Insurance Corporation (June 1974); J. Boorman, "The Prospects for Minority-Owned Banks: A Comparative Analysis," *Journal of Bank Research* (June 1974).

[4] J. Boorman and M. Kwast, "The Start-Up Experience of Minority-Owned Commercial Banks: A Comparative Analysis," *Journal of Finance* (June 1974).

[5] W. Bradford, *Minority Financial Institutions: Performance, Prospects, and Role in Business Capital Formation* (Los Angeles: University of California at Los Angeles, 1988).

[6] T. Bates, "Lending Activities of Black-Owned Commercial Banks," *Review of Black Political Economy* (Winter 1976).

[7] T. Bates and W. Bradford, "An Analysis of the Portfolio Behavior of Black-Owned Commercial Banks," *Journal of Finance* (June 1980); T. Bates and W. Bradford, "Lending Activities of Black-Owned and -Controlled Savings and Loan Associations," *Review of Black Political Economy* (Winter 1978).

[8] H. Black, "Analysis of Minority Commercial Banks," *Magazine of Bank Administration* (Fall 1978).

[9] A. Doctors, A. Drebin, and E. Irons, "The Impact of Minority Banks on Communities," *Bankers Magazine* (Spring 1975).

[10] J. Ducker and T. Morton, "Black-Owned Banks: Issues and Recommendations," *California Management Review* (Fall 1974).

[11] B. Summers and J. Tucker, "Performance Characteristics of High Earning Minority Banks," *Review of Black Political Economy* (Summer 1977).

[12] M. Kwast, "New Minority-Owned Commercial Banks: A Statistical Analysis," *Journal of Bank Research* (Spring 1981).

[13] M. Gardner, "Black-Owned Commercial Banks: A New Look at Their Performance and Management," *Review of Black Political Economy* (Fall 1982).

[14] R. Clair, "The Performance of Black-Owned Banks in Their Primary Market Areas," Research Working Paper, Federal Reserve Bank of Dallas (1986).

[15] T. Wright, "Minority Banks: An Intra-Group Comparison of Performance," Unpublished Manuscript, Wright State University, 1983.

[16]J. Cole, A. Edwards, E. Hamilton, and L. Reuben, "Black Banks: A Survey and Analysis of the Literature," *Review of Black Political Economy* (Fall 1984).

[17]M. Kwast and H. Black, "An Analysis of the Behavior of Mature Black-Owned Commercial Banks," *Journal of Economics and Business* (January 1983).

[18] T. Bates and W. Bradford, "Lending Activities of Black-Owned and -Controlled Savings and Loan Associations," *Review of Black Political Economy* (Winter 1978); W. Bradford, "The Performance and Problems of Minority-Controlled Savings and Loan Associations," *Federal Home Loan Bank Board Journal* (August 1976); W. Bradford, "The Viability and Performance of Minority-Controlled Savings and Loan Associations," *Federal Home Loan Bank Board Journal* (December 1975); W. Bradford, "Minority Savings and Loan Associations: Hypothesis and Tests," *Journal of Financial and Quantitative Analysis* (September 1978); W. Bradford, "The Deposit Demand of Minority Savings and Loan Associations," *Journal of Bank Research* (Spring 1982); W. Bradford, "A Financial Analysis of Minority Savings and Loan Associations," in B. Bobo and A. Osborne, eds., *Emerging Issues in Black Economic Development* (New York: Lexington Books, Inc., 1976); and W. Bradford, A. Osborne, and L. Spellman, "The Efficiency and Profitability of Minority Controlled Savings and Loan Associations," *Journal of Money, Credit, and Banking* (February 1978).

[19]W. Bradford, "Recent Experience of Minority Savings and Loan Associations of California," *Special Publications Series Research Report,* Federal Home Loan Bank of San Francisco (February 1980).

[20]A. King, "The Performance of Minority-Controlled Savings and Loan Associations," *Federal Home Loan Bank Board Journal* (November 1980).

The Economic Base of African-American Communities: A Study of Consumption Patterns

Marcus Alexis, Ph.D.
and
Geraldine R. Henderson

INTRODUCTION

In this paper we study the African-American economic base: those aspects of economic activity which generate income and employment and have the potential for wealth accumulation. Those segments are the one-quarter trillion-dollar consumer base and the smaller $19.7 billion business base, respectively.

We begin with the consumer base in part because this is familiar territory. Alexis and Smith (1973) established benchmarks which we reexamine here. We extend the earlier analysis to the three largest U.S. cities—New York, Los Angeles, and Chicago—and find many similarities. We also find some changes which have taken place in the African-American consumer market such as a relative decline in alcohol consumption. There are some constants as well—greater African-American propensity to spend on apparel. We try to identify commercial opportunities for African-American vendors.

Next we turn to the African-American business base. We note its relatively small size and the under representation of African Americans in the U.S. business sector. Great variation in the business communities of several cities with large African-American concentrations is found. This section concludes with suggestions for African-American business growth.

AFRICAN-AMERICAN CONSUMER SPENDING

According to the 1990 Census, there are approximately 30 million (29,930,524) African Americans in the United States. Because the Census misses many African Americans, experts estimate an undercount of 2 million, making for a total of 32 million African Americans.[1] Although we agree that 30 million is a conservative estimate, it will be the one used throughout this chapter since Census data are also used for many of our analyses. As in the case of the population count, various estimates have been made of the buying power of African Americans, based on either spending or income. In terms of spending, *African-American MONITOR*, a Yankelovich Partners and Burrell

Communications Group Joint Venture, reports that African Americans spend more than $175 billion a year on goods and services.[2] According to the Bureau of Labor Statistics' (BLS) *Expenditure Survey*, African Americans spent $216 billion in 1991 (the latest year for which data are available).[3] *Black Enterprise* reports African Americans spend $223 billion annually.[4] *Target Market News*, a Chicago-based publication that tracks minority markets, reports that African-American consumers spend more than $280 billion annually.[5] In terms of income, *Minority Markets Alert* says that the African-American community has a combined annual income of $284 billion, which is equivalent to a country with the fourteenth largest gross national product (GNP) in the world.[6] The Joint Center for Political and Economic Studies says that African Americans represent over $350 billion in household income annually, which is equivalent to the ninth wealthiest country (bigger than Canada, Australia, or a combination of Israel and South Africa).[7] Such a range in the measure of spending by and income of African Americans could be due to several factors, including their underrepresentation in population surveys and scanner and diary panels.[8] We adopt the conservative estimate for spending and base our analysis on the data provided by BLS *Consumer Expenditures* reports. We next discuss the distribution of dollars spent by African Americans and comparable spending by white and other consumer counterparts.

What Do African Americans Buy?

Table 1 contains data gathered from the U.S. Department of Labor Bureau of Labor Statistics (BLS) Report 835, December 1992, entitled *Consumer Expenditures in 1991*. This is the latest report available at the time of publication. In addition, we use summary information from the "BLS Reports on Chicago Area Consumer Expenditures, 1990-91" (dated May 14, 1993).

Table 1

Item	All Consumer Units 1991[a]		White and Other		Af-Am		Af-Am % to White %[d]	Af-Am Consumer Market[e]	White and Other[f] 1970[b,c]	Af-Am	Af-Am % to White %[d]
	$	%	$	%	$	%	Ratio	($mil)	%	%	Ratio
Income before taxes (per consumer unit)	33,901		35,311		21,929		0.62[g]	236,022			
Average annual expenditures	29,614	100.0	30,794	100.0	20,091	100.0	0.65[h]	216,239	100.1	100.3	
Food	4,271	14.4	4,387	14.2	3,352	16.7	1.17	36,078	25.7	24.4	0.95
Food at home	2,651	9.0	2,676	8.7	2,448	12.2	1.40	26,348	20.7	20.0	0.97
Food away from home	1,620	5.5	1,711	5.6	904	4.5	0.81	9,730	5.1	4.4	0.86
Alcoholic beverages	297	1.0	314	1.0	159	0.8	0.78	1,711	1.7	2.3	1.35
Housing	9,252	31..2	9,570	31.1	6,692	33.3	1.07	72,026	26.7	27.0	1.01
Shelter	5,191	17.5	5,389	17.5	3,585	17.8	1.02	38,585	16.1	16.1	1.00
Owned dwellings	3,280	11.1	3,512	11.4	1,409	7.0	0.61	15,165	7.1	4.7	0.66
Rented dwellings	1,588	5.4	1,525	5.0	2,093	10.4	2.10	22,527	8.5	11.3	1.33
Other lodging	323	1.1	353	1.1	83	0.4	0.36	893	0.5	0.1	0.20
Utilities, fuels, and public services	1,990	6.7	2,005	6.5	1,866	9.3	1.43	20,084	4.8	4.6	0.96
Household operations (includes housekeeping supplies and household furnishings and equipment)	2,072	7.0	2,176	7.1	1,241	6.2	0.87	13,357	5.8	6.3	1.09
Apparel and services	1,735	5.9	1,726	5.6	1,803	9.0	1.60	19,406	8.9	12.5	1.40
Transportation	5,151	17.4	5,413	17.6	3,029	15.1	0.86	32,601	13.1	11.9	0.91
Automobiles (includes net outlay for vehicle purchases, gasoline and motor oil, and other vehicle expenses)	4,847	16.4	5,101	16.6	2,797	13.9	0.84	30,104	11.4	9.5	0.83
Other transportation (includes public transportation)	304	1.0	313	1.0	232	1.2	1.14	2,497	1.8	2.4	1.33
Health care	1,554	5.3	1,640	5.3	857	4.3	0.80	9,224	7.1	4.5	0.63
Entertainment (includes Recreation)	1,472	5.0	1,578	5.1	620	3.1	0.60	6,673	3.5	3.7	1.06
Personal care products and services	399	1.4	404	1.3	352	1.8	1.34	3,789	2.8	3.8	1.36
Reading	163	0.6	174	0.6	74	0.4	0.65	796	1.0	0.9	0.90
Education	447	1.5	476	1.5	206	1.0	0.66	2,217	0.9	0.5	0.56
Tobacco products and smoking supplies	276	0.9	282	0.9	228	1.1	1.24	2,454	1.8	2.0	1.11
Miscellaneous	860	2.9	903	2.9	517	2.6	0.88	5,564	2.2	1.4	0.64
Cash contributions	950	3.2	1,001	3.3	536	2.7	0.82	5,769			
Personal insurance and pensions	2,787	9.4	2,925	9.5	1,665	8.3	0.87	17,920			
Life and other personal insurance	356	1.2	363	1.2	302	1.5	1.28	3,250			
Pensions and Social Security	2,431	8.2	2,563	8.3	1,364	6.8	0.82	14,681			

Source: "Consumer Expenditures in 1991," U.S. Department of Labor, Bureau of Labor Statistics, Report 835, December 1992, pp. 1-17.

Source: Raymond A. Bauer and Scott M. Cunningham, "The Negro Market," *Journal of Advertising Research* (April 1970), p. 10., as cited in Alexis and Smith, 1973.

Controlled for income: $1,000-$14,999 income inclusive. Income control was obtained by "averaging averages"—i.e., the percent for each income group was weighted by 1, summed and divided by 8, the number of income categories. Income categories under $1,000 and over $15,000 were excluded from the analysis. Total sample size was 8,000 families.

Represents the ratio of African-American % spending to white and other % spending

Represents the African-American $ spending per consumer unit multiplied by the number of consumer units (10,763,000)

For Whites (controlled for income), 25.7% of the total expenditures for current consumption was spent on food.

Represents a ratio of income levels in $

Represents ratio of expenditures in $

53

The information is presented in terms of average spending for a consumer unit. BLS defines a *consumer unit* as follows:

> a single person living alone or sharing a household with others but who is financially independent; members of a household related by blood, marriage, adoption, or other legal arrangement; or two or more persons living together who share responsibility for at least two out of three major types of expenses—food, housing, and other expenses.

The shaded rows within the table represent summary categories. For instance, the food category consists of both money spent to provide food for home as well as food away from home.

Food. In terms of absolute dollars, African Americans spend less than whites on food, which is to be expected since, on the average, whites have higher incomes than African Americans. However, in relative terms, African Americans spend more from their budget on food at home than whites, a reversal from 1970. African Americans spent 20 percent of their incomes on food at home in 1970 as compared to whites, who spent 20.7 percent. On the other hand, the 12.2 percent spent by African Americans for food at home is high when compared to the 8.7 percent spent by whites. For instance, one food item heavily consumed by African Americans is soft drinks. According to Dennis Kimbro, African Americans spend more than $6 billion annually on this category alone.[9] In terms of food away from home, African-American consumers spend about the same relative amount today as they did 20 years earlier, 4.4 percent in 1970 and 4.5 percent in 1991, about 20 percent less than whites, who spent 5.6 percent of their 1991 income for food away from home. This could be due to the relative frequency with which the two groups dine out or the type of establishments at which they eat. If whites are more prone to eat at full-service restaurants versus fast food and the opposite is true for African Americans, then one would expect the average bill to be larger for the former. African Americans are estimated to spend more than $500 million per year on McDonald's fast food.[10]

Alcoholic Beverages, Tobacco Products, and Smoking Supplies. Alcoholic beverages represented 2.3 percent of African-American expenditures in 1970; this percentage fell to 0.8 percent in 1991. Although whites experienced a similar decrease in consumption, from 1.7 percent in 1970 to 1.0 percent in 1991, their decrease was not as steep as in the case of African Americans; the black-to-white ratio decreased from 1.35 to 0.78.[11] However, there is disproportionate spending on particular alcoholic beverages. For instance, African Americans consume 32 percent of all malt liquor products and 20 percent of the scotch whiskey market.[12] Although tobacco consumption as a percentage of the overall budget has decreased significantly for both African Americans and whites over the past 20 years, African-American consumption relative to whites has increased. The ratio, which was 1.11 in 1970, increased to 1.24 in 1991.

Housing. Of the $216 billion that African Americans spend, over $72 billion, or 33 percent, go toward housing, which includes shelter, utilities, and household operations. Shelter—which includes owned and rented dwellings as well as other lodging, such as hotels and motels—accounted for the bulk of housing expenses: $39 billion. African Americans spend 2.1 times the amount of money on rented dwellings as white and other Americans, up from 1.33 in 1970. On an absolute basis, in 1991, African Americans spent more ($2,093 vs. $1,525) per year.

In terms of home ownership, African Americans have made some improvement, but not nearly as much as their white counterparts. In 1970, owned dwellings accounted for 4.7 percent of the budget for African Americans as compared to 7.0 percent in 1991, an increase of 49 percent. However, for whites, owned dwellings accounted for 7.1 percent of the budget in 1970 and 11.4 percent in 1991, an increase of 60 percent. Therefore, the ratio of income spent by African Americans to whites for homes owned in 1991 was 0.61 versus 0.66 in 1970.

Spending by African Americans on other lodging, as a percentage of total expenditures, increased by 300 percent to 0.4 percent of their budgets between 1970 and 1991. This expenditure is still only a third of what white Americans spend (1.1 percent). African Americans appear to be spending more now to stay at commercial lodging establishments such as national hotel chains rather than with friends and relatives when they go out of town on business or for pleasure. This is due to both the growth of the African-American middle class and the decrease in discriminatory practices by commercial establishments.

In relative terms, African Americans are spending almost 1.5 times the amount spent by whites on utilities, fuels, and public services. This is a great change from 1970, when whites and African Americans spent about the same percent of their budget on this category.

Between 1970 and 1991, African Americans maintained a steady percentage budget allocation for household operations, which includes housekeeping supplies and household furnishings and equipment, while relative white expenditures increased by nearly a quarter. In 1970, African Americans spent 6.3 percent on this category, whereas whites spent 5.8 percent. By contrast, in 1991, African Americans spent 6.2 percent as compared to the 7.1 percent spent by whites.

Apparel and Services. In absolute dollars, African Americans spend more than whites on apparel and services each year. This is the only other category besides rented dwellings where this occurs. This finding is consistent with earlier ones reported by Alexis (1962, 1970). Over time, African Americans have demonstrated a strong propensity to spend disproportionately more for clothing than do whites. In relative terms, African Americans spend 1.6 times that of whites and others on apparel and services. This is up 14 percent over the relative comparison in 1970. Kimbro reports that African-American males between the ages of 13 and 24, who are less than 3 percent of the total U.S. population, account for 10 percent of the $12 billion athletic shoe market, purchasing more than 1 out of 5 pairs of shoes made by Nike; they also account for 55 percent of the $275 million starter jacket market.[13]

Transportation. African Americans spend more than $30 billion per year to acquire and maintain an automobile.[14] They are also twice as likely as whites to own an Audi, a BMW, or a Mercedes.[15] African Americans also spend more of their budget on other transportation, including public transportation. The latter is similar in direction and magnitude to that reported in Alexis (1959). This makes sense since African Americans are more likely to populate highly urban settings. However, in the years since 1970, expenditures on private automobiles have grown from 9.5 percent to 13.9 percent of the budget (4.6 percent increase) and expenditures on nonprivate transportation have halved, falling from 2.4 percent in 1970 to 1.2 percent in 1991.

Health Care. Health care spending for African Americans has remained fairly steady, 4.5 percent of the household budget in 1970 versus 4.3 percent in 1991. Whites, however, have decreased spending in this category, from 7.1 percent in 1970 to 5.3 percent in 1991. Expenditures for health increase with income but not proportionally; the lower white percentage in 1991 could be due to a faster relative rise in income and to greater third-party paying.

Entertainment. According to *Black Enterprise*, African Americans spend over $4 billion on consumer electronics.[16] Kimbro reports that one-fifth of all portable televisions are purchased by African Americans. Perhaps this spending pattern is related to the overall spending decrease for entertainment (including recreation) experienced by African Americans relative to whites. Whereas the percent of income spent on entertainment by African Americans fell from 3.7 percent in 1970 to 3.1 percent in 1991, the ratio of white income spent for entertainment increased from 3.5 percent in 1970 to 5.1 percent in 1991. Because of discriminatory treatment, African Americans have traditionally spent proportionately more of their entertainment dollars at home (consistent with larger expenditures on electronic equipment) or close to home. The latter could explain why African-American consumers, who make up only 12 percent of the population, are estimated to buy 50 percent of the movie tickets.[17]

Personal Care Products and Services. In relative terms, African Americans spend more on personal care products and services: one-third more than whites. However, both groups have experienced a significant decline in this category over the past 20 years. For African Americans, spending has decreased 53 percent, from 3.8 percent of their overall budget to 1.8 percent. African-American consumers reportedly buy 36 percent of all hair care conditioners and 25 to 35 percent of all detergent and toothpaste. African-

American females, who equal approximately 6 percent of the total U.S. population, purchase 15 percent of the $4 billion cosmetics industry, or $600 million, and spend 26 percent more on perfume than any other group of females.[18]

Education and Reading. The good news is that the percent of income spent on education by African Americans has increased by 100 percent over the past 20 years. The bad news is that this relative spending increase still represents only two-thirds of the percentage spent by whites and others. Reading has decreased for all Americans over the past 20 years. The percent of income spent for reading items has declined by 56 percent for African Americans and 40 percent for whites and others since 1970, perhaps reflecting the competition from television (network and cable) and the explosive growth in the movie video business.

Personal Insurance and Pensions. Although blacks spend slightly less than whites on life insurance and other personal insurance, their spending is almost a third higher than whites when one controls for level of income. The predisposition of African Americans to spend a higher proportion of their income for insurance helps to explain why black-owned insurance firms such as Golden State and North Carolina Mutual have been so successful. On the other hand, there are not many firms in the property and casualty business, due in part to the underrepresentation of African Americans in business in general (discussed later in this paper) and perhaps to the more risky character of the property and casualty insurance business, in particular.

Cash Contributions and Savings. Cash contributions reflect the philanthropic allocation of households. African Americans allocate less in cash contributions on an absolute and relative basis. This is to be expected, given the lower incomes of blacks; they have less discretionary income. It is not possible to comment on savings because of the lack of information on taxes. There is a difference between average income before taxes and total expenditures; however, we are not able to determine how much of the difference is taxes and how much is savings.

Comparison by Income Level

African Americans had higher relative expenditures in 1991 for food (1.17), housing (1.07), rented dwellings (2.10), utilities, fuels, and public services (1.43), apparel and services (1.60), personal care products and services (1.34), tobacco products and smoking supplies (1.24), and life and other personal insurance (1.28) (ratios of African-American to white percentage of income spent are found in column 7 of Table 1). The two largest categories, food and housing, account for 45 percent of white budgets and 50 percent of African-American budgets. The relatively high expenditures on these items by African Americans mean proportionately less is available for those items representing the other 50 percent. The only category in which

African Americans had higher relative spending in 1991 versus 1970 is utilities, fuels, and public services. The reason for this change is not clear; it could be due to changes in relative prices being higher in areas with larger concentrations of African Americans or to changes in responsibilities for paying utilities, particularly after the energy price increases which began with the oil import embargo of 1973. We cannot say with confidence if these or other factors are at work.

The largest change in relative spending between 1970 and 1991 occurred in rented dwellings, increasing from 1.33 in 1970 to 2.1 in 1991. African Americans have a lower home ownership rate than whites, so their relative spending for rented dwellings has been higher since at least 1970. The magnitude of the increase signals that rental costs increased faster for African Americans than for whites. Home-owning African Americans had a slight decrease in relative expenditures, from 0.66 in 1970 to 0.61 in 1991. The sharp increase in the relative African-American expenditures for rented dwellings reflects the increased difficulty experienced by blacks in becoming home buyers as housing prices soared, coupled with the high mortgage rates of the 1970s and 1980s.

An area in which African Americans maintained a large relative spending ratio was personal care products and services, which remained virtually flat between 1970 (1.36) and 1991 (1.34). The relatively high spending on personal care products and services specifically designed for African Americans has been an important part of the enormous success of beauty care firms owned by African Americans such as Fashion Fair Cosmetics, Johnson Products, and Soft Sheen.

The largest change in relative spending between 1970 and 1991, in those categories where the ratio of African American to white spending is less than 1.0, is in alcoholic beverages, where the ratio fell from 1.35 in 1970 to 0.78 in 1991, a very welcome change. Relative entertainment spending also declined, from 1.06 in 1970 to 0.60 in 1991, reflecting the changes previously discussed. Relative spending on education edged up for African Americans, from 0.56 in 1970 to 0.66 in 1991, another favorable change. But relative spending on reading shrank 0.25 points, from 0.90 in 1970 to 0.65 in 1991— an unfavorable change.

Consumer Spending in Three Selected Areas

There are few changes of note in relative spending nationally by African Americans between 1970 and 1991. What stands out is the relative stability (at least directionally) of the 1970 findings reported in Alexis and Smith (1973). The Chicago, New York, and Los Angeles spending data which follow display a striking similarity across the cities as well. Tables 2 through 4 provide estimated categorical spending for African Americans and whites for each of these three metropolitan statistical areas (MSAs).[19]

Table 2

Item	All Consumer Units		White and Other[c]		Af-Am[c]		Af-Am % to White %[d]	Af-Am Consumer Market[e]
	%[a]	Chi-U.S. Ratio[b]	$	%	$	%	Ratio	($mil)
Income before taxes			35,448		22,234		0.63[f]	
Average annual expenditures	100.0		30,914	100.0	20,371	100.0	0.66[g]	9,681
Food	15.7	1.0608	4,648	15.0	3,490	17.1	1.14	1,658
Food at home	8.9	1.0000	2,676	8.7	2,448	12.0	1.39	1,163
Food away from home	6.8	1.1525	1,972	6.4	1,042	5.1	0.80	495
Alcoholic beverages	1.2	1.2000	377	1.2	191	0.9	0.77	91
Housing	32.4	1.0452	10,027	32.4	6,905	33.9	1.05	3,281
Shelter	19.6	1.1329	6,091	19.7	3,981	19.5	0.99	1,892
Owned dwellings	12.7	1.1759	4,130	13.4	1,657	8.1	0.61	787
Rented dwellings	5.8	1.0741	1,638	5.3	2,248	11.0	2.08	1,068
Other lodging	1.1	0.9167	324	1.0	76	0.4	0.36	36
Utilities, fuels, and public services	6.3	0.9403	1,885	6.1	1,755	8.6	1.41	834
Household operations (includes Housekeeping supplies and Household furnishings and equipment)	6.5	0.9420	2,050	6.6	1,169	5.7	0.87	556
Apparel and services	7.1	1.2241	2,113	6.8	2,207	10.8	1.59	1,049
Transportation	15.2	0.8588	4,680	15.1	2,663	13.1	0.86	1,265
Automobiles (includes net outlay for vehicle purchases, gasoline and motor oil, and other vehicle expenses)	13.6	0.8193	4,179	13.5	2,292	11.2	0.83	1,089
Other transportation (includes public transportation)	1.6	1.6000	501	1.6	371	1.8	1.12	176
Health care	4.4	0.8462	1,388	4.5	725	3.6	0.79	345
Entertainment(includes Recreation)	5.0	1.0000	1,578	5.1	620	3.0	0.60	295
Personal care products and services	1.4	1.0769	435	1.4	379	1.9	1.32	180
Reading	0.6	1.2000	209	0.7	89	0.4	0.65	42
Education	1.3	0.8667	413	1.3	179	0.9	0.66	85
Tobacco products and smoking supplies	1.2	1.3333	376	1.2	304	1.5	1.23	144
Miscellaneous	3.2	1.1034	996	3.2	570	2.8	0.87	271
Cash contributions	2.9	0.9667	968	3.1	518	2.5	0.81	246
Personal insurance and pensions	8.6	0.9247	2,707	8.8	1,531	7.5	0.86	728
Life and other personal insurance	1.0	0.8333	303	1.0	252	1.2	1.26	120
Pensions and Social Security	7.6	0.9383	2,405	7.8	1,280	6.3	0.81	608

Chicago Metropolitan Statistical Area — 1991

a	Source: "Consumer Expenditures in 1991," U.S. Department of Labor, Bureau of Labor Statistics, Report 835, December 1992, pp.1-17.
b	Chi-U.S. Ratio represents the ratio of spending % for Chicago consumer units to total U.S. spending %.
c	Represents the Chicago-U.S. ratio multiplied by the comparable U.S. spending level
d	Represents the ratio of African-American % spending to White and Other % spending
e	Represents the African-American $ spending per consumer unit multiplied by the number of consumer units (475,227)
f	Represents a ratio of income levels in $
g	Represents ratio of expenditures in $

Table 3

Item	All Consumer Units		White and Other[c]		Af-Am[c]		Af-Am % to White %[d]	Af-Am Consumer Market[e]
	%[a]	NYC-U.S. Ratio[b]	$	%	$	%	Ratio	($mil)
Income before taxes			35,317		22,441		0.64[f]	
Average annual expenditures	100.0		30,799	100.0	20,560	100.0	0.67[g]	17,828
Food	14.9	1.0068	4,405	14.3	3,245	15.8	1.10	2,814
Food at home	7.9	0.8876	2,375	7.7	2,173	10.6	1.37	1,884
Food away from home	7.0	1.1864	2,030	6.6	1,073	5.2	0.79	930
Alcoholic beverages	1.2	1.2000	377	1.2	191	0.9	0.76	165
Housing	35.0	1.1290	10,805	35.1	7,687	37.4	1.07	6,665
Shelter	22.5	1.3006	6,936	22.5	4,779	23.2	1.03	4,144
Owned dwellings	13.1	1.2130	4,260	13.8	1,709	8.3	0.60	1,482
Rented dwellings	7.6	1.4074	2,146	7.0	2,946	14.3	2.06	2,554
Other lodging	1.8	1.5000	530	1.7	125	0.6	0.35	108
Utilities, fuels, and public services	6.5	0.9701	1,945	6.3	1,810	8.8	1.39	1,570
Household operations (includes Housekeeping supplies and Household furnishings and equipment)	6.1	0.8841	1,924	6.2	1,097	5.3	0.85	951
Apparel and services	6.8	1.1724	2,024	6.6	2,114	10.3	1.56	1,833
Transportation	14.1	0.7966	4,346	14.1	2,528	12.3	0.87	2,192
Automobiles (includes net outlay for vehicle purchases, gasoline and motor oil, and other vehicle expenses)	11.7	0.7048	3,595	11.7	1,971	9.6	0.82	1,709
Other transportation (includes public transportation)	2.4	2.4000	751	2.4	557	2.7	1.11	483
Health care	4.4	0.8462	1,388	4.5	725	3.5	0.78	629
Entertainment(includes Recreation)	4.5	0.9000	1,420	4.6	558	2.7	0.59	484
Personal care products and services	1.4	1.0769	435	1.4	379	1.8	1.31	329
Reading	0.5	1.0000	174	0.6	74	0.4	0.64	64
Education	1.7	1.1333	539	1.8	233	1.1	0.65	202
Tobacco products and smoking supplies	0.9	1.0000	282	0.9	228	1.1	1.21	198
Miscellaneous	2.8	0.9655	872	2.8	499	2.4	0.86	433
Cash contributions	2.7	0.9000	901	2.9	482	2.3	0.80	418
Personal insurance and pensions	9.0	0.9677	2,831	9.2	1,615	7.9	0.85	1,401
Life and other personal insurance	1.2	1.0000	363	1.2	302	1.5	1.25	262
Pensions and Social Security	7.8	0.9630	2,468	8.0	1,313	6.4	0.80	1,139

a   Source: "Consumer Expenditures in 1991," U.S. Department of Labor, Bureau of Labor Statistics, Report 835, December 1992, pp.1-17.

b   NYC-U.S. Ratio represents the ratio of spending % for NYC consumer units to total U.S. spending %.

c   Represents the NYC-U.S. ratio multiplied by the comparable U.S. spending level

d   Represents the ratio of African-American % spending to White and Other % spending

e   Represents the African-American $ spending per consumer unit multiplied by the number of consumer units (867,145)

f   Represents a ratio of income levels in $

g   Represents ratio of expenditures in $

Table 4

	Los Angeles Metropolitan Statistical Area							
	1991							
Item	All Consumer Units		White and Other[c]		Af-Am[c]		Af-Am % to White %[d]	Af-Am Consumer Market[e]
	%[a]	L.A.-U.S. Ratio[b]	$	%	$	%	Ratio	($mil)
Income before taxes			35,434		22,365		0.63[f]	
Average annual expenditures	100.0		30,901	100.0	20,491	100.0	0.66[g]	7,248
Food	14.2	0.9595	4,209	13.6	3,211	15.7	1.15	1,136
Food at home	8.5	0.9551	2,556	8.3	2,338	11.4	1.38	827
Food away from home	5.7	0.9661	1,653	5.3	873	4.3	0.80	309
Alcoholic beverages	1.0	1.0000	314	1.0	159	0.8	0.76	56
Housing	36.3	1.1710	11,249	36.4	7,908	38.6	1.06	2,797
Shelter	22.4	1.2948	6,919	22.4	4,867	23.8	1.06	1,721
Owned dwellings	13.6	1.2593	4,423	14.3	1,774	8.7	0.61	628
Rented dwellings	7.8	1.4444	2,203	7.1	3,023	14.8	2.07	1,069
Other lodging	1.0	0.8333	294	1.0	69	0.3	0.35	24
Utilities, fuels, and public services	5.3	0.7910	1,586	5.1	1,476	7.2	1.40	522
Household operations (includes Housekeeping supplies and Household furnishings and equipment)	8.7	1.2609	2,744	8.9	1,565	7.6	0.86	553
Apparel and services	6.9	1.1897	2,053	6.6	2,145	10.5	1.58	759
Transportation	15.1	0.8531	4,676	15.1	2,618	12.8	0.84	926
Automobiles (includes net outlay for vehicle purchases, gasoline and motor oil, and other vehicle expenses)	14.3	0.8614	4,394	14.2	2,409	11.8	0.83	852
Other transportation (includes public transportation)	0.9	0.9000	282	0.9	209	1.0	1.12	74
Health care	4.2	0.8077	1,325	4.3	692	3.4	0.79	245
Entertainment(includes Recreation)	5.3	1.0600	1,673	5.4	657	3.2	0.59	232
Personal care products and services	1.5	1.1538	466	1.5	406	2.0	1.31	144
Reading	0.4	0.8000	139	0.5	59	0.3	0.64	21
Education	1.5	1.0000	476	1.5	206	1.0	0.65	73
Tobacco products and smoking supplies	0.5	0.5556	157	0.5	127	0.6	1.22	45
Miscellaneous	2.3	0.7931	716	2.3	410	2.0	0.86	145
Cash contributions	2.3	0.7667	767	2.5	411	2.0	0.81	145
Personal insurance and pensions	8.5	0.9140	2,681	8.7	1,481	7.2	0.83	524
Life and other personal insurance	0.6	0.5000	182	0.6	151	0.7	1.25	53
Pensions and Social Security	7.9	0.9753	2,500	8.1	1,330	6.5	0.80	471

a   Source: "Consumer Expenditures in 1991," U.S. Department of Labor, Bureau of Labor Statistics, Report 835, December 1992, pp.1-17.

b   LA-U.S. Ratio represents the ratio of spending % for LA consumer units to total U.S. spending %.

c   Represents the LA-U.S. ratio multiplied by the comparable U.S. spending level

d   Represents the ratio of African-American % spending to White and Other % spending

e   Represents the African-American $ spending per consumer unit multiplied by the number of consumer units (353,716)

f   Represents a ratio of income levels in $

g   Represents ratio of expenditures in $

Figure 1

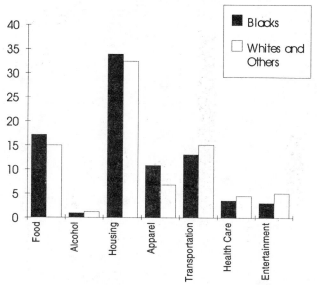

Chicago 1991
Relative Consumer Expenditures (%)

Figure 2

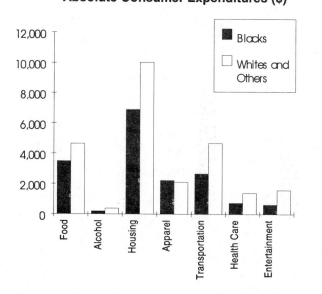

Chicago 1991
Absolute Consumer Expenditures ($)

Figure 3

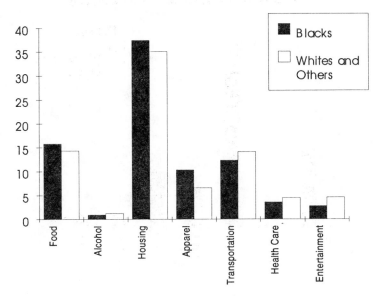

**New York City 1991
Relative Consumer Expenditures (%)**

Figure 4

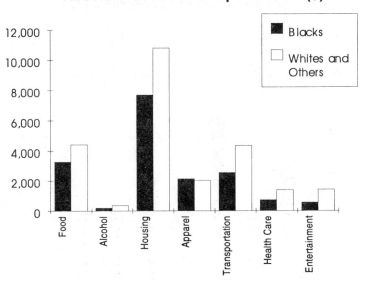

**New York City 1991
Absolute Consumer Expenditures ($)**

Figure 5

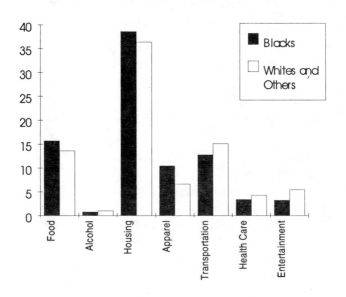

**Los Angeles 1991
Relative Consumer Expenditures (%)**

Figure 6

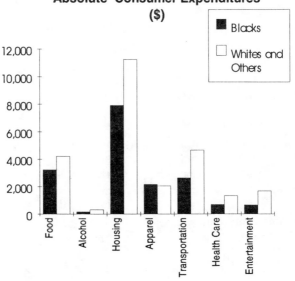

**Los Angeles 1991
Absolute Consumer Expenditures
($)**

The three chosen MSAs—Chicago, New York, and Los Angeles—have relative spending percentages similar to those for the United States discussed earlier.[20] Figures 1, 3, and 5 depict differences in relative spending for the three MSAs. Figures 2, 4, and 6 provide the same information on the absolute spending levels.

When the diagrams depicting the relative spending by African Americans and whites are compared (Figures 1, 3, and 5) to those portraying absolute expenditures by these two groups in those cities (Figures 2, 4, and 6), the striking similarity of the spending profiles across cities virtually jumps out at you. There is apparently a consistent urban spending profile for both African Americans and whites; this profile is quite similar to the national data discussed earlier.

In these three cities, African Americans spend proportionately more for apparel than whites. African Americans also spend a larger absolute amount per household on apparel, even though their annual incomes are lower. This persistent tendency in national and city data highlights a significant difference in black and white spending behavior and identifies an area of potential African-American entrepreneurial opportunity since the deficiency in African-American incomes (compared to whites) is not matched by lower spending levels. The propensity of blacks to spend more on apparel at comparable incomes was first noted by Alexis (1959). Explanations for the earlier findings included the supposed need of affluent black women to buy clothing at better stores (and one assumes at higher prices) because they were not permitted to try on clothing in many southern and border-city stores. To assure proper sizing, these women shopped and purchased their garments at select stores where they knew how size related to fit. Another explanation advanced then was that African Americans acquired a taste for more expensive attire because of the concentration in domestic employment in affluent white homes. The first explanation, even if true, does not hold today. The second explanation is also suspect because of the substantial decline in domestic employment. Thus, one has to find another explanation.

A tenable hypothesis is that African Americans are denied many symbols of success and status and use outwardly visible ways (quality fashionable clothing) to compensate. (For example, no African-American male in Cook County, which includes Chicago, was permitted to join a golf-playing country club until last year, despite the large number who sought such membership and could afford it.) The wearing of fashionable, high-quality clothing is said to confer status in the African-American community. This hypothesis has not been tested, but it is at least consistent with the persisting propensity of African Americans to outspend whites for apparel. Shopping rates second only to television viewing as a favorite African-American pastime (see Table 5).

Table 5

African Americans' second favorite pastime is shopping:

Watch television	66%
Go shopping	50%
Read	48%
Party	39%
Cook	37%

Source: Market Segment Research Inc.,
The 1993 MSR Minority Market Report:
A Portrait of The New America, Florida, as cited in Reynolds (1993).

Blacks are also twice as likely as whites to be interested in low prices and are half again as much inclined to buy a known or trusted brand name (see Table 8). This latter tendency is not inconsistent with the first explanation given for why affluent African-American women patronized better stores.

Advertising to African Americans

In 1992, Madison Avenue spent $785 million trying to reach the 32 million African-American shoppers.[21] The impact of this advertising is difficult to estimate because, although African Americans pay more attention to advertising than whites do,[22] African Americans are often turned off by the advertising they encounter. In a survey reported in *Black Enterprise* magazine, 60 percent of African Americans reported being alienated by most advertisers because they felt that television commercials and print ads are "designed for whites."[23] The Burrell/Yankelovich study which made these findings based them on one-hour, in-home interviews with 1,000 blacks. African Americans are more media-involved than the general public, partly because blacks watch television more. Despite the finding that 60 percent of African Americans think ads are designed for whites, blacks as a group rate media higher than whites do.[24] African Americans are more prone than whites to watch cable movie channels; whites are more likely to watch CNN and The Discovery Channel (see Table 6).[25]

Table 6

Cable Channels Currently Watched, African Americans vs. Others

	Af-Am	Others
Black Entertainment Television (BET)	69%	7%
Home Box Office (HBO)	51%	31%
Cable News Network (CNN)	50%	60%
Showtime	34%	14%
MTV-Music Television	34%	29%
The Discovery Channel	31%	44%
The Movie Channel	28%	14%

Source: Burrell/Yankelovich *African American MONITOR* as cited in *Minority Markets Alert*, May 1993.

Patronage Factors Which Impact Purchasing Decisions

Tables 7, 8, and 9 present information on factors of interest and influence for African Americans when making shopping/buying decisions.

Contrary to popular opinion, rational and prudent motives for buying rank

Table 7

Issues African Americans consider when deciding where to shop.

Treats African-Americans the same as other people	61%
Has African-American salespeople	43%
Other African-Americans shop there	31%
Is owned by African-Americans	26%

Source: Burrell/Yankelovich *African-American MONITOR* as cited in Reynolds (1993).

Table 8

WHY AFRICAN AMERICANS BUY WHAT THEY BUY[a]

	Total U.S.	African-American population						
		total	sex		age			
			male	female	14 to 20	21 to 29	30 to 49	50 and older
long lasting	70 %	82%	79%	85%	81%	80%	82%	84%
reliable	75	74	73	75	65	67	78	78
low price	38	67	69	64	65	60	69	70
easy to use	41	62	56	67	63	68	60	62
easy to maintain	47	55	59	51	47	46	63	52
known or trusted brand name	34	54	56	52	58	53	52	53
simple to purchase	30	41	46	36	57	27	39	28
many features	17	36	37	36	57	27	39	28
latest style	18	34	39	30	49	33	35	25
made in U.S.	na	33	31	36	24	30	33	43

Source: Burrell/Yankelovich African-American MONITOR as cited in *The Numbers News*, August 1993.

[a] percent of total U.S. population and percent of African-American population whose purchase decisions are strongly influenced by selected factors, by sex and age, 1992.

Table 9

WHAT'S IMPORTANT IN DECIDING WHERE TO SHOP, BASED ON A NATIONWIDE SURVEY

	African-Americans	Others
	14 and older	16 and older
Has reasonable prices	78%	77%
Carries quality merchandise	66%	73%
Can always find what I want	69%	58%
Has knowledgeable salespeople	66%	51%
Has lots of sale items in stock	57%	47%
Makes it quick and easy to shop	49%	62%

Source: Burrell/Yankelovich *African-American MONITOR* as cited in Poole (1993).

high with African-American consumers as is evident in the top six reasons cited in Table 8. Over half of the African-American sample (more than in the white sample) was strongly influenced by these factors. Only one in four black shoppers said African-American ownership of a business was an important factor in deciding where to shop, according to a study by the Burrell/Yankelovich *African-American MONITOR* (see Table 7).[26] This confirms a view held by many that there is not much vendor loyalty based on race. Comparison data for other races and ethnic groups are not available. It would be more informative to find out how much loyalty other groups express for vendors from their own group. Another clue to factors which influence African-American buying behavior is the relative importance given to knowledgeable salespeople; it is as important as reasonable prices.[27]

Prices emerge as the dominant factor in African-American buying decisions. When it comes to deciding where to shop, African Americans place a strong emphasis on reasonable prices as an important factor—78 percent of African Americans compared to 77 percent of the total population (see Table 9). A related study reveals that reasonable prices are slightly more important to black women than to black men, 80 percent compared with 77 percent.[28] The importance of reasonableness of prices, together with the importance of knowledgeable sales people and absence of strong racial influences, means that for African-American retailers to be successful, they cannot rely on race alone; they must be competitive.

Although Table 9 seems to indicate that whites are just as price-conscious as blacks when determining where to shop, it must be noted that the information presented is not controlled for income. If money is scarce, one would expect people to be more careful in their buying. It is rational that people with fewer assets are more cautious in spending. If African Americans earn less money, the value of time is less; therefore, they will have more time relative to dollars and will be willing to give up more time to shop. In other words, given the income per household and the available resources of blacks relative to nonblacks, African Americans can expend more time and effort shopping since their opportunity cost is lower. Hence, the data presented in Table 5 which indicate that shopping is the second favorite pastime of African Americans is put into a new light.

Brand vs. Nonbrand Products

"African Americans are quality conscious and status conscious," notes Byron Lewis, chairman and CEO of UniWorld Group, Inc., a New York City advertising firm which ranks 14th on the 1993 *Black Enterprise* 100 Industrial/Service List. "Not only do we prefer to buy top-shelf, we tend to use 'the purchase' as one way of gaining equality in the marketplace—whether we can afford it or not."[29] Younger African Americans are more willing than other age groups to buy a brand they believe is the "best," even if the brand is not known to most people. This strongly suggests that if status is associated with purchases, then that status could be conferred by a small in-group. This age group also likes to be among the first to try new products. Sixty-one percent say they like to try new products before others do, compared with just 32 percent of African Americans aged 21 to 29, 34 percent of those aged 30 to 49, and 26 percent of those aged 50 and older. For the population as a whole, 33 percent like to be the first with new products.[30] African Americans are brand loyal at all age levels. Over half (56 percent) of young African Americans (21-29) and 73 percent of African Americans 50 and over say it is difficult to get them to change brands once they find a brand they like.[31] For sellers this means once these buyers accept a product, they will be repeat purchasers and hence loyal customers.

Treatment of Black Consumers

A recent nationwide lifestyle survey of more than 1,000 African-American consumers over the age of 14 indicates that fair treatment is the most important factor of all. A crucial test of how much progress has been made by African Americans is how much they get for their money. Do they obtain the same values for their dollars in terms of quality, service, and convenience of outlets? If they do not, then the approximate 30 percent by which their incomes fall below incomes of other Americans understates how less well off they are. Unfortunately, what evidence exists is not positive. Fifty-nine percent of the African Americans who consult sales staff report being disrespected by them, and four-fifths of those who say they were disrespected (48 out of 59) indicate that reporting the slight is a waste of time.[32]

One of the more careful studies of how African Americans fare in the marketplace, which appeared in a 1991 *Harvard Law Review* article, examined how blacks and whites come out in the market for cars. The study revealed that, when test shoppers negotiated prices on 180 cars in 90 showrooms in the Chicago area, the final offer for African-American men was double the markup for white men, and the work-up for African-American women was three times the markup for white men. Thus, blacks routinely pay more for cars than do whites.[33]

The Home Mortgage Disclosure Act (HMDA) data for 1990 and 1991, published by the Federal Reserve, reveal disproportionately high rejection rates for African Americans of all income levels and in all types of neighborhoods (classified by income and racial composition). The highest-income African Americans are less likely to secure mortgage financing or refinancing than the lowest-income whites. When data are adjusted for credit history, loan-to-value ratio, and other financing criteria, two-thirds of the difference—which a Boston Federal Reserve study classifies as discrimination—persist. Inability to finance home purchases must certainly depreciate the value of income to African-American households. What the HMDA data reveal are common to the experiences of many African Americans.[34]

BLACK-OWNED BUSINESSES

African Americans are underrepresented as business owners. Additionally, most of the firms owned by African Americans are small; only TLC Beatrice, whose business is European-based, tops $1 billion in annual sales. How African Americans fare in business is important for several reasons: (1) private businesses, particularly small- and medium-sized businesses, are responsible for most of the employment growth of the past decade; (2) business ownership is an important source of wealth accumulation; (3) business contributes to social and civic needs of communities—Little League, Community Chest/Crusade of Mercy, scholarships, etc.; and (4) business owners occupy a highly visible place in the social and leadership structure of communities. For years, African Americans have been excluded from many lucrative business fields—public contracting, interstate transportation, and corporate and business finance. The Small Business Administration's 8(a) program, which qualifies minority-owned firms for preferential treatment, is an attempt to redress the underrepresentation of African Americans. But legal setbacks such as the U.S. Supreme Court's *City of Richmond* decision have undone some public programs designed to assist African-American entrepreneurs. As Maxima Corporation Chairman Joshua Smith stated in a recent keynote address to the National Black MBA Association, minority business enterprises (MBEs) represent about 10 percent of the number of businesses, but only 4 percent of the revenues, and "minority" and "black" are going in different directions.[35]

In 1987, 35 percent of the number of MBEs were black-owned; they accounted for 25 percent of the revenues. However, by the year 2000, the projection is that 18 percent of the number of MBEs will be black-owned, accounting for only 12 percent of the receipts. Also, over 90 percent of black-owned businesses have no paid employees as compared to 82 percent for all firms.

We have studied the African-American business community in the United States and found it to be (1) geographically diverse and (2) highly varied by industry sector. Table 10 presents data for the ten metropolitan statistical areas (MSAs) with the highest number of African-American firms and sales as well as population information for the MSAs and the major city within the MSAs. Sales per firm range from a low of $28,659 in Houston to $63,315 in Atlanta. The percentage of sales attributed to the cities within the MSAs ranges from 39 in Atlanta to 86 in New York. With the exception of Chicago, the tendency is that the higher the percent sales in the city, the lower the average sale per firm. The obvious implication is that African-American firms that have found customers outside the city get larger. Accomplishing

Table 10

Geographic Distribution of African-American Owned Firms

MSA/City	MSA Rank[a]	# of Af-Am Firms In MSA	Sales ($1000) In MSA	Size of Af-Am Population In MSA	Average Sales per firm ($)	# of Af-Ams In the pop. per Af-Am-Owned Firm	City Rank[a]	# of Af-Am Firms In City	Sales ($1000) In City	Size of Af-Am Population In City	% of Af-Ams In MSA who live In the City	% of Af-Am-Owned Firms In MSA located In the City	% of the Sales of Af-Am-Owned Firms In MSA due to firms In the City
Total U.S.	na	424,165	19,762,876	29,930,524	46,592	71	na	na	na	na	na	na	na
NYC	1	28,063	1,234,910	2,254,576	44,005	80	1	25,256	1,065,032	2,107,137	93	90	86
LA	2	23,932	1,300,336	990,406	54,335	41	2	11,607	721,958	485,949	49	48	56
DC	3	23,046	951,945	1,042,210	41,306	45	5	8,275	411,941	399,751	38	36	43
Chicago	4	15,374	908,500	1,330,636	59,093	87	3	11,156	670,369	1,086,389	82	73	74
Houston	5	12,989	372,256	610,377	28,659	47	4	10,025	288,897	457,574	75	77	78
Atlanta	6	11,804	747,367	735,477	63,315	62	na	3,869	290,702	264,213	36	33	39
Philadelphia	7	10,249	612,995	930,017	59,810	91	8	5,540	255,907	632,430	68	54	42
Detroit	8	9,852	514,324	942,450	52,205	96	6	7,116	258,375	778,456	83	72	50
Baltimore	9	8,593	331,493	615,218	38,577	72	9	5,044	165,350	435,619	71	59	50
Dallas	10	7,857	234,823	410,458	29,887	52	7	5,633	157,962	297,018	72	72	67
Memphis	na	4,937	190,108	399,325	38,507	81	10	4,225	147,861	334,981	84	86	78
Average (of the above MSAs)	na	14,245	672,642	932,832	46,336	69	na	8,886	403,123	661,774	68	64	60

Source: 1987 Economic Censuses, Survey of Minority-Owned Business Enterprises

a   rank based on number of African-American firms located within MSA or city

Table 11

Distribution by Industry of African-American-Owned Firms for Selected Metropolitan Statistical Areas

Industry	All Firms in U.S.			African-American-Owned Firms in U.S.			African-American-Owned Firms in Chicago			African-American-Owned Firms in NYC			African-American-Owned Firms in LA		
	# of Firms	Sales ($mil)	Sales per Firm	# of Firms	Sales ($1,000)	Sales per Firm	# of Firms	Sales	Sales per Firm	# of Firms	Sales	Sales per Firm	# of Firms	Sales	Sales per Firm
All Industries	13,695,480	1,994,808	145,654	424,165	19,762,876	46,592	15,374	908,500	59,093	28,063	1,234,910	44,005	23,932	1,300,336	54,335
Agriculture/Mining	478,042	35,669	74,615	7,638	270,813	35,456	66	5,795	87,803	67	2,825	42,164	253	8,091	31,980
Construction	1,651,102	232,372	140,738	36,763	2,174,399	59,146	802	47,449	59,163	1,623	139,324	85,843	1228	60,861	49,561
Manufacturing	432,971	226,824	523,878	8,004	1,023,104	127,824	206	45,974	223,175	326	54,910	168,436	400	123,620	309,050
Transportation/Public Utilities	592,751	76,355	128,815	36,958	1,573,342	42,571	1,612	72,718	45,110	3,834	112,303	29,291	1364	66,074	48,441
Wholesale	439,200	298,264	679,107	5,519	1,327,479	240,529	248	45,036	181,597	345	59,871	173,539	397	55,675	140,239
Retail	2,241,494	544,768	243,038	66,229	5,889,654	88,929	2,654	358,927	135,240	2,861	256,903	89,795	3511	241,540	68,795
Finance/Insurance/Real Estate	1,227,215	123,710	100,805	26,989	804,252	29,799	1,267	41,067	32,413	1,313	76,534	58,289	2266	80,792	35,654
Services	5,937,671	417,105	70,247	209,547	6,120,084	29,206	7,562	268,912	35,561	15,177	480,169	31,638	12764	607,562	47,600
Industries not classified	695,034	39,741	57,178	26,518	579,749	21,862	957	22,622	23,638	2,517	52,071	20,688	1749	56,121	32,087

this is not as difficult as might first appear. Note that for the United States as a whole and for Chicago, New York, and Los Angeles (Table 11), firms in the services industry are more than half the total. Many of these services firms offer business services which are not dependent on a large African-American population base.

Table 10 ranks MSAs by the number of firms. Table 12 is an alternative ranking, based on the number of *Black Enterprise* (BE) 100 industrial firms in the MSA.

Figures 7 through 16 show the number of U.S. firms and sales by industry, the number of African-American firms nationwide and sales by industry (see also Table 13), and the respective information for African-American firms in Chicago, New York, and Los Angeles. There is a close match between the distribution of African-American firms in Chicago and African-American firms throughout the United States.

The patterns in New York and Los Angeles are very different. For the United States as a whole, for African-American firms nationally, and for African-American firms in Chicago, New York, and Los Angeles, retailing services dominate in terms of both number of firms and revenues.

Retailing accounts for 30 percent of African-American firms nationally, 39 percent in Chicago, 21 percent in New York City, and 19 percent in Los Angeles. These sales are highly vulnerable because of the weak attachments of African-American purchasers to African-American sellers. In New York, Chicago, and Los Angeles, Middle Easterners and Asians have entered the markets and won marketshare because they have been able to provide merchandise at quality/price combination levels superior to others. In many cases, these venturesome retailers have replaced Europeans who formerly were the retailers. Tensions similar to those that gripped inner cities in the 1960s have flared recently in Brooklyn and in Central Los Angeles. African-American retailers with good offerings and who respect their customers and are part of the civic and social life stand a good chance of success in these areas.

Figure 7

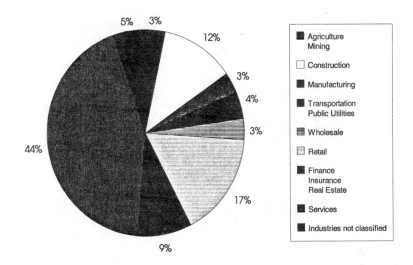

Distribution of All U.S. Firms by Industry
by Number of Firms

5% 3%
12%
3%
4%
3%
44%
17%
9%

Legend:
- Agriculture Mining
- Construction
- Manufacturing
- Transportation Public Utilities
- Wholesale
- Retail
- Finance Insurance Real Estate
- Services
- Industries not classified

Figure 8

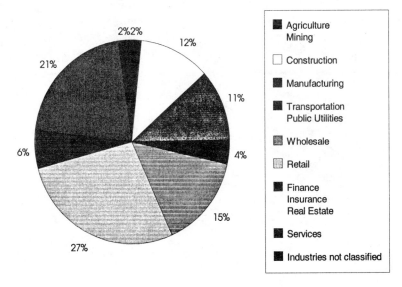

Distribution of All U.S. Firms by Industry
by Sales

2% 2%
12%
21%
11%
6%
4%
15%
27%

Legend:
- Agriculture Mining
- Construction
- Manufacturing
- Transportation Public Utilities
- Wholesale
- Retail
- Finance Insurance Real Estate
- Services
- Industries not classified

Figure 9

Distribution of All Af-Am Owned Firms by Industry by Number of Firms

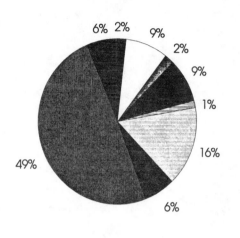

Figure 10

Distribution of All Af-Am Owned Firms by Industry by Sales

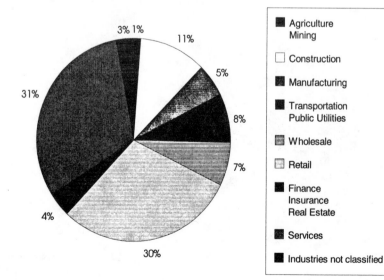

Figure 11

Distribution of Af-Am Owned Firms in Chicago by Industry by Number of Firms

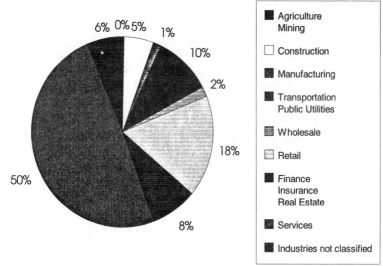

Figure 12

Distribution of Af-Am Owned Firms in Chicago by Industry by Sales

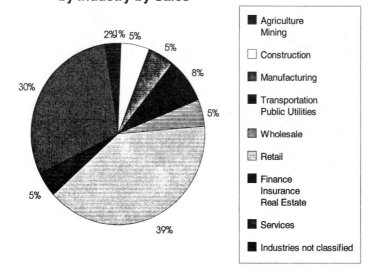

Figure 13

Distribution of Af-Am Owned Firms in NYC by Industry by Number of Firms

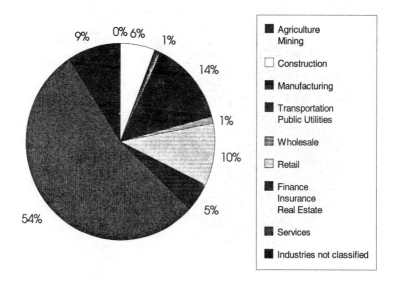

Agriculture Mining

Construction

Manufacturing

Transportation Public Utilities

Wholesale

Retail

Finance Insurance Real Estate

Services

Industries not classified

Figure 14

Distribution of Af-Am Owned Firms in NYC by Industry by Sales

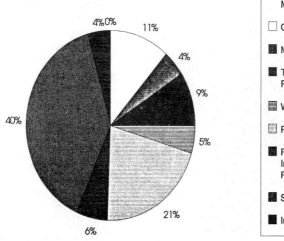

Agriculture Mining

Construction

Manufacturing

Transportation Public Utilities

Wholesale

Retail

Finance Insurance Real Estate

Services

Industries not classified

78

Figure 15

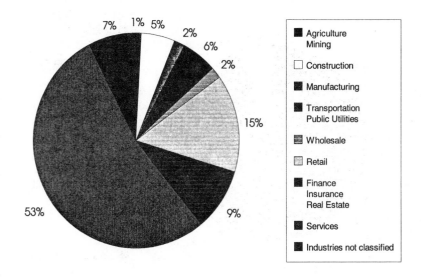

Distribution of Af-Am Owned Firms in LA by Industry by Number of Firms

- Agriculture Mining
- Construction
- Manufacturing
- Transportation Public Utilities
- Wholesale
- Retail
- Finance Insurance Real Estate
- Services
- Industries not classified

Figure 16

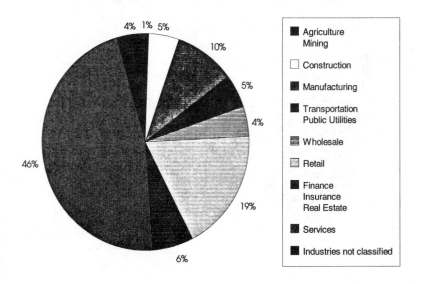

Distribution of Af-Am Owned Firms in LA by Industry by Sales

- Agriculture Mining
- Construction
- Manufacturing
- Transportation Public Utilities
- Wholesale
- Retail
- Finance Insurance Real Estate
- Services
- Industries not classified

Table 12

Metro Area	Sales (BE Total in $1000)	Average BE Rank	Number of BE Firms	Average Sales per BE Firm (in $1000)
New York City	2,073,535	45	13	159,503
Chicago	692,299	39	11	62,936
Washington, DC	504,725	51	16	31,545
Detroit	297,645	44	7	42,521
Atlanta	280,310	60	7	40,044
Philadelphia	279,891	47	2	139,946
Los Angeles	262,231	36	7	37,462
Baltimore	138,300	32	3	46,100
Houston	91,880	7	1	91,880
Dallas	72,874	38	2	36,437
Memphis	na	na	na	na

Source: 1993 *Black Enterprise* 100 Industrial/Service Company Ranking

Table 13

Ten Largest Major Industry Groups in Receipts for African-American-Owned Firms: 1987					
SIC Code	Major Industry Group	Industry Division	Firms (number)	Receipts ($mil)	Average Receipts ($)
55	Automotive Dealers and Service Stations	Retail Trade	3,690	2,156	584,282
73	Business Services	Services	59,177	1,570	26,531
80	Health Services	Services	30,026	1,351	44,994
17	Special Trade Contractors	Construction	29,631	1,314	44,354
59	Misc. Retail	Retail	34,870	1,086	31,144
58	Eating and drinking places	Retail	11,834	1,084	91,601
42	Trucking and warehousing	Transportation	19,663	1,010	51,366
54	Food Stores	Retail	8,952	1,001	111,819
72	Personal Services	Services	56,772	960	16,910
51	Wholesale Trade - nondurable goods	Wholesale	2,727	699	256,326

Source: 1987 Economic Censuses, Survey of Minority-Owned Business Enterprises

OPPORTUNITIES

Fairlie (1993) identifies five factors which contribute to the differences in transition rates to self-employment between whites and African Americans.[36] These factors are the level of education, level of assets, level of education of the reference person's father, the probability of having a self-employed father, and the group of variables measuring the individual's work history. In addition, Fairlie mentions other factors that he did not study which may affect the black self-employment rate: consumer discrimination, lending discrimination, and lack of access to co-ethnic resources.

Despite the difficulty in changing some of these historical and/or environmental factors, the outlook for black-owned businesses is promising. Most Americans are aware that by the year 2000, 85 percent of the new entrants into the work force will be either minorities or women.[37] The underlying reason for this trend is the overall population growth of African Americans, Hispanics, and Asians relative to the total. If current growth patterns continue, nonwhite consumers will comprise about 30 percent of the U.S. population by 2002, the largest portion of which will be African Americans.[38] As the size of the African-American consumer market increases, so do the opportunities for African-American entrepreneurship. However, black entrepreneurs should not limit themselves to African-American consumers. The larger community—with its greater wealth—offers opportunities in business services, construction, transportation, and FIRE (Finance, Insurance, and Real Estate). Some of this might take the form of joint ventures with whites and others (e.g., as was done in the case of Black Entertainment Television).

CONCLUSION

African Americans are a large market, about one-quarter of $1 trillion per year—more than most countries in the world. This market, for the most part, is not being served by African-American businesses, whose sales are less than one-tenth of African-American purchases ($19.7 billion for businesses versus $216 billion for households). Much of the income that enters African-American communities soon leaves them. Whereas a dollar is estimated to change hands 7 times in white communities, it does so only 1.5 times in African-American communities.[39] Middle Eastern and Asian merchants have won significant marketshares in the Bedford-Stuyvesant section of Brooklyn and in South Central Los Angeles, despite large African-American populations there. African-American sellers cannot rely on race alone to attract patronage; the race-patronage link is not strong in African-American communities. Black consumers desire quality goods at reasonable prices, knowledgeable sales people, and respect. These should be readily available from motivated African Americans.

The economic base of communities is based on their income-generating potential. Income derives from employment for most African Americans.

Entrepreneurship is one area in which African Americans have yet to establish themselves firmly; they are underrepresented, and the firms owned are, on average, about one-third in sales that of firms in the nation. The good news is that there is lots of room for growth. To make the most of opportunities, African Americans must expand into nontraditional fields because there are no safe havens. Whites have entered the African-American beauty care industries (cosmetics, hair care, etc.), and Middle Easterners and Asians successfully challenge African-American retailers. Growth opportunities exist in the larger market—the U.S. economy—and African Americans should vigorously pursue them as well as those in their own backyards.

REFERENCES

Alexis, Marcus. 1970. "Patterns of Black Consumption, 1935-1960," *Journal of Black Studies*, pp. 55-74.

_____. 1962. "Some Negro-White Differences in Consumption," *The American Journal of Economics and Sociology* 21:1, pp. 1-28.

_____. 1959. "Some Negro-White Differences in Consumption," Ph.D. dissertation, Department of Economics, University of Minnesota.

_____ and Smith, Clyde M. 1973. "Marketing and the Inner-City Consumer," *Journal of Contemporary Business*, Autumn, pp. 45-80.

Bureau of the Census. 1987. "1987 Economic Censuses: Survey of Minority-Owned Business Enterprises—Black." U.S. Department of Commerce Report Number MB87-1.

_____. 1987. "1987 Economic Censuses: Survey of Minority-Owned Business Enterprises." U.S. Department of Commerce Report Number MB87-4.

Fairlie, Robert W. 1993. "The Absence of the African-American Owned Business: An Analysis of the Dynamics of Self-Employment." Paper presented to Labor Workshop, Department of Economics, Northwestern University, October 13.

Kimbro, Dennis. 1993. National Black MBA Association National Conference and Exposition, Tape #KBS01, Atlanta, GA, September 25.

Poole, Sheila M. 1993. "Atlanta Business: The World of Business: The Southeast Buy Black Regularly, Activists Urge," *The Atlanta Journal and Constitution*, Business Section H, April 25, p. 6.

Reynolds, Rhonda. 1993. "Courting Black Consumers," *Black Enterprise*, Facts and Figures Section, September, p. 43.

"21st Annual Report on Black Business." 1993. *Black Enterprise* 23:11, pp. 91-98.

ENDNOTES

[1] Rhonda Reynolds, "Courting Black Consumers," *Black Enterprise*, Facts and Figures Section, September 1993, p. 43.

[2] "Young, Black, and Born to Shop," *The Numbers News* 13: 8, August 1993, p. 2.

[3]Leslie Vreeland, "How to be a Smart Shopper," *Black Enterprise*, Money Management Section, August 1993, p. 84.

[4]Reynolds, *op. cit.*

[5]Sheila M. Poole, "Atlanta Business: The World of Business: The Southeast Buy Black Regularly, Activists Urge," *The Atlanta Journal and Constitution*, Business Section H, April 25, 1993, p. 6.

[6]"African-American Consumers Exhibit Market Savvy and Zest for Shopping," *Minority Markets Alert*, May 1993.

[7]Dennis Kimbro, National Black MBA Association National Conference and Exposition, Tape #KBS01, Atlanta, GA, September 25, 1993.

[8]*Scanner panels* are groups of consumers who agree to have their purchases monitored at checkout counters through electronic scanners. *Diary panels* are groups of consumers who complete diaries of their purchases and submit them for use by marketing research concerns.

[9]Kimbro, *op. cit.*

[10]*Ibid.*

[11]The terms "African American" and "black" are used interchangeably throughout this chapter.

[12]Kimbro, *op. cit.*

[13]*Ibid.*

[14]Research memorandum compiled by DE Research, January 1994, from *Average Annual Expenditures and Characteristics, Consumer Expenditures Survey 1991*, U.S. Labor Department, Bureau of Labor Statistics, November 30, 1992.

[15]"Trendy Transport: Comparisons of Car Ownership for Blacks and Whites, " *Black Enterprise*, November 1990, p. 49.

[16]Vreeland, *op. cit.*

[17]Kimbro, *op. cit.*

[18]*Ibid.*

[19]The U.S. Office of Management and Budget defines a *metropolitan statistical area* (MSA) as an integrated economic and social unit with a population nucleus of at least 50,000 inhabitants. Each MSA consists of one or more counties meeting standards of metropolitan character. For instance, the Chicago MSA includes the counties of Cook, Du Page, Grundy, Kane, Kendall, Lake, McHenry, and Will in Illinois; Lake and Porter in Indiana; and Kenosha in Wisconsin.

[20]"BLS Reports on Chicago Area Consumer Expenditures 1990-91," *Bureau of Labor Statistics News*, U. S. Department of Labor, Chicago, IL, May 14, 1993, pp. 1-6.

[21]Reynolds, *op. cit.*

[22]*Ibid.*

[23]*Ibid.*

[24]Burrell/Yankelovich, *African-American MONITOR*, as cited in "Greater Media Involvement," *Minority Markets Alert*, May 1993.

[25]*Ibid.*

[26]*Ibid.*

[27]Reynolds, *op. cit.*

[28]"Young, Black, and Born to Shop," *op. cit.*

[29]Vreeland, *op. cit.*

[30]"Young, Black, and Born to Shop," *op. cit.*

[31]*Ibid.*

[32]Reynolds, *op. cit.*

[33]Vreeland, *op. cit.*

[34]*Ibid.*

[35]Joshua Smith, "Retooling the African-American Business Community," National Black MBA Association Annual Conference and Exposition, Tape #KLT01, September 23, 1993.

[36]Robert W. Fairlie, "The Absence of the African-American Owned Business: An Analysis of the Dynamics of Self-Employment," Northwestern University Labor Workshop, October 13, 1993.

[37]"BLS Previews the Economy of the Year 2000," *Bureau of Labor Statistics News*, U.S. Department of Labor, June 25, 1987.

[38]Marilyn Kern-Foxworth, "Black, Brown, Red, and Yellow Markets Equal Green Power," *Public Relations Quarterly* 36:1, Spring 1991, pp. 27-30.

[39]Poole, *op. cit.*

PLAYOFFS AND PAYOFFS:
THE AFRICAN-AMERICAN
ATHLETE AS AN
INSTITUTIONAL RESOURCE

Harry Edwards, Ph.D.

Notwithstanding sports' reputation as a realm of frivolous activity that is isolated and insulated from the more serious concerns and interests of society, it is in fact a national institution that both reflects and recapitulates the established and evolving realities of social life in this nation. The validity of this proposition is demonstrably evident in the analysis of African-American athletes' potential as institutional resources within black society. The forces determining the course and character of black involvement in mainstream integrated sport and the extent of black society's control over its sports resources are shown to be identical with or to overlap substantially those historical and ongoing influences that have molded and configured black life overall. In the decades since World War II, the looming permanence of racism as an integral component of American liberal democracy combined with radical integrationist black advancement strategies have given rise to the erosion and, in some instances, the outright destruction of black institutional viability. While some black institutions were sacrificed or allowed to collapse in the interest of what was presumed to be the greater good and promise of radical integration, others were essentially taken over by mainstream interests and, in effect, reconfigured to maximize black exploitability. The outcome of this **advancement** process has been the evolution of a **plantation system** of black-white status and authority relations in both sports and society accomplished through a shift from the black collective exclusion and subordination of segregation to the black selective inclusion and subordination of radical integration. Because of its highly public profile, sports more than any other arena displays this characteristic process of change without commensurate progress, of transition without substantive transformation.

Only through a thorough understanding of the tangle of confluent and contradictory forces impacting the black sports experience is there any hope of even **salvaging** black sports traditions, much less controlling black human and material athletic resources in the interest of black society. The critical factors in either case are black people's capacities to engineer a resurgence in the viability of black institutions and, by extension, in traditional black communities even as they intensify the struggle to broaden black access and opportunity in the American mainstream. It is not now and nor has it ever been a case of *either* black institutional development *or* mainstream integrated access. Rather, it is a case of black institutional and community development *as a condition* of black competence and competitiveness in and dependable access to an integrated but still highly racist American mainstream.

Given that black sports involvement reflects in microcosm the broader reality of black life in America as well as the morass of contradictions and continuities characteristic of that reality in the post-integration era, black athletes' greatest current value as an institutional resource might well lie with their less obvious potential as barometers of the state of Black America and its potential—that is, both as *canaries in the mineshaft* forewarning disaster, and as *heralds on the mountain top* signaling the proper path of black development and advancement.

All institutional arrangements are by definition components of a broader system of patterned relationships. Irrespective of the specific arena or focus of the social discourse involved, the pattern prevails. Thus, in *Reading Jazz*, David Meltzer observes that:

> Racism . . . weighs upon and within American life, a deeply imprinted and inalienable truism hiding in the large shadows of blazingly huge myths . . . What is 'the myth of jazz'? A circular process where . . . oppressed peoples subvert and transform the master's music of definition into a defiance that, in turn, becomes a mystery to the master class who sets out to learn its secrets and, as with other property, to own it, control it . . . In turn, the music is reclaimed, resubverted, re-syncopated, harmonized, like be-bop, and again, in turn, the defiant intelligence is sapped of force and focus . . . jazz [becomes] a white discourse, a white mythology, a white form of control over its production, reproduction, history, and economics; a white reverie over blackness sustained and contained within the cultural plantation system of late capitalism . . . Yet, I insist that jazz is highly resistant and durable. Jazz . . . cannot only be seen as reflecting institutional racism but as posing creatively resilient answers to the transcendence of racism.[1]

Like the arts (or education, government, the economy, the mass media, or even religion, for that matter), sports is but another institutional arena of black-white interaction evidencing a **plantation** structure of authority and power relationships. Inherent in sports, conversely—as in education, the economy, the mass media, and especially in religion—is a liberating potential accessible to those who explore beyond the superficialities of institutionally contrived and propagated myths and **conventional wisdom,** and who, in turn, act, based upon the realities revealed.

86

In America, sports by long-standing tradition has been regarded as frivolous, as legitimately belonging to the *toy department* of human affairs. However, notwithstanding this presumption of sports' isolation from the more serious concerns and interests of American society, it is in fact a national institution. As such it reflects much of the established and developing character of human and social organizational relationships in this nation as well as the values and beliefs—the ideology—legitimizing and otherwise rationalizing and supporting those patterned relationships. In essence, American sports invariably, unavoidably, and quite predictably looks, sounds, and behaves very much like American society. Since sports neither evolved, exists, nor functions in a vacuum, it cannot be fully understood aside from the dynamics of the social cultural matrix and political contexts out of which it evolved and within which it remains inextricably embedded.

Commensurate with this reality, any creditable exploration of African-American athletes' potential as institutional resources within black society compels some consideration of related forces determining black experiences and outcomes overall.

Since emancipation, black life in America has been significantly contoured and configured both by committed struggle for black advancement and by powerful and deeply engrained counterforces of antiblack racism usually institutionally abetted and broadly subscribed to in the American mainstream. In the face of diverse and recurring black freedom movements, racism has proved to be not only a multifaceted and multifunctional dimension of mainstream life but also one that is malleable to the point of accommodating transitions in black-white relations while typically frustrating any substantive transformations of those relations. Far from constituting an aberrant countercurrent of social sentiments existing in opposition to liberal democratic values prescribing freedom and equality of opportunity—a supposed contradiction long termed the "American Dilemma"—racism is today a highly mutable constituent feature of American liberal democracy.[2] Moreover, changes in the domestic and global economies, racially conservative trends in the national political climate, shifts in judicial vision and temperament relative to race-related issues, and—most importantly—a continuing deterioration in the viability and integrity of institutions and cultural support processes within black society are clearly exacerbating and compounding the problems traditionally posed by racism for African-Americans. Under the circumstances, racism is not only likely to persist in a multiplicity of forms, but—contrary to declarations popular in some academic and political circles alleging the **declining significance of race** as a factor determining black life chances—it is likely to survive for all practical purposes as an integral and permanent feature of the American social landscape. Recognition that racism in whatever guise or degree must be regarded as no less a changeable constant in America than the weather—and so must be monitored and transcended in perpetuity—is neither defeatist nor victimist. Rather, such recognition is a necessary step toward consigning racism to its proper priority within the full constellation of problems (political, economic, cultural, educational, moral, spiritual, etc.) challenging Black America. This relegation of racism to its proper place is imperative to the development of viable modern-day strategies and vehicles capable of generating at least representative black advancement across the spectrum of mainstream institutional life.

It follows then that reassessment of prevailing black perspectives on racism, and its appropriate place and priority as a focal concern of the struggle for black advancement, invites reconsideration also of established black responses to racism and its various manifestations. The pervasiveness and intractability of racism might well have justified adoption of a *radical integrationist* emphasis in assaulting those features of American life founded upon racist prescriptions—particularly features such as de jure segregation. But along with and even in consequence of its significant accomplishments, the almost singular emphasis upon an integrationist strategy (often interpreted to mandate black assimilation virtually to the point of black cultural, institutional, and ethnic annihilation) also generated residues of stigmata and degradation that yet burden and afflict the traditional black community.

The combined impact of entrenched racism and radical integrationism (henceforth termed simply integration) has been to erode and undermine the integrity of black institutions and thereby black people's capacities to control, develop, and direct systematically black resources—human, material, and institutional.

RACE-RELATED CHANGE IN SPORTS AND SOCIETY

What follows is by no means intended as an exhaustive presentation of change forces influencing social developments at the interface of race, sports, and society. Neither space nor mandate will accommodate elaboration, for instance, upon such important influences as the revolution in black music that was be-bop, rhythm and blues, hard bop, and free jazz; or the mainstream's discovery and selective sponsorship of black literature, arts, and lifestyles that was subsumed under the label of the "Harlem Renaissance"; or the emergence of new black African nations in the 1950s and 1960s. For purposes here, it is sufficient to highlight a few of the more directly seminal developments that illustrate the scope, pattern, and interdependence of change factors impacting sports and society, and that **demonstrate, therefore, the range of forces potentially germane to any proposed change strategy or goals targeting sports and black athletes.**

A national black sports institution paralleling that of mainstream white society evolved after the Civil War and was sustained well into the 1950s. This was principally the result of the racist exclusion of black Americans from sports involvement that would have brought them into contact and competition with whites as equals. Significant impetus toward change in this state of affairs did not occur until the post-World War II years, and then only in response to converging global and domestic developments buttressed by an intensification of threatened and actual protests and other intervention strategies on the parts of black Americans and their allies.

It was initially President Franklin D. Roosevelt who breached the nearly solid wall of racial segregation in national life by issuing Executive Order 8802 on June 25, 1941. This order prohibited discrimination in certain areas of federal employment including in the defense industry. On July 26, 1948, President Harry S Truman signed Executive Order 9981 requiring equal treatment for all military personnel without regard to race, color, religion, or ethnic identity. Irrespective of the degree of presidential goodwill involved, the predisposing weight and influence of broad scale objective conditions operating in conjunction with black protest activism cannot be overestimated as factors motivating the signing of these edicts.

By the onset of the 1940s, the adoption and application of Keynesian economic regimes and the use of forceful executive action in response to problems associated with the economic depression of the 1930s had accustomed the society to bold and aggressive government intervention schemes and strategies in addressing national institutional problems. To mainstream America, this made executive orders mandating racial desegregation appear more proper in form if no less unpalatable in substance.

It was World War II that provided what was perhaps the chief predisposing impetus behind the desegregation orders issued by Roosevelt and Truman. As the war evolved, the stark contradiction of the United States fighting for democracy and *against* racist tyranny abroad while maintaining a race-based oppressive caste system at home became ever more politically untenable. In U.S. defense industries and eventually in the military itself, it also became increasingly less practical. The war generated labor needs that prompted massive black migrations to northern urban centers. As the war wore on and military needs drained the civilian labor force, color (like gender) tended to recede somewhat as a priority concern in favor of production skills in the factories. The expanded opportunities created by the human resource demands of the war, in combination with the inexorable erosion of southern social and cultural prescriptions among black migrants under the pervasive influences of northern city life, gave rise to black impressions of more race-neutral circumstances and diminished race-based stigmata. This stood in direct contrast to black experiences in southern rural and small town environments where black life was so frequently dominated by laws, customs, and conventions that blatantly and unambiguously demarcated the color line and enforced black subordination.

The war effort also generated extensive government and corporate propaganda programs aimed at spurring greater worker productivity and patriotism, propaganda extolling the virtues of human freedom and equality and urging sacrifice toward the end of victory over the racist Axis powers and their notions of racial supremacy and ethnic superiority.

As a consequence of such influences, by the end of World War II, black people had developed expectations relative to the expansion of black freedom that were unprecedented since the post-Civil War years, and nowhere were these expectations higher and more intense than with regard to the issue of racial desegregation. Even greater urgency was brought to the situation by returning black soldiers who literally demonstrated their disinclination to tolerate traditions of racist segregation by participating in picketing and other protest efforts—often attired in their military uniforms and bedecked with medals for meritorious service. Popular identification with the push for desegregation was spurred on yet further by the black and liberal white press. Typical was the sentiment expressed by black columnist Ralph Matthews who wrote:

> After our armies have marched on Berlin and Tokyo, if the G.I. Joes, both colored and White, don't turn around and march on Washington and drive out the Fascist coalition of Southern Democrats and Republicans who are trying to Nazify America, they will not have learned what they were fighting for.[3]

Black America responded to such urgings with a dual mindset epitomized by the organization of the *Double V* campaign stipulating the goal of victory over racism both abroad and at home.

And then there was the post-World War II advent of the Cold War, that global political, economic, and military struggle between Western capitalist nations headed by the United States and Eastern bloc socialist countries led by China and the former Soviet Union. The specter of this nation's Cold War adversaries accruing any measure of geopolitical influence or advantage—particularly in the so-called Third World—as a consequence of U.S. laws and official policies that tolerated and frequently mandated racial segregation was not a welcome prospect in the view of the Truman administration and its cadres of emerging cold warriors. Even less appealing was the absolutely ludicrous and transparently contradictory prospect of sending racially segregated military units abroad to fight or to provide military assistance to Third World people in defense of freedom and democracy.

Notwithstanding the gravity of the objective conditions confronting the Roosevelt and Truman administrations and favoring desegregation measures, in and of themselves they were insufficient to precipitate timely government action. It was not until the black labor leader, A. Philip Randolph—with an acute sense and appreciation of the grassroots strength and political potential of desegregation sentiment in Black America—threatened in 1940 to organize 100,000 people and stage a march on Washington, DC, that President Roosevelt undertook to fashion the executive order that he finally signed in 1941. Further capitalizing upon the black masses' growing intolerance for segregationist laws and official policies, Randolph again threatened a massive protest march and demonstration against the federal government in 1948, precipitating President Truman's signing of Executive Order 9981. And still, the military was not significantly desegregated until the onset of the Korean War and the military personnel demands that it created. Moreover, desegregation did not occur through wholesale infusions of Black and white troops into formerly unmixed segregated units. Rather, white casualties and soldiers rotating out of front-line duty were replaced by black soldiers and vice versa—the prevailing wisdom being that there are no bigots in foxholes once the shooting starts.

So What?

Race-related developments in the national defense realm overlapped, interfaced with, influenced, and gave momentum to developments toward the desegregation of American sports. During the 1930s and into the 1940s, black people and their liberal white allies protested segregation in professional sports and worked diligently to eliminate the color barrier. Civil rights organizations, the black press (led by, among others, Wendell Smith of the *Pittsburgh Courier*), and a few liberal white columnists and sports writers—all with the adamant support of black baseball players—urged desegregation of the major leagues. They rhetorically and persistently queried owners as to why skilled black baseball players were snubbed, especially those who had served honorably in the military. And they agitated for city and county governments to cancel stadium use contracts with segregated Major League Baseball teams. World War II and its aftermath added the force of practical need to these essentially moral and political entreaties.

Sports, like every other aspect of American life, was seriously disrupted by war-time hardships and sacrifices. Manpower difficulties forced the National Football League to cut its team rosters from 33 to 25 players, while Major League Baseball was threatened with the prospect that the much more established national pastime would not be able to field baseball players capable of playing up to traditional professional competitive standards.

The war had decimated the player talent of Major League Baseball, while segregation, the restriction of blacks to noncombat roles in some cases, and the virtual exclusion of blacks from service by some military branches contributed to sustaining the stability of the player pool in the Negro Leagues. Given the talent that was available, even during the war, there were games between such stellar teams as the "Washington, DC Homestead Grays" and the "Kansas City Monarchs" that regularly attracted thousands of fans.

The Negro League East-West All-Star Game had been known to draw over 50,000 fans. It was, therefore, perhaps inevitable that rumors eventually began to circulate that there was unprecedented internal league pressures to eliminate the color bar to compensate for war-related player personnel deficits and to garner a larger share of the dollars spent on baseball entertainment by black fans. Between 1944 and 1946, such speculation was rampant; it was also quite accurate.

As was the case with the aforementioned presidential executive orders desegregating certain areas of federal employment and the military, in Major League Baseball— irrespective of the degree of owner goodwill motivating the lifting of the ban against black players, the seminal influence of objective conditions cannot be overstated. Quite simply, the color ban in professional baseball locker rooms was lifted more as a result of Major League Baseball's Achilles' wallet than its conscience. It was business not brotherhood that was the principal incentive motivating Branch Rickey to reach into the Kansas City Monarchs franchise of the Negro Leagues and sign Jackie Robinson to a contract with the Brooklyn Dodgers' minor league Montreal Royals, thereby initiating the desegregation of Major League Baseball.

The desegregation of professional football evolved under influences similar to those impacting the major leagues. It is a seldom acknowledged fact that in the 1920s, professional football was somewhat integrated only to be resegregated by the onset of the 1930s. Fritz Pallard, one of a handful of black athletes who played in the National Football League (NFL) in its early days of sparse integration and the league's first black head coach, probably characterizes the evolution of the situation quite accurately when he suggested that the NFL signed a few black players to expand league recognition and gain fan support in the 1920s. But having established its fan base and consolidated its franchises into a viable league by the 1930s, and facing a deepening economic depression that had put millions of whites among others out of work, NFL owners felt it neither necessary nor particularly prudent to hire blacks to play professional football.[4] The heightened interracial sensitivities brought on by the economic depression apparently also prompted NFL owners to question whether it was worth having black players on their teams given recurrent difficulties over racial discrimination in lodging, travel, and dining accommodations.

The democratic idealism spawned by World War II and the extensive propagandization of the problem of racial segregation in professional football by black leadership organizations and black and liberal white journalists, all with the staunch support of black football players and a politicized and aroused black public, emerged as the predisposing factors behind the desegregation of professional football. However, the precipitating factors were the prospects for financial gain, combined with black and white liberal protest efforts. The color ban was finally lifted in March of 1946 when several black journalists, at a meeting of the Los Angeles Coliseum Commission, objected to the use of the public facility by any organization that practiced racial segregation. Representatives from the Los Angeles Rams of the NFL and from the Los Angeles Dons of the competing professional football league, the All-America Football Conference, immediately agreed to sign black players—later conceding that they did so to secure their leases on the coliseum and to boost gate receipts by attracting black fans.[5]

By the mid-1950s, the third major spectator team sport was well down the road toward desegregating its locker rooms. The color ban in the National Basketball Association (NBA) was lifted during the NBA's 1950 college draft, when Boston Celtics owner Walter Brown picked Charles Cooper, a 6-foot, 5-inch black forward from Duquesne University, in the second round. In a later round, the Washington Capitals took Earl Lloyd, a 6-foot, 6-inch forward from West Virginia State. There were also factors beyond goodwill motivating desegregation. First, NBA owners did not relish the notion of professional basketball being the nation's only remaining major professional sport that was segregated. Secondly, five or six years after World War II, the NBA playoffs attracted less fan support and attention than either the collegiate National Invitational Tournament or National Collegiate Athletic Association (NCAA) Championship tournament. Compounding the NBA's status and prestige problems was the popularity of black professional basketball teams such as the Harlem Globetrotters and the Renaissance Big Five. Though these teams were compelled to barnstorm around the country in search of games since—unlike black baseball—they had no organized league, they often generated huge gates, especially when they played white teams from the segregated NBA. The recruitment of black professional and college players contributed to a surge in the popularity of professional basketball that, combined with a series of gambling and point-shaving scandals in the collegiate ranks, enabled the professional game to develop and eventually to catch up to its collegiate counterpart in popularity.

The next wave of influences determining the course and character of black advancement in sports again emanated from beyond the sports realm: U.S. Supreme Court decisions ultimately ordering the desegregation of public education; congressional civil rights legislation expanding the scope of anti-discrimination laws and regulations; and most significantly, the evolution of television, its technology and its broadcast techniques in directions that were ever more compatible with the needs and demands of sport as a mass entertainment business enterprise.

After a series of cases that paved the way for a favorable ruling, in 1954, of the U.S. Supreme Court ruled in Brown v. Board of Education of Topeka, Kansas that racially segregated public education was inherently unequal and therefore unconstitutional. In ordering school desegregation, the Supreme Court also accelerated the desegregation of football and basketball locker rooms at every level in sports. For example, as a result of one-way integration where black schools were either closed or, less frequently, merged with previously all-white institutions under white administrations and faculties, White coaches gained a windfall of black athlete talent. For—like black teachers and principals—most African-American coaches and athletic administrators were not transferred with their students to the integrated schools.

Subsequently, this development contributed to the integration of college locker rooms because it was inevitable that white high school coaches would begin to funnel what had been a largely untapped and excluded pool of black athletic talent toward the traditionally white collegiate institutions with which these coaches had long-standing athletic recruitment relationships.

The impact of Brown v. Board of Education was buttressed by Supreme Court rulings specifically dealing with issues of segregation and other forms of racial discrimination in college education. But it was the Civil Rights Act of 1964 that consolidated the integrationist thrust in sports by prohibiting discrimination on the basis of race or color in a host of areas that interfaced with the sports enterprise, e.g., Title II, public accommodations; Title IV, public education; and Title VII, employment. In combination, these judicial and legislative developments provided a legal push toward more racially integrated sports. It was television, however, that provided the pull.

In the mid-1950s, at the onset of the era of widely televised sports events, there was the prevalent fear that this new technology would ultimately prove detrimental to sports by encouraging people to stay home and watch sporting events free on television rather than paying to see them at the stadium or pavilion. If there was ever any real threat that television would undermine gate receipts, it was short-lived. Not only did television draw viewers and spur increased gate receipts by broadening fan interest in sports (to no small degree owing to the abilities of increasingly more sophisticated broadcast personnel to dramatize and *sell* sports events to mass audiences as entertainment spectacles), but also in consequence of its success, televised sports programming attracted unprecedented corporate sponsorship and advertising dollars. For the sports enterprise, gaining access to those dollars came to be most directly dependent upon mainstream athletic competitiveness and success.

Since the post-World War II onset of locker room integration in sports, black athletes—for reasons that are social and cultural, not biological— have shown themselves to be demonstrably superior relative to the development of winning sports programs. In consequence, the business motive precipitating the mainstreaming of black athletic talent in major sports has intensified immeasurably. At both the professional and collegiate levels, the presence of the black athlete has become a competitive imperative. As television technology and broadcast techniques have advanced and improved (giving rise to more portable and powerful cameras and sound reproduction systems, to live satellite and cable broadcast capabilities, to color, instant replay, split screen, picture-in-a-picture, and more), fan attention and allegiance has intensified; the revenues that television networks and sports interest could command from corporate advertisers have ballooned; and there have been even greater pressures to garner the talented black athlete.

LOCKER ROOM INTEGRATION AND ITS AFTERMATH: MARCHING UP THE DOWN ESCALATOR

The benefits of racially desegregated locker rooms in major sports have been significant and substantially uniform for mainstream white sports interests in the sense of generating little in the way of tangible *down-side* consequences. Black sports outcomes, on the other hand, have been nowhere near as unmixed or beneficent. In order to grasp the implications of the circumstances alluded to here and to understand them in relation to black athletes' potential as institutional resources, it is necessary to situate properly black sports experiences within the context of some key post-integration developments in black society overall. Again, the effort here is merely to illuminate a few seminal developments that influenced the emerging character of black sports involvement, not to present an exhaustive analysis.

From the outset, integration in both sports and society was mostly one-way and individual as opposed to two-way and institutional in focus. That is to say, while there was an emphasis upon blacks accessing previously all-white settings, there was no comparable emphasis upon whites moving into greater affiliation and involvement with previous all-black social structures and arrangements. And though there was some limited merging of institutional structures such as schools (and even these mergers were most often consolidated under white-dominated authority arrangements), racial desegregation as conceived and implemented typically had the goal of mixing people, not the symbiotic amalgamation of black and white institutions under shared authority and control.

In the final analysis, the methods of integration had several critical consequences for the black community. First, integration exacerbated long-standing class distinctions and divisions within the black community. Though many in black society—particularly within the black leadership and the higher classes—had presumed that black political, social, and cultural solidarity were either impervious to integration's potentially corrosive impact or that such solidarity would become increasingly irrelevant as integration progressed, the reality has been that integration as implemented has fueled the expansion of black interclass divisions, alienation, and estrangement to the detriment of all classes in black society.[6] Individual focused one-way integration enabled the more affluent members of black society to more easily distance themselves from the traditional black community, its institutions and, many presumed, its problems. Indeed, moving up and out of the black community—and away from the black lower classes and its problems—came to be by definition synonymous with making it. Consider, for instance, the message of such productions as Lorraine Hainsberry's *A Raisin In The Sun* in which the Youngers—a stable black working class family literally oozing with middle-class virtues and values—ultimately abandoned their black community to move into a white neighborhood. Presented on Broadway in 1959 at the height of black radical integrationist fever, neither in the script of the play nor in the grossly patronizing acclaim that it received from a normally crass and almost obscenely commercial corps of Broadway theater critics was there even so much as an inference that perhaps the Younger family's integrationist aspirations could have down-side consequences far beyond the white hostility highlighted in the production. To utterly abandon the black community, its institutions, and its people for life on the periphery of mainstream white society was projected as the normal, natural, and logical next step in black Americans' pursuit of the American Dream.

Commensurably—and quite predictably—the legitimacy and integrity even of black institutional structures, social arrangements, and cultural processes not specifically targeted for sacrifice upon the altar of integration were severely eroded, owing to diminished affiliation, identification, respect, and support by the more affluent classes of black society. Over ensuing years, even as the increasingly more integrated and suburbanized black higher classes grew in both numbers and affluence, there was a corresponding and ever-deepening spiral of cultural, racial, and institutional degradation and desperation among those left behind within the confines of the traditional black community. In essence, the sociocultural and institutional impoverishment and bankruptcy at the root of much of the crime, violence, hopelessness, and futurelessness today besetting so many traditionally black communities arise not from a failure of integrationist strategies and goals but, in substantial measure, precisely from integrationist successes **in the absence of viable safeguards assuring black sociocultural integrity and institutional viability.**

No institution more than sports reflects the tangled web of contradictions confronting black Americans in the wake of integration. Consistent with prevailing practice, the desegregation of sports was one-way and individual in focus (Jackie Robinson's debut in pro baseball). As a result of this method of integration, key components of the black sports institution—such as the Negro League and black professional football and professional basketball enterprises—disintegrated. Other components, such as the athletic programs at traditionally black colleges and universities, were severely diminished in stature and prestige in black society, owing to their decreased access to blue-chip black athletes and insufficient mainstream media exposure—and therefore insufficient funding—to compete with traditionally white integrated institutions.

At the high school and junior high school levels, resegregation by race and class became increasingly more widespread as both whites and the more affluent classes of black society recurrently fled schools that tipped relative to tolerance levels for race and class diversity, respectively. This, combined with the persistence of traditionally black communities, contributed to sustaining the functional foundations of the black sports institution in lower class African-American culture, even as the institution's collegiate and professional components eroded and, in the case of the latter, collapsed.

Black neighborhood playgrounds, sandlots, recreation facilities, and school-based sports programs continued to be developmental and staging areas for Black athletic talent. Because the majority of successful black athletes have always emerged out of the lower classes where families are more likely to believe that sports provide significant black upward mobility opportunities, the resegregation of the black lower classes helped to sustain and even intensify (in the absence of the black higher classes) the cultural milieu that has nourished a greater emphasis on sports achievement at least since Jackie Robinson's entry into Major League Baseball. But as black post-integration circumstances evolved in sports, the impact of the contradictions inherent in the method of integration began to surface in conjunction with the consequences of black institutional degradation.

In a majority of cases in the post-integration era, black athletes have pursued their sports dreams under the tutelage of entrepreneurial coaches—white and black—who, owing to differences in race or class, residence, and community affiliation, have had little in the way of involvement with these athletes or the traditional black community beyond the sports enterprise connection. The mentorship, the role modeling, the sociocultural *bridging* among the demands and traditions of life in the black community and the expectations of the American mainstream and other role functions long fulfilled by the higher classes of black society significantly disappeared with affluent Black America into the mainstream. For perspective, definitions, and direction relative to sports, its potential, and proper priority, the black athlete has, therefore, become increasingly more reliant upon conventional wisdom, coaches, athletic boosters, recruiters, and school alumni, and an impersonal (which is not to say impartial) mainstream sports media which are the most influential force defining sports-related realities.

Dependence upon parents and other close relations frequently provides only uneven and inconsistent guidance for young black athletes at best since these sources typically have little in the way of an informed up-to-date understanding of the sports enterprise and—like coaches and other interested parties—often subscribe to notions supporting sports-reputed potential as a socioeconomic mobility vehicle for significant numbers of black youths. It is precisely this definition and vision of sports that incites disproportionately high numbers of black youth to irrational, almost single-minded pursuit of sports fame and fortune and that, in turn, gives rise to the channeling process that is responsible for black athletes' domination of all sports to which they have access in numbers. With so much talent and potential channeled into one area of competitive achievement, the demonstrable superiority of the relatively few black athletes who ultimately realize their greatest aspirations is virtually preordained. And such athletes are indeed few.

Only five percent of black athletes who compete in high school football and basketball ever compete in those sports as collegiate varsity athletes. A black high school football player has only 1 chance in 43 of playing for a Division I collegiate football team. His chances of playing in the NFL are 1 in 6,318. A black male high school basketball player has 1 chance in 130 of playing for a Division I collegiate basketball team and only 1 chance in 10,345 of playing in the NBA. Aside from the revenue-producing sports of basketball and football and to a lesser extent track (since over 80 percent of America's Olympic contingent has consistently come from the college ranks, track has been somewhat more open to black participation than other nonrevenue sports), black athletes' opportunities to participate in collegiate sports are negligible. In all other sports combined, including the non-revenue producing sport of collegiate baseball, black athletes get fewer than 5 percent of the athletic grants-in-aid awarded by Division I colleges and universities. In contrast, at these same institutions—where the percentage of black students overall averages 4 percent and where black faculty have hovered right at 2 percent for more than a decade—blacks make up 37 percent and 56 percent of the athletes in the revenue-producing sports of football and men's basketball, respectively, while 33 percent of the players in the preeminent women's sports of basketball are black.[7] In short, black athletes have been mainly integrated into those mainstream sports where whites had the most to gain through the exploitation of black athletic talent.

Failing athletic stardom and typically having emphasized the achievement of sports success to the detriment of other critically vital spheres of personal development—intellectual, cultural, political, etc.—many black would-be beneficiaries of the American sports dream drop to the very bottom of the status hierarchy in the black community. Nothing is more in the tradition of the dramatic tragedy than the legions of black former athletes whose high hopes and futures have been dashed against the realities of modern sports. Sports' promise as a mobility escalator proves disappointingly hollow, even perverse for these athletes whose faith in the sports dream, whose hard work and sacrifices never take them beyond the boundaries of the lower-class communities that they (and with them their families) seek to escape via athletic prowess. For most among the minority of black athletes who do eventually advance to Division I collegiate athletic participation, outcomes are not so much different as they are merely delayed. And they are no less devastating.

Owing to accumulated academic deficiencies, the majority of black athletes enter college under *special action* or *special admission* auspices. For example, in the first two years of NCAA Proposition 48 implementation, there were 410 football players who were declared ineligible to participate in varsity sports as freshmen due to high school grade and aptitude test score deficiencies. Eighty-four percent or 346 of these athletes were black. Of 150 basketball players who were ineligible, 138 or 92 percent were black.[8] When these marginal students but phenomenally competitive and accomplished athletes arrive on the integrated campus, they typically encounter a maze of institutional and cultural obstacles to their development outside of the athletic realm. The athlete is, first of all, likely to spend much more time on sports (about 28 hours per week of supervised practice, games, and individual work and preparation) as opposed to attending class and studying (from 12 to 24 hours per week). If time expended on other sports-related activities (such as travel and extended tournament play during the season in basketball, for example) is also considered, the hours consumed by sports can go from 28 to as much as 60 in some weeks. Moreover, on the average, Division I basketball and football players miss two class sessions per week and 40 percent of class instruction during the season.[9] Among the most visible members of black society in general and the campus community in particular, many black athletes' poor preparation for college academic matriculation, their classroom absenteeism, and an average post-enrollment grade point average of 2.14 (barely above the 2.00 necessary to maintain athletic eligibility) combine with low academic expectations for black students overall on the traditionally white integrated campus to reinforce both the "dumb jock" caricature and the stereotype of the dumb black student condemned by racial heritage to intellectual inferiority.

Beyond the classroom and the sports arena, life for black athletes on the integrated campus can become a morass of contradictions and confusion. For example, black athletes can feel broad acceptance **as athletes** on the one hand while sharing feelings with black non-athlete students of cultural isolation and psychological alienation in the white-dominated campus environment. As a consequence of their academic circumstances, the majority of black student athletes never graduate from the schools that they represent in sports. In 1990, for example, only 26.6 percent of black athletes graduated as compared with 52.2 percent of white athletes after five years of college matriculation. Another 5.4 percent of black athletes remained in school beyond the fifth year. Thus, 68 percent of black athletes left the schools that they represented in sports at the end of their athletic eligibility without their degrees.[10] This figure is consistent with data indicating that nearly two-thirds of Division I black athletes drafted in the spring of 1990 by professional football and basketball teams had not completed their degrees.[11]

Only 1.6 percent of black college athletes eventually end up on a professional sports roster; on the average, even this extremely talented and fortunate minority survives for fewer than four years in the professional ranks. Furthermore, the average black professional athlete earns less than his nonminority counterpart. Black athletes also earn less than whites with comparable skills, productivity, and years of service. At the conclusion of their athletic careers, few black athletes move on to other roles within the sports institution. First of all, at the collegiate level, most athletic personnel have college degrees—even coaches. A significant proportion of black former athletes would be eliminated from candidacy for collegiate coaching and other athletic department jobs on these grounds alone. (How could a college coach logically tout the importance of athletes completing their degrees if the coach has no degree?) Be this as it may, the fact is that few black former athletes **with or without** degrees ever get the opportunity to present themselves as candidates for coaching jobs—particularly head coaching jobs—at the Division I level. In 1976, of 276 Division I programs, there were seven black head basketball coaches. By 1982, the number had risen to 13. By 1991, there were 35 black head coaches at Division I schools but only 13 held position at schools affiliated with major conferences. The majority of these had little or no head coaching experience, and half of the 35 black head coaches have been hired within the past three years by schools often desperately seeking advantage in the recruitment of blue-chip black athletic talent.[12]

By 1981, two black head football coaches had been hired at traditionally white Division I colleges: at what was then the school with the most penalized football program in NCAA history, Wichita State University, and the school with the longest football losing streak in NCAA history, Northwestern University. By the fall of 1992, there were no black head football coaches in Division IA collegiate football. One year later, three black head football coaches had been hired in Division I—all at colleges with football programs in disastrous decline, so-called death bed cases at Temple, Wake Forest, and Eastern Michigan. Parenthetically, the fluctuation in the presence of black head football coaches (even in these negligible numbers as compared to the 295 Division I football head coach job openings since 1977), and the tendency, with few exceptions, for blacks to be offered the top coaching job principally with death bed or low profile programs are instructive. These developments are indicative of the typical course and character of black outcomes when those outcomes are substantially products of mainstream goodwill or, conversely, of mainstream desperation or of temporary embarrassment over race-related improprieties (e.g., the Al Campanis and Marge Schott incidents) as opposed to being rooted in compelling objective conditions buttressed by black competitive competence and committed action around the issues in question.

Only two of the 105 athletic directors in Division I NCAA institutions are black, while no major athletic conference outside of those involving the traditionally black colleges has a black commissioner.[13] By contrast, blacks are substantially represented among the ranks of Division I football and basketball assistant coaches. But here it must be understood that, in many cases, their primary function is to recruit black athletic talent—a mandate which has generated both job opportunities and job restrictions because all too frequently the successful black recruiter is not taken seriously as a coach.

In professional basketball, football, and baseball, there are no black franchise presidents or chief executive officers, while 99 percent of the ownership in baseball, 100 percent of the ownership in basketball, and 100 percent of the ownership in professional football is other than black. In the NBA, nine of 52 vice-presidents are black, as are three of 46 in the NFL and four of 97 in Major League Baseball. In all three professional sports leagues, the front office position most frequently held by blacks at the franchise level is that of Community Relations Director. It is this individual who generally represents the franchise in dealings with grassroots community organizations and at franchise-area community events. Under circumstances where franchise areas often encompass large minority populations, it is both politically expedient and economically prudent for such franchises to have the option of presenting a minority face to some sectors of the local public. Thus, minorities—mostly blacks—represent 41 percent of community relations directors in the NBA, 33 percent in Major League Baseball, and 31 percent in the NFL.

On the other hand, negligible numbers of blacks hold the position of Public Relations Director. This position is critically central and important in franchise efforts to influence and, in some instances, to script and choreograph information disseminated through the print and broadcast media about the franchise organization, its personnel, its course of development, and its progress. There is a combined total of only three black public relations directors employed in professional basketball and football, while Major League Baseball employs none. This is consistent with overall black access to mainstream media-related sports roles in the wake of integration.[14] Among some 724 beat writers and columnists covering the three major sports for daily newspapers and major sports magazines in this nation, fewer than 30 are black. In the broadcast media, things are even more dismal. Though black ex-jocks serving as analysts and color commentators are commonplace, neither NBC nor ABC has a black play-by-play announcer, while CBS employs two. Still, the number-one analyst or color commentator on all broadcast and cable networks is always white. Of some 60 sports producers and directors at ABC, NBC and CBS, only *one* is black.[15]

Diminished black control and influence over black athletic resources and outcomes in the post-integration era has been severely compounded by a loss of definitional control relative to characterizing and portraying the black American experience in integrated sports. Differences in awareness, culture-based value orientations, and political sensibilities and commitments more frequently than not prevent nonblack sports journalists and other sports media personnel from completely comprehending, much less accurately reporting, black perspectives and definitions in the sports realm. And even where blacks hold mainstream sports media positions, a lack of production, editorial, or other authoritative control and power often limits black latitude in covering and projecting black perspectives—particularly on racially sensitive or other controversial issues. The close symbiotic, mutually supportive relationship between the mainstream sports media and major sports organizations further consolidates both the need and the capability of tightly controlling access to definitional authority and power over sports. It is unfortunately all too often the case in the sports media that even when there is a black physical presence, white definitional domination and hegemony are merely replaced by white definitional ventriloquism.

THE AFRICAN-AMERICAN ATHLETE AS AN INSTITUTIONAL RESOURCE

Though the analysis here has explored only the most obvious dimensions of the complex tangle of factors generating the evolved and ongoing circumstances of blacks in integrated mainstream sport, it should nonetheless be quite clear that any proposed changes or shifts in the established character of black sports involvement will entail a good deal more than moral appeals and political posturing—even when supported by incontrovertible evidence of the need for change. In the absence of the combined force of objective conditions conducive to desired changes, of black competence and commitment relative to meeting the demands of proposed changes, and of serious black political organization and initiatives toward realizing such changes, moral and political entreaties alone amount to little more than a wish list. Under circumstances that prevail today, the vision of African-American athletes as a potential black institutional resource is clearly at best a wish list item.

The ubiquitous and perplexing outcome of the sociopolitical dynamics of black-white relations in post-integration America has been a shift not from black segregation—or collective exclusion and subordination—to collective inclusion and equality, but rather, from black segregation to selective inclusion and subordination. The resulting structure of black-white role and authority relationships in consequence has come to approximate nothing so much as a plantation system of mainstream social and institutional organization. Consistent with this reality, in most mainstream sports, African Americans are woefully underrepresented or completely absent. In sports to which they do have access in numbers, African Americans tend to be significantly underrepresented in authority, policy, and decision-making positions, while being greatly overrepresented in the least powerful, most exploitable, and most expendable production roles—principally that of athlete. This fact alone compels very careful assessment relative to determining the potential of African-American athletes as black institutional resources because they are so firmly controlled and dominated by interests outside of black society.

The challenge of converting African-American athlete talent into a black institutional resource is made all the more difficult because typically these athletes either consciously or unwittingly—like so many other upwardly mobile affluent blacks—accept the notion that the abandonment of traditional black communities to abide even in subordinated—though often materially rewarding—roles within mainstream America is simply a necessary step toward achieving the American dream. This and related "escape the black community" radical integrationist definitions of appropriate black advancement strategies and goals have become embedded in black individual and collective consciousness and accepted as common-sense and conventional wisdom that appear to be substantially reinforced and validated by the ordinary observations, experiences, and relationships of everyday life. In short, African-American athletes for the most part believe and act in accordance with what they see, hear, read, experience, and so forth as the prevailing truths and realities of their social and cultural environments. Thus, if the black doctor, the black lawyer, the black engineer, the black teacher, the black entertainer, and other talented, upwardly mobile, and affluent blacks are seen to abandon the traditional black community, its institutions, and its people and to move into or onto the periphery of mainstream society, why should black athletes logically opt to do otherwise? Why would black athletes, in the face of virtual ideological consensus and behavioral unanimity to the contrary, sustain their affiliation, identity, and involvement with and their commitment to the traditional black community in the collective capacity of an institutional resource? Not surprisingly, therefore, today there is no broad base of support among black athletes for any strategy that would encumber their individual prerogatives within the existing plantation system of sports organization with the additional burdens and obligations of black institutional resource status. Furthermore, both the black press—owing largely to advertising concerns—and black journalists working in the mainstream media lack the independent *clout* enjoyed by their pre-integration predecessors to persistently and uncompromisingly press for the changes in sports and society that would predispose the black athlete—as well as other affluent, mobile blacks—toward a closer involvement and identification with traditional black communities. In consequence, as John Thompson, head coach of men's basketball at Georgetown University, passionately argued during a panel of the 1993 convention of the National Association of Black Journalists:

> Most black journalists, both inside and outside of the sports media, have no idea what's going on with black athletes, black coaches, and other black people involved in mainstream athletics. You are too busy trying to please your editors and your producers. You're too busy trying to be just a regular journalist, to advance yourselves, to not make waves—especially over racial issues. There is literally nobody that I can consistently call to get my side of an issue out— accurately, completely and with the slant on it that reflects my vision and version of the problem I'm talking about. I couldn't call anybody in the black press when Proposition 48 broke. I couldn't call any one of you in the black press when I walked out over Proposition

42 and truly feel that my position would be accurately represented in the newspapers and on the television airwaves.[16]

Specifically, with regard to the material dimension of black athletes' potential as an institutional resource, on the one hand, the circumstances of the majority of black athletes reduce the issue to a moot point. On the other hand, the lack of compelling objective conditions and ideological definitions broadly subscribed to among black athletes means that those black athletes with sufficient discretionary assets and the latitude and inclination to invest those assets in some measure within the traditional black community do so purely by virtue of individual idiosyncratic prerogative, not out of any ingrained sense of categorical institutionalized duty. The analogous difference here is that between making a donation to the church and tithing—the former being an individual option, the latter being an institutionalized duty and obligation.

It must also be recognized that most mainstream parties having vested interests in maintaining the status quo relative to black subordination in sports are likely to look suspiciously at best upon any black orchestrated change effort of a type and caliber sufficient to transform black athletes collectively into a black institutional resource. Quite simply, any breach in the systematic domination and control of prime black athletic talent is likely to be perceived as a potentially disruptive black power resource and, as such, to constitute a palpable threat to the entire plantation system of sports organization. Therefore, no matter how logical, justifiable, or critically urgent the need might be from the perspective of black people and black communities to capitalize upon black athletes as an institutional resource, there is absolutely no basis to expect anything short of noncooperation (if not active opposition) from the sports establishment given objective conditions today. (This most certainly has been the experience of black student organizations, for example, that have solicited the support of black athletes in campaigns to leverage change in black circumstances on traditionally white campuses.)

For the overwhelming majority of black athletes, the issue is not one of becoming an institutional resource, but rather, it is one of looking to institutions for resources. Most of the 65-70 percent of black scholarship athletes who never graduate from the schools that they represent in sports and who never make a professional sports roster usually command no discretionary resources and often are hard put even to support themselves. After their collegiate sports careers are over, many end up back in the communities from which they emerged, in their parents' homes where they started, with no degree, no professional sports career, and little hope of achieving even a decent job, much less the fame and fortune that they had dreamed of since they first came to define themselves as athletes.

Most of the black athletes who do make it into the professional ranks are in many instances only slightly better off. As has been stated, the average black professional athlete will make less than the average salary in a team sport, and if he is in a sport such as golf, tennis, or automobile racing—not to speak of boxing—he will typically profit nothing at all, or worse, must often go into debt simply to continue pursuing his sports career.

There are tremendous pressures on black professional athletes to share whatever financial resources they do command. Often operating under woefully ill-informed assumptions and expectations relative to the amount of money that an athlete has at his disposal, family members and other relatives will typically besiege him with requests for what is often desperately needed financial assistance. The parents and siblings of most black athletes expect that professional sports success will raise the entire family above their accustomed circumstances and stations in life. Seldom do they seriously consider that the *face value* of an athlete's contract constitutes in most cases a *best of all worlds, optimal outcome* projection, i.e., the full amount is paid only if the athlete meets the performance standards stipulated in the contract's incentive clauses, only if he does not suffer some seriously debilitating or career-ending injury, and so forth. Seldom do family members consider the tax bill and agents' fees confronting the average black professional athlete, or the athlete's own lifestyle aspirations, or his own plans for the use of his money. Seldom is there much consideration given to the fact that the average black professional athlete is out of professional sports within four years of signing his first contract, and so, lacking a college degree or marketable skills outside of sports, will need whatever funds he might secure as he struggles to develop and sustain a future for himself.

As for the relatively few black athletes who do make enough money to secure their own futures, accommodate family expectations, and invest in the black community, there is—as has been stated—no sense of collective duty or obligation to undertake the latter. At best, there exists today a philanthropic disposition toward the black community on the part of some few black star and superstar athletes. Because there is no institutionalized imperative for black athletes to collectively identify with and support the black community, as time passes, there may be a few more or a few less who see black community involvement and development as a priority obligation. But the mere passage of time and political pleading will not transform black athletes into an institutionalized material resource in the service of black society.

In the capacity of role models black athletes are also less than ideal insofar as their potential is concerned for becoming an institutional resource. Largely as a result of media choreographed and projected life images of the rich and famous and Madison Avenue's penchant for casting celebrities as experts in realms far removed from the spheres in which they achieved their fame,

Americans have developed this predilection for assuming—if not insisting—that people who are very talented and accomplished in one area of their lives be equally exemplary in all areas. In reality, of course, no life is so evenly and uniformly consistent. It is no more reasonable to expect that a great basketball player should be a role model than to argue that Vincent van Gogh should have been a role model because he was a great painter, or that Charlie Parker should have been a role model because he was a great jazz musician. To the extent that black athletes have become positive and active role models within the black community, they have done so of their own volition—not owing to any compelling institutionalized imperative for affluent and successful blacks to serve that function in the post-integration era. To the contrary, as integration has preceded over the decades and the gap between the lower and upper classes of black society has widened, the ethic and admonition to *lift as we climb* has come to be honored less in practice than in the breach. Lacking broad spectrum cultural and ideological renovation of black sociopolitical perspectives and priorities that would place black community and institutional development and self-reliance on an equal footing with integrationist aspirations and efforts, and that would claim the allegiance of *all* sectors of Black America—not merely successful athletes—the notion of black athletes collectively becoming an institutional resource as role models emerges as a groundless wish at best.

Not only do current circumstances militate against the potential of black athletes becoming an institutional resource, but the conditions in traditional black communities are deteriorating so precipitously that the very foundations of black athlete development are today collapsing. The impact of a priority emphasis upon achieving integration combined with a concomitant neglect and abandonment of black institutions and the black lower classes, all occurring against a background of persistent and unrelenting racism has been to spur unprecedented social instability in the black community. According to data results reported in the *San Francisco Chronicle*, January 28, 1987, by the year 2000—if conditions evident then persist—70 percent of all black adult males will be either dead, in jail, or otherwise institutionally controlled (in the military, in hospitals, etc.), or hopelessly addicted to alcohol or drugs. Today, there are more black males incarcerated in the jails of this nation than enrolled in its colleges. When the number of black males under indictment, on probation, on parole, or otherwise constrained by the legal system are added to those in jail, a portrait emerges of a black male population already significantly under institutional control.

Sports in black society reflects and recapitulates this state of affairs so thoroughly and directly that the black athlete might well be viewed as the proverbial canary in the mineshaft, forewarning a broader disaster. Crime, drugs, random violence, gangs, and gang warfare have virtually destroyed the cultural and institutional infrastructure supporting black athletic development in many communities. Playgrounds, sandlots, parks, and even back-

106

yard recreational sites in many instances have been taken over by drug dealers, or these places have become battlegrounds in disputes between competing drug traffickers or gangs, or they have simply become too dangerously exposed to eruptions of violence to be used for play or practice. Also, cutbacks in education budgets have meant less money for organized sports programs in schools. Where school sports programs have survived in the black community, security problems and fears of gang violence and other disruptions in an increasing number of cases have restricted both the scheduling of events and spectator attendance.

But in some schools, it is no longer a question of scheduling, security, or spectator access relative to sports events because not enough students are signing up for sports participation to allow these schools to field teams. Crime, gang membership, drugs, student drop-out rates, and death are decimating the athletic resources of far too many black communities. Some potential athletes have simply traded team colors for gang colors. Others have dropped out of sports rather than cross gang turf boundaries to participate in athletic events. Yet other potential athletes never had the opportunity to make a choice relative to athletic participation because they fell victim to homicide or were jailed as a result of gang involvement, drug activity, or other criminal behavior.

In the fall of 1993, Richmond High School in Richmond, California, provided a chilling profile of what the future may be for school sports in troubled black communities. In Richmond, crime, drugs, and gang problems are pervasive. Homicide is the leading cause of death among black males in the 12- to 15-year-old age group—the same age group within which sports aspirations and interests typically escalate along with testosterone levels and physical development. Richmond High School also has a student drop-out rate well in excess of 50 percent. Given these facts, no one should have been surprised when only five—5!—students signed up to try out for the football team.[17] When black children are discarded, jailed, and buried, we are discarding, jailing, and burying our future black running backs, wide receivers, point guards, and power forwards—right along with our future black lawyers, doctors, teachers, engineers, entrepreneurs, and others critically vital to the future of Black America. It just happens that owing to the highly public nature of every level of sports participation, the tragic personnel deficits in black sports become evident much earlier than black human resource deficits in other areas. Thus, what is happening in sports clearly presages and portends the future of Black America across the spectrum of occupational and career endeavors. The black athlete may indeed be the canary in the mineshaft.

On the other hand, there is much to be learned from the serious study of black athletes, their circumstances, and the approach taken by the greatest among them in pursuing their goals in sports. It is, first of all, critically important to recognize that black athletes' domination of those sports to which they have significant access would have been impossible in the absence of a viable black sociocultural and institutional sports infrastructure supporting black athletic development within the traditional black community. As the viability of that supportive infrastructure has deteriorated under the burdens of racism, radical integrationism and related epidemics of crime, violence, drug trafficking and use, gang-related pathologies, and other social afflictions, the black community's capacity to develop black athletic talent has likewise deteriorated--a situation that will ultimately and inevitably be reflected at the more advanced levels of black sports participation.

Secondly, in the normal course of their development black athletes typically have not allowed racism to distract them from commitment to athletic excellence. On a day-to-day basis, they are typically painfully aware of the racism in their sports and the threat and potential it holds for limiting and restricting their opportunities and outcomes. Yet they do not become preoccupied with this racism or make it a principal focus of their athletic involvement. They strive instead to become the best and most proficient athletes that they can be, to constantly elevate and advance their athletic competence and skills toward the end of doing everything in their power as athletes to realize their full productive potential. Racism is, therefore, placed in proper perspective as a factor to be contended with on the same level and in the same context as any other *constant* in the competitive sports environment, e.g., opposing athletes, hostile fans, or the weather. Great black athletes are not able to transcend racism because they are great athletes, they are great athletes at least in part because on a day-to-day basis they are able to transcend racism by placing it in its proper place and priority relative to the full constellation of concerns and challenges confronting them in the development of their athletic careers. Indeed, some—though as has been suggested, by no means all—of the reluctance of black athletes to become involved in antiracism activism stems not from some inherent conservatism or Uncle Tomism, but from an honest, almost intuitive difference of perspective with non-athletes over the value of targeting racism as **the** priority concern in black advancement strategies. Now, this by no means is to suggest that the battle against racism is futile, unnecessary, or that it should not be waged. The point here is that a major factor determining the success of any battle against racism—irrespective of the arena involved—has always been the capability and readiness of black people to take advantage of any opportunity space created in the wake of that struggle even as they struggle.

So in those cases where the battle against racism in sports has been actively and openly waged as a priority concern by such black athletes as Jackie Robinson, Bill Russell, Jim Brown, Tommie Smith, and John Carlos, Kareem Abdul Jabbar, Mike Warren, Lucius Allen, Arthur Ashe, Muhammad Ali, and, of course, Paul Robeson, their concern with racism never eclipsed their pursuit of athletic excellence. Indeed, in virtually every case, this pursuit intensified owing to the certainty that an unsympathetic sports establishment likely would look upon any diminution of athletic competence as an opportunity to dismiss both the antiracist struggle and the athlete waging it. These athletes met the challenges of racism along with, not in lieu of, meeting the challenges of athletic participation. They struggled against racism in sports toward the end of creating the opportunity space to express and demonstrate their excellence, competence, and competitiveness. The goal of the antiracism struggle in sports has never been to lower the standards or dilute the challenges of athletic competition. So despite the fact that sport today is more competitive than ever, and that neither the NFL the NBA, Major League Baseball, nor any Division I NCAA football or basketball program has ever staged an affirmative action athlete draft or recruitment effort targeting black athletes, black athletes are not only represented in disproportionately high numbers but they also dominate in all of these arenas of mainstream sports. Thus, while the black athlete **role** today can be validly seen as a barometer of African-American circumstances, the disposition and approach that the greatest of black athletes have taken to meeting the challenges of both the athlete role and racism might well herald the proper disposition toward the challenges confronting black Americans in all spheres of endeavor.

So, notwithstanding the currently minimal collective potential of black athletes as institutional resources, there is still a great deal to be gained from an understanding of the black athlete's promise and circumstances—whether as the proverbial canary in the mineshaft or as the herald on the mountain top signaling a more promising approach to black advancement.

CONCLUSION: NOW'S THE TIME

Nothing in this presentation should be construed as being anti-integration. And there most certainly is no suggestion that there was or is currently any redeeming virtue or value in segregation. To the contrary, not only is rational integration imperative to stability in our multiracial pluralistic society, but it is absolutely necessary to the realization of the full potential of this nation's human resources. Here, it has been the method of integration and the corresponding almost obligatory degradation of black institutional development that have been placed at issue. In sports, the benefits of integration as implemented must be weighed against its costs relative to black institutional erosion and collapse; relative to the outcomes of thousands of black athletes now on the streets without college degrees or job skills after earning tens of millions of dollars for the colleges and universities that they represented in sports; and relative to the black interclass estrangement and alienation that have left millions of black youths without the requisite spectrum of mentors and role models, increasing their vulnerability to influences antithetical to their interests and, by extension, to those of black society. In the final analysis, athletes will emerge collectively as black institutional resources only when black leadership and black people place equal priority upon developing programmatic strategies to both combat racism through committed creative struggle and to transcend racism through excellence and competence, to both achieve integration into the national life of this society and to develop the institutions of the traditional black community. This both-and (as opposed to either-or) approach to the problems of black human resource development and control is imperative—not merely another option. Black people must be able to transcend racist obstacles to goal achievement especially when objective conditions are not optimally conducive to successfully combating those conditions. In this society, with its long history of anti-black racism, any potential for full black equality of opportunity in a racially integrated pluralistic American mainstream rests strongly upon the capabilities of institutions within the black community to incite, nurture, and sustain black aspirations toward excellence, competence, and achievement. Only under these circumstances can it be expected that black athletes—along with black lawyers, black doctors, black teachers, black ministers, black politicians, and blacks from all other potentially contributory walks and stations of life—will collectively accept the privileged calling to serve black people as an institutional resource, to lift as they climb.

NOTES

[1]David Meltzer, ed., *Reading Jazz*, (San Francisco: Mercury Haise, Inc., 1993), pp. 11-12, 30.

[2]For several provocative analyses relating to the conception of racism as a permanent and integral feature of American life, see Derrick Bell, *Faces At The Bottom Of The Well* (New York: Basic Books, 1992); Jennifer Hochschild, *The New American Dilemma* (New Haven: Yale University Press, 1984); George M. Fredrickson, *The Black Image in the White Mind* (Middletown, CT: Wesleyan University Press, 1987); Jack Levin and William Levin, *The Functions of Discrimination and Prejudice* (New York: Harper and Row 1975); and Theodore Cross, *The Black Power Imperative* (New York: Faulkner, 1984).

[3]See Thomas Smith, "Outside The Pale: The Exclusion of Blacks from the National Football League, 1934-1946," *Journal of Sport History*, Vol. 15, No. 3, 1988 p. 275.

[4]*Ibid.* p. 259

[5]*Ibid.* p. 277

[6]See Raymond Franklin, *Shadows of Race and Class* (Minneapolis: University of Minnesota Press, 1991); Ray L. Brooks, *Rethinking the American Race Problem* (Berkeley: University of California Press, 1990); Theodore Cross, *The Black Power Imperative* (1984); Mike Davis, *City of Quartz* (New York: Vintage Books, 1992).

[7]See Robert M. Sellers, "Black Student Athletes: Reaping the Benefits or Recovering From Exploitation," Dana Brooks and Ronald Althouse, eds., *Racism in College Athletics: The African-American Athlete's Experience* (Morgantown, WV: Fitness Information Technologies, Inc., 1993), p. 144.

[8]See Edwin Anderson and Donald South, "Racial Differences in Collegiate Recruiting, Retention and Graduate Rates,"Brooks and Althouse, eds., *Racism in College Athletics, op. cit.*, p. 88.

[9]See Othello Harris, "African-American Predominance in Collegiate Sport" in Brooks and Althouse, eds., p. 67.

[10]Anderson and South, "Racial Differences," p. 93.

[11]Harris, "African-American Predominance," p. 64.

[12]Brooks and Althouse, *Racism in College*, p. 123.

[13]*Ibid.*, p. 127.

[14]"1993 Racial Report Card," *Center for the Study of Sport in Society Digest,* Vol. 4, No. 2 Summer 1993, pp. 6-7.

[15]Norma Chad, "Balance of Power Affects Balance of Color," *The Washington Post*, Sports Section, June 22, 1989, p. 1.

[16]From minutes of National Association of Black Journalists, section on Sport and Black America, Houston, TX, July 24, 1993.

[17]See Yumi L. Wilson, "Richmond High Drops Varsity Football", *San Francisco Chronicle*, September 8, 1993, p. 1.

Mission to Mandate: Self-Development through the Black Church

W. Franklyn Richardson

THE BLACK CHURCH: THE CORNERSTONE OF THE AFRICAN-AMERICAN COMMUNITY

Even before Dr. Martin Luther King, Jr.'s death in 1968, there was a growing realization that the frontier area for the civil rights movement concerned economic justice and equal opportunity.[1] Since then, African Americans have learned, by trial and error, that waiting for the abundant blessings over Jordan were not sufficient for their Sitz-em-Leben and that "no one will help us, for us, but us." This is not to negate the progress made on the social and educational fronts by blacks in America; however, experience has taught us that when it comes to economic revitalization and investment, charity always begins at home. Thus, in a society that continues to live by (sociopolitical and economic) double standards based not on "the content of character, but on the color of one's skin" (M.L. King, Jr.), African Americans must turn inward to find the needed strength to define their own economic destiny through self-help programs and cooperative partnerships and initiatives. "For no man or community of men can elevate another. Elevation must always come from within."[2] The African-American church past and present continues to serve as the cornerstone of the African-American community, liberating it from the crucible of economic deprivation, dehumanization, depression, and oppression. Today upon this rock, African-American people are building their communities into economic enterprises.

> "The Negro churches were the birthplaces of Negro schools and of all agencies which sought to promote the intelligence of the masses; and even today, no agency serves to disseminate news or information so quickly and effectively among Negroes as the church. . . . Consequently, all movements for social betterment are apt to center in the churches. Beneficial societies keep in touch; cooperative and building associations have lately sprung up; the minister acts as an employment agent; considerable charitable and relief work is done; and special meetings are held to aid special projects. Moreover, the race problem in all its phases is continually discussed, and indeed from this forum many a youth go forth inspired to work."[3]

The black church was the birth canal through which the African-American community's identity was born; just as a mother continues to nourish her newborn child with the milk from her breasts through maturity into adulthood, so the black church continues to function as the surrogate mother to the African-American community in the world. It was in the black church that African Americans were first accepted and affirmed when there was no other hiding place or citadel of hope to be found. It was in the black church that African-American men and women, boys and girls learned the three Rs: reading, writing, and arithmetic, when the doors to public schools and colleges were barred by segregation and discrimination. It was the African-American church that was the first and last hope for African-American people who were viewed as three-fifths of a man by white society and denied access to jobs because they were considered intellectually inferior, insignificant, and invisible as a race. It was the African-American church that first contributed to the

> "formation of the black self-help tradition and to the establishment of an economic ethos of uplift for the race that emphasized the following virtues and moral values: industry, thrift, discipline, sobriety, and long-term sublimation rather than immediate gratification. Black churches led in the spreading of this ethic of economic nationality among newly freed masses during the Reconstruction period. Thus, the African-American church functioned as the first (economic sociopolitical) liberation movement in the self-defining of African-American people in the United States. The black church had a major role in establishing the self-help tradition during a time when there were no social welfare agencies, and private philanthropy was reserved for other groups. Black churches and their allied institutions, like the mutual aid societies, the quasi-religious fraternal lodges, and the benevolent and burial associations, which often met in the churches, helped to create the first major black financial institutions: the black-owned banks and the black life insurance companies."[4]

While many hurdles have been overcome in the advancement of African-American people, the black community at large is in a state of chaos. "A staggering 44,428 black males were murdered between 1980 and 1985—nearly equal the total number of Americans killed during the entire Vietnam conflict. In 1990, African Americans stand a 10 times greater chance of being murdered than whites. Moreover, blacks stand: a 40 percent greater chance of being burglarized than whites and a 25 percent greater chance of being assaulted than whites."[5] Today, when one in four black males is incarcerated or on parole, and where a disproportionate number of black men is addicted to or sells drugs, not to mention teenage pregnancy, single parenting, divorce, unemployment, poverty, and the overwhelming sense of hopelessness and helplessness, the African-American church must once again rise and provide the catalyst for change necessary for the revitalization of the African-American community. This stimulus must be holistic in its approach, but it necessitates an infusion of economic development and self-help programs geared toward black enterprise in the African-American community. "This vision for community development can be attributed to three key elements of the African-American church tradition: (1) the strong sense of cooperative economics fostered by the influence of West African culture; (2) the authenticating of the Judeo-Christian tradition, which calls for justice and righteousness; and (3) the creation of a religious system grounded in ministry to both the spiritual and social needs of the community."[6]

In retrospect, African-American people have learned that citizenship and education are not enough to survive in America. Since African Americans' beginnings in this country, there has been an incessant desire on their part to prove to their oppressors that they were capable of "manhood Christianity" and citizenship. They sought to gain whites' approval through means of education and moral development. Moreover,

"it was generally agreed among black churches that the economic standing of the race was directly proportional to the level of educational development. Hence, they believed that improvement in the latter would result in a corresponding improvement in the former. Although many black economic enterprises had their beginnings in the black churches, and although the churches themselves constituted major economic institutions, they never gave high institutional priority to black economic development. Hence, the churches expended much less energy in that sphere of their life than in education, moral training, and civil rights. The reasons for this are certainly multiple, but a major one is that blacks viewed education and civil rights as necessary conditions for economic development. To combat racial discrimination and segregation in education, the black churches established a variety of schools, many of which were partially supported by monies from white churches and liberal philanthropists. Several of those schools continue, a few of the most prominent being Lane College (Christian Methodist Episcopal), Wilberforce University (African Methodist Episcopal), Livingstone College (African Methodist Episcopal Zion), and American Baptist College of the Bible in the South (National Baptist Convention, U.S.A., Inc.). Each of these schools comprised a theological seminary as well."[7]

Needless to say, more than 30 years since the civil rights movement began that stimulated African Americans into creative thinking and academic pursuits, a disproportionate number of African-American communities remains in a state of economic deprivation. The past has taught us that citizenship—however we may choose to quantify it—and educational developments are not sufficient to ensure African Americans a viable economic future in a country that in theory cares for all its citizens but in practice shuns those who are largely responsible for building it.

HOW FAR WE HAVE COME BY FAITH

Historically, the black church has been the preeminent institution in the black community for strengthening and stabilizing black families. As its moral teacher, guardian, and financial advisor, the black church has provided African Americans with the means necessary to not only survive but also to thrive in White America. When there were no outside educational opportunities offered, the black church rose to teach its own. When wages were low and resources were depleted, the black church rose and provided for its own. When racist propaganda tried to annihilate African Americans' self-consciousness, self-identity, and dignity, it was the black church that arose with a message of hope and courage. The black church has secured the African-American community on every leaning side and has stood perpetually as its refuge and strength. Truly, the black church is the life-blood and hallmark of character and fortitude in the African-American community. According to *Emerging Trends*, 78 percent of African Americans are "churched" compared to 72 percent nationwide; 37 percent of African Americans are "superchurched" compared to 31 percent nationwide; the "unchurched" rate among black people is 22 percent compared to 28 percent nationwide; and 3 percent of black people claim to be "totally nonreligious" compared to 4 percent nationwide (see Figure 1). All of the church affiliation

Figure 1

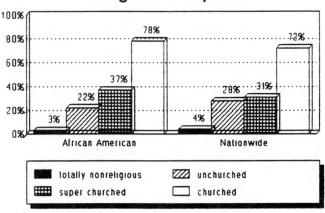

African American vs. Nationwide Religious Comparison

Source: *Emerging Trends*, Vol. 9, No. 5 (May 1987).

116

rates of African Americans tend to be slightly higher than the national rate. The weekly church attendance rate of black people at 43 percent in 1986 is also slightly above the national average of 40 percent.[8]

The data suggest that African Americans are more likely to be part of a local congregation than not. Moreover, given the relationship between the pastor and the pew, it is a given that an indelible bond is present upon which to build an empowerment program.

Stephen L. Carter, in *The Culture of Disbelief: How American Law And Politics Trivialize Religious Devotion,* discusses the religious nature of the civil rights movement and the fact that it was led by a minister whose motivation was religious in nature. Carter reminds us of how easy it is to trivialize the fact that Dr. King was a minister or the strength of the church, for that matter. "When pundits discuss the work of Dr. Martin Luther King, Jr.—the only member of the clergy whose life we celebrate with a national holiday—the fact of his religious calling is usually treated as a relatively unimportant aspect of his career if, indeed, it is mentioned at all. The liberal reluctance to acknowledge the religious aspect of the civil rights movement is a close cousin to another societal blind spot: the refusal to admit the centrality of religion to most of the black community itself. As a group, black Americans are significantly more devout than white Americans. By some measures, a recent study concluded black Americans are 'the most religious people in the world.' For example, black Americans are more likely than any other Americans to have a high level of confidence in the church or organized religion and are much more likely than other Americans to be church members and to attend church weekly."[9]

The African-American church, by the magnitude of its size and the overwhelming commitment of its constituency, has been an effective platform from which to be the catalyst for change. The black church has at its beckoning call the economic strength of some small countries when pooled and resourced properly. It is a dynamic force.

The church and, by implication, African Americans have leverage with which to induce white corporate America into a bargaining position. In a 1993 random survey conducted by the National Baptist Convention's New York Entertainment Committee, it was discovered that "in the New York metropolitan area, 600 churches deposit $152 million annually in 21 banks, and they have $40 million in loans. That means that each Monday morning, these churches deposit over $3 million in New York banks. With this kind of capital, the necessary leverage to facilitate policy changes and [to] eliminate discrimination in lending and hiring practices already exist[s]. Ergo, with this one sampling, we can see that the conservative updated numbers reflect-

Figure 2

Blacks Distribution Of Charitable Giving Comparison (Religious Category)

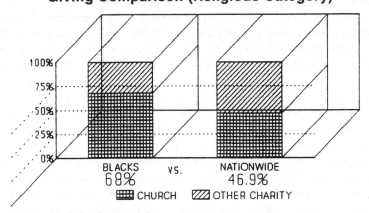

Source: *The Black Church & Economics* as reported by Emmett Carson for the Joint Center for Political Studies.

ing the income of the black church as $2 billion annually"[10] listed by the Lincoln and Mamiya study could well be as high as $3 billion.

It is clear that enormous economic resources pass through our hands. There are 65,000 churches connected with the Congress of National Black Churches, Inc. (CNBC), alone (see Figure 3). The Congress is composed of

Figure 3

The Congress of National Black Churches Inc. (CNBC)

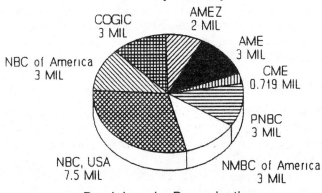

Breakdown by Denominations

Note: CNBC uses a conservative figure of 19 ML (million) to compensate for dual affililation within the Baptist Convention.

eight historically black denominations representing 250,000 church employees and in excess of 19 million worshippers.

These resources, coupled with the tremendous financial expertise that has been developed in our black men and women, make it conceivable that we can do much to assure our economic viability. The elections of African Americans—more than 330 mayors, 40 U. S. Congresspersons, a U.S. Senator, and a governor—all attest to what we can accomplish when we lock our arms.

The societal and political gains which have been the result of earnest cooperation can be enhanced by a renewal of our collective consciousness toward empowerment. However, the economic empowerment we seek must have a broad-based focus. We must seek empowerment which enhances not some individuals and elitist contingents but that which is intentional in improving the plight of many in the African-American community. As we seek self-empowerment, we must avoid being swept into the European or Western notion of nonintegrated or fragmented aspects of our struggle. We must recognize the interrelatedness of aspects of our struggle. The social, political, and economic factors must be held in tension with the spiritual, moral, and ethical principles. Our community needs a holistic healing.

Our liberation must be multidimensional. In his 1967 speech, "Where Do We Go From Here?," Dr. Martin Luther King, Jr., issued this economic challenge to the black middle class: "It is time for the Negro middle class to rise up from its stool of indifference, to retreat from its flight into unreality, and to bring its full resources, its heart, its mind, and its checkbook to the aid of the less fortunate brother."[11] Until we accept the challenge that a few privileged African Americans do not constitute a community, we will continually suffer as a people. We must not compromise our ethics or morality for material gains. History has shown us what happens to a people who compromise their values. We must have a theology and a way of living informed by an understanding that God is on the side of our empowerment, and that heaven is not only a destination to be reached in the "then and there" but also a vision to be realized in the "here and now."

AFRICAN-AMERICAN COMMUNITY INVESTMENT

African-American community investment is a crucial form of the ministry of self-help and -empowerment. It is paramount to the vitality and sustaining power of the black church as well as of the African-American community's present economic plight. History has taught that "we cannot live by prayer and fasting alone"; we need economic empowerment. The black church has awakened to the realization that we are our own greatest asset, and "community investment is a strategy that can help people at the grass-roots level while providing models that can be used on a broader level. Community investment not only helps members of local congregations learn about poverty and wealth, examine their understanding of stewardship, and put capital at the service of the gospel,"[12] but it also serves as a way of mobilizing African Americans' consciousness and promoting the black church as a viable part of the African-American community.

Community investment can take the form of financing community land trusts, housing cooperatives, community loan funds, community credit unions, and worker-owned businesses. These ideas are exemplified by several African-American congregations of varying sizes from the inner city to the rural South, as reported by *The Wall Street Journal* in an article entitled "More Black Churches Go Into Business" (January 1993).

According to the *Journal*:

> Most members of Hartford Memorial Baptist Church in Detroit's Northwest side aren't on welfare. In fact, many are doctors, lawyers, accountants, and teachers. Hartford's pastor, the Rev. Charles Adams, was confronted by a challenge. A decade ago, his sprawling church was surrounded by bottle-strewn dirt lots, abandoned buildings, drug houses, and plots of wildly growing grass. Today, however, the neighborhood is bustling with activity. Numerous shops line the main thoroughfare, and more businesses are popping up. The 7,200 members of Hartford Memorial are largely responsible for the change. The church opened a social service center in 1977, and it provides food, clothing, medical help, and emotional counseling to the under-privileged. It also started a school to train former criminals and drug addicts to be auto mechanics. Next, Rev. Adams assessed $1 million from his congregation to buy lots that he described as sitting foul and unused.

The church leased those lots to Kentucky Fried Chicken and McDonald's restaurants, which quickly built large franchises and hired workers from the community. Once those businesses opened, other companies began investing in the area. The neighborhood is now home to, among other businesses, a Pizza Hut, Rally's hamburger restaurant, a record shop, and numerous convenience stores. Hartford also owns several small auto repair shops in the neighborhood. "The church awakened the financial community to the value of the property," says Rev. Adams. In addition, Hartford Memorial works with a coalition of area hospitals and colleges to invest further in the community. With their help, it plans to open a "car care mall."

Another example of African-American churches investing in the community is Chicago's Christ Universal Temple. It owns a large banquet facility that it rents to businesses and schools. The church is also building a school and a bookstore.

In addition to the above-mentioned black church enterprises is the monumental effort at Greater Christ Temple Church in Meridian, MS. It dates back to 1977, when Bishop Luke Edwards gathered his 200-member congregation to discuss salvaging his parishioners' pride and their decaying community. The bishop's task was formidable. Back then, 96 percent of the congregation was on welfare. "I talked to them about helping themselves," says Bishop Edwards. "I showed the congregation that they have the buying power to deliver themselves if they spend their money right." **Bishop Edwards combined church members' food stamps and purchased items from a wholesale grocer.** The church then began running a grocery store out of its auditorium. After four months, the members had earned enough money to purchase a supermarket.

Today, the church owns a 4,000-acre farm, seven tractors, hundreds of cattle, two meat processing plants, a bakery, three restaurants, and an auto repair shop. It has also expanded its ministry to Alabama. **And none of its members is on welfare because they have been given jobs by the church.**

Greater Christ Temple uses the profits from its businesses to invest in other ventures. It owns several dormitories, where most church members live. Young people who have problems at home or who have been in trouble with the law also live there. The church operates office buildings, a computer room, a nursery, a cafeteria, a medical clinic, a library, a machine shop, and a school. In short, it has created its own community.

Another African-American church that is community minded and putting its money where its mouth is is New Sunny Mount Baptist Church in St. Louis, MO. It has created 15 jobs in its struggling community and owns a bus rental company and a parking lot that it leases to schools and businesses. It also owns a 328-acre retreat that it rents to various groups. As evidenced by these models, economic liberation and self-empowerment through community investments by black churches in the African-American community are possible and financially rewarding. These models are proof-positive paradigms of self-development projects for other black churches.

AFRICAN-AMERICAN COLLECTIVE CONSCIOUSNESS

The collective consciousness of African-American people stemmed from their forefathers' struggle for emancipation from the crucible of slavery. Although few crosses are burned today and lynching is nonexistent, and although few Ku Klux Klan members wear their white robes publicly, the impetus behind the system of slavery remains. The collective consciousness of African-American people was therefore a coping mechanism developed to survive their dehumanizing circumstance. This strength, born out of weakness, was crystallized in 1787, when Richard Allen, Absalom Jones, and other black worshippers withdrew from St. George's Methodist Episcopal Church in Philadelphia, PA, after being pulled from their knees during a worship service in a gallery they did not know was closed to black Christians. In protest, they all left the church in a body and began the African Methodist Episcopal Church with their own financial resources.

This incident, though far removed in time from African-American people's experience today, still stands as a watershed for the mandate of economic collective consciousness. It is no sin to seek one's own self-betterment, for "no one is going to help us, for us, but us." Therefore, the proverb that says, "If we don't think of ourselves, we're nothing; but if we think only of ourselves, we're worse," not only resonates the African-American collective consciousness but also moves forward towards bridge-building through co-operative links with private banks, insurance companies, and other federally funded agencies.

As a part of fulfilling its mandate (Luke 4:19-23), the church must continue to seek ways in which it may open the doors to financial empowerment for African Americans. Today, many African-American clergy are reading Peter Drucker and are getting acquainted with the language of the nonprofits. Churches have found an avenue of development funding beyond Sunday collections by responding to RFPs (request for proposals). Moreover, foundations, philanthropists, and the federal government have found that the church is in touch with the community and has a better understanding of community assessments and strategies for productive development.

Many churches have created or are in the process of creating 501(c)3 non-profit foundations or community development corporations. These corporations provide churches with a streamlined approach to pragmatic outreach programs. The National Congress for Community Economic Development has compiled a fairly extensive and diverse list of case studies of church-based programs in *Restoring Broken Places and Rebuilding Communities.* The models included in this book are helpful both for knowing what has been done and following along the development process of how it can be replicated. These cooperative development projects are individual church efforts as well as venture partnerships with other African-American congregations. Under the aegis of a collaborative effort, the Memphis Church and Community Investment Fund (CCIF), comprised of 22 churches, created a venture capital fund to stimulate a "warning level" of economic activity in African-American communities. The fund was capitalized at an "effective level" with each church contributing $1,200 per year to the enterprise. The churches invested $24,000 and selected Valley Management, a subsidiary of the Tennessee Valley Center for Minority Business Development, to manage the fund. Although this program has not been fully successful, its implications are far-reaching. Currently, there is $90,000 in assets. Considering the initial investment, the positive returns illustrate that the venture has had a modest success. If allowed to grow, this fund could become a strong resource for serious new business proposals.

All of these case studies are promising, but none is as amazing as the development of Hope Plaza Shopping Center in Philadelphia. Hope Plaza is a model for effective ministry and a symbol of the credibility of the black church's economic power. This remarkable facility of 50,000 square feet boasts as its tenants Thriftway Supermarket and a two-story McDonald's restaurant. Each of these tenants has been locked in with a long-term (50 years) lease. Hope Plaza, Inc. (HPI), operates a productive center and has been able to turn marginal profits toward other outreach programs. HPI was able to construct its mammoth facility with a U.S. Housing and Urban Development (HUD) grant. The repayment terms of the $1.150 million Urban Development Action Grant (UDAG) required **zero percent** interest the first 10 years, 3 percent the second 10 years, and 5 percent for the last 10 years. "Never before in Philadelphia had a city development project received a zero % interest loan."[13]

HPI then obtained $2.8 million in project financing, and the Deliverance Evangelistic Church completed the financing with a $1.33 million loan of its own. This project, with its hefty sum of money, demonstrates the significant leverage the church has and the leverage it can extend to programs aligned with it. The project has provided employment opportunities on the north end of the city. Moreover, it has removed urban blight and replaced it with a strong infrastructure for the future.

Recently, *Black Enterprise* published a special report: "The New Agenda of the Black Church."[14] It is an exceptional look at what churches are doing all over the country. What is clear is that these churches have been forced to enter the secular "public square" in order to serve their constituencies. From Los Angeles to New York, the economic plight of the African-American community has become a major priority; "the black church recognizes that it has to be in the forefront of economic development. It has become evident that black people are simply going to have to stand on their own feet and the black church, with all of its economic power, can help facilitate that by creating businesses.[15]

At present, Allen African Methodist Episcopal Church of Queens, NY, is negotiating to buy a Burger King and a Ben and Jerry's ice cream franchise. In Los Angeles, First African Methodist Episcopal (FAME) Church, under the leadership of Rev. Cecil Murray, has formed the "FAME Renaissance Program to fund community services, business and economic development programs through private and public sources. FAME Corp. is a nonprofit organization established by the church. Shortly after the Renaissance Program was formed, church officials competed for and received a $1 million grant from the Walt Disney Co., leading to the creation of the Micro Loan Program, which supplies low-interest loans of $2,000 to $20,000 to minority entrepreneurs in the area. So far, the program has approved about 34 loans totaling more than $500,000."[16]

The church has created a ready resource for a community often passed over by traditional funding sources. The long-range goal of the church is to capitalize its program with $10 million from the business and private sector.

"While a number of African-American churches have just begun to launch the economic redevelopment projects for their communities, Atlanta's Wheat Street Baptist Church began changing the face of its historically black neighborhood in the early '60s. Today, it boasts more than $33 million in real estate holdings, making it one of the wealthiest African-American churches in the nation."[17] This is without a doubt true economic clout. The church as a whole is in the process of gaining its practical equilibrium in this ever-expanding area. The year 2000 may prove that the church is the most adaptable institution ever.

The Congress of National Black Churches (CNBC) has created a Church Insurance Partnership Agency (CIPA). This multi-line insurance agency is a wholly owned subsidiary of the Congress. Its economic empowerment plan offers property casualty and life insurance for churches of CNBC's member denominations. This endeavor will facilitate the ability of African-American churches to receive affordable coverage and loans. The Congress is also developing agreements with long-distance telephone carriers for reduced rates.

The collective buying power of the black community has been estimated at $400 billion, more than the gross national product of Canada. If we work cooperatively, we have the leverage to broker any deal and secure credit for any project we desire.

Recently, the courts have come down hard on the banking industry for its selective racist lending practices. The banking industry has made it very difficult if not impossible for minorities to secure the start-up capital for new business ventures. The African-American church will have to begin to flex its collective muscle to ensure that we receive our fair share. The Community Reinvestment Act (CRA) of 1977 must be pushed to the limit in order to see measurable change for individual entrepreneurs.

Martin Luther King, Jr., reminded us of a two-pronged economic power: "There exists two other areas where Negroes can exert substantial influence on the broader economy. As employees and consumers, Negroes' numbers and their strategic disposition endows them with a certain bargaining strength."[18] This is the leverage the black church can employ. Since the civil rights movement, no institution has channeled the collective power of African Americans as the black church has. It is reasonable and practical to use our strength to make positive change.

Facing the year 2000 in America, we as African Americans must grapple with the problems of economic misfortune that our forefathers were trying to grapple with throughout history. It is evident in America that it is no longer a matter of economic fairness or equality for African Americans but a matter of self-help and survival. The African-American community is realizing more and more that it is dependent on the black church not only for guidance and hope but also for economic stability and community investment. The black church's mission and mandate are inextricably connected to the African-American community. It is the talisman and anchor that will keep African-American people from sinking in the quicksand of economic deprivation. The black church will provide the transforming, life-giving power and opportunities whereby black men, women, boys, and girls can live in the mainstream of economic independence with self-pride and confidence. The new mission and mandate of the black church no longer solely minister to the spiritual and educational well-being of the African-American community but are committed to the third dimension that has eluded us for so long—self-help through economic black enterprise.

ENDNOTES

[1]C. Eric Lincoln and Lawrence H. Mamiya, eds., *The Black Church in the African-American Experience* (Durham: Duke University Press, 1990), p. 273.

[2]Bishop C.M. Tanner, "Education, Economics, Civil Rights," in Peter Paris, ed., *The Social Teaching of the Black Churches* (Philadelphia: Fortress Press, 1985), p. 69.

[3]W.E.B. Du Bois, "The Economic Roles and Functions of the Black Church in the Past: A Historical Overview," in C. Eric Lincoln and Lawrence H. Mamiya, eds., *The Black Church in the African-American Experience* (Durham: Duke University Press, 1990), p. 250.

[4]Lincoln, *The Black Church*, p. 243.

[5]Earl Hutchinson, *The Mugging of Black America* (Chicago: African American Images, 1990), p. x.

[6]Robert A. Clemetson, ed., *Restoring Broken Places and Rebuilding Communities: A Casebook on African-American Church Involvement in Community Economic Development* (Washington, DC: The National Congress for Community Economic Development, 1993), p. iii.

[7]Paris, *The Social Teaching of the Black Churches*, p. 70.

[8]Lincoln, *op. cit.*, p. 261.

[9]Stephen L. Carter, *The Culture of Disbelief: How American Law and Politics Trivialize Religious Devotion* (New York: Basic Books, A Division of HarperCollins Publishers, Inc., 1993), pp. 59-60.

[10]Lincoln, *The Black Church*, p. 260.

[11]James M. Washington, *A Testament of Hope: The Essential Writings of Martin Luther King, Jr.* (San Francisco: Harper and Row Publishers, 1986), p. 600.

[12]Julia Weaver, "Community Investment: The Ministry of Empowerment," *The Christian Century*, April 1991.

[13]All of the case studies in this section are reprinted with permission from *Restoring Broken Places and Rebuilding Communities,* published by the National Congress for Community Economic Development.

[14]Lloyd Gite, "The New Agenda of the Black Church: Economic Development for Black America," *Black Enterprise* 24:5, December 1993, pp. 54-59.

[15]C. Eric Lincoln, *The Black Church*, as quoted by Gite, "The New Agenda of the Black Church," p. 56.

[16]Gite, *op. cit.*, p. 57.

[17]*Ibid.*, p. 58.

[18]Washington, *op. cit.*

Historically Black Colleges and Universities: Taking Care of Home

Mary E. Dilworth, Ed.D.

Institutions of higher education (IHE), by nature, are typically perceived to be essential components in the advancement of society. Although many historically black colleges and universities (HBCUs) were established amidst legal segregation, they are no exception. More than a century after many HBCUs were established, they remain—by and large—the source for leadership, culturally responsive thought, and action for the African-American community. The challenge for the coming decades is to advance and propagate these attributes beyond the African-American community, while at the same time acknowledging and accommodating their primary mission and audience. In noting HBCUs' well-documented successes, this chapter will also focus on issues and conditions that appear to impede HBCUs' growth and to stifle their establishment as power brokers within the educational arena and beyond the African-American community.

HBCUs: A HISTORICAL PERSPECTIVE

There are approximately 105 colleges and universities in this nation that were established for and/or by residential coincidence which have predominantly black student bodies. They are typically referred to as historically or traditionally black colleges and universities.* Aside from the fact that the vast majority of these institutions are located in the South, their profiles mirror those of majority/white higher education institutions in this country. Specifically, HBCUs include college and university total enrollments ranging from 384 to 12,000 students; rely on public, private, and/or religious organizations for support; provide academic programs ranging from marine biology to clothing and textiles; and award degrees ranging from associate of

---

* The precise number of these institutions varies for a number of reasons. A distinction is typically drawn between those institutions established prior to 1964, whose principal mission was (and continues to be) the education of black Americans and those colleges and universities that emerged or were established in predominantly black communities during the '60s, '70s, and '80s. Certain of these institutions are further distinguished as they were established with the intent of educating blacks, but whose enrollments have since become predominantly white. A 1992 National Center for Education Statistics publication reports 105 HBCUs, 40 public four-year colleges and universities, 11 public two-year colleges, 46 private four-year colleges, five private two-year colleges, and three private professional institutions (Hoffman, Snyder, and Sonnenberg, 1992).

arts (AA) to doctor of philosophy (Ph.D.).   As Garibaldi (1991, 104) notes, ". . . these institutions cannot be viewed as monolithic."

Perhaps the most consistently compelling argument for the maintenance of HBCUs is their level of productivity throughout history, despite constraining economic and societal conditions. For instance, during the great economic Depression between 1929-1940, enrollment at HBCUs rose by 66 percent compared to a rise of 36 percent at all colleges. By 1940 current expenditures at HBCUs were more than double the amounts expended in 1929, after adjustment for inflation (Hoffman, Snyder, and Sonnenberg, 1992).

More recent testaments to these institutions' value and tenacity include the following:

- HBCUs constitute only 3 percent of the nation's 3,559 institutions of higher education; however, they enroll over 17 percent of the black students in college.
- In 1989-90, more than 1 in 4 black bachelor degree recipients earned their degrees from an HBCU.
- Compared to other IHEs, a larger proportion of students at HBCUs enrolls in four-year and private institutions.
- Nearly 1 in 7 blacks receives his/her first professional degree from an HBCU; e.g., veterinary medicine (63 percent), and at least 25 percent of blacks receiving degrees in 1989-90 in theology, dentistry, and pharmacy attended HBCUs.
- HBCUs have provided undergraduate training for three-fourths of all black persons holding a doctorate degree; three-fourths of all black officers in the armed services; and four-fifths of all black federal judges (C.M. Hoffman, T.D. Snyder, and B. Sonnenberg, 1992). Enrollment at the majority of private HBCUs (represented by the 43 colleges and universities that are members of the United Negro College Fund (UNCF)) reached an all-time high of 53,179 in fall 1992.
- Although the number of African Americans graduating from public high schools declined by 8 percent during 1986-1991, applications to UNCF institutions increased by 27 percent (Fordyce and Kirschner, 1993).

Certain disciplines are particularly fortified by HBCUs, e.g., approximately 45 percent of black bachelor degree recipients in agriculture and at least 35 percent of the degrees issued in physical sciences, mathematics, computer and information sciences, life sciences, education, and theology are awarded by HBCUs. Lastly, it is important to note that in some disciplines, e.g., teacher education, HBCUs are more "integrated" than majority institutions enrolling greater proportions of Hispanics, Native Americans, and Asians than their majority counterparts (AACTE, 1993).

Generally speaking, HBCUs have more programs, more faculty, and currently enroll more and better academically prepared students than at any other point in their history. The challenge is to build and expand on this momentum.

THE NEED FOR HBCUs: THE PERCEPTIONS, THE REALITY

To some, it may appear that HBCUs are perennially dissatisfied—complaining of a racist society that deprives and limits opportunity on the basis of race—justifying their existence on missions that are no longer relevant and on the distinctive accomplishments of alumni who have long since gone. On the other hand, the informed observer recognizes that these institutions do indeed operate in a racist society, but excel in spite of it and strongly embrace their missions to educate African Americans who, as a group, are still underserved as they were a century ago. Those with insight understand that HBCUs rightfully take pride in adding to their lists of distinguished graduates names of men and women, alive and well, born after the *Brown v. Board of Education* decision, after the civil rights movement of the '60s, and some even after the Black Power movement of the '70s. These colleges and universities continue to achieve beyond their means, advancing not just individuals but also communities as well.

Historically black colleges and universities have always had proponents and detractors. As John B. Williams (1984) notes, "Ever since the late nineteenth century, when most of the black colleges were founded, government leaders and public policymakers have been ambivalent about the prospects of their continued growth and expansion." Possibly it is this ambivalence that makes many HBCUs apprehensive or cautious in aggressively moving forward and/or in different directions to engage individuals, communities, and nations other than their own and of Africa and of the Caribbean. While HBCUs represent widely diverse faculty and student bodies, there are few examples of HBCU program initiatives with other communities.

History will attest to the tremendous difficulty of these institutions to establish a safe, secure place within academia and society. Throughout their century-old existence, HBCUs have been repeatedly asked the same question: do HBCUs serve a purpose to this society? As Blake (1991, 555) explains, "Desegregation does not necessarily produce movement toward educational equality. It is a means to a specific end—more and better education for children, youth, and adults—not an end in and of itself." Until the nation is willing and able to negotiate a firm and actual commitment to the equality end, the answer must be yes—HBCUs have a place.

The legal desegregation of higher education, particularly in southern and border states, suggests that all is well. It leads one to believe that the doors of colleges and universities are open to all who are prepared and that institutions catering to certain groups, HBCUs in particular, are no longer needed or viable. To some, the pooling of resources, the uniting of forces for equal educational opportunity, is in the common good and that African Americans and their institutions most certainly are on the list of beneficiaries. Consequently, recognizing that equal educational opportunity is a significant part of this century's civil rights struggle, HBCUs are in a compromising situation: either rely on the good will of the nation, i.e., close their doors; accept a partial installment on the education of black students until the nation's majority institutions become credit-worthy, i.e., allow the institutions to close by neglect; or tough it out, i.e., remain open and viable, recognizing that full payment may never come. Clearly, HBCUs have taken the last high road.

Currently, HBCUs are in a battle for what some perceive to be self-survival and others perceive to be a necessary period of reexamination and/or restructuring. In many ways, this decade's most compelling legal challenge, that of the U.S. Supreme Court's June 26, 1992, decision in *United States v. Fordice,* parallels legal challenges of previous decades, especially as it relates to purpose and survival. For instance, in 1973 black college students—supported by the NAACP Legal Defense Fund—successfully sued the federal government for its failure to enforce Title VI of the 1964 Civil Rights Act by issuing grants to institutions that discriminated on the basis of race. As a result of the *Adams v. Richardson* case, a number of southern and border states were issued strict guidelines and timetables to dismantle their dual systems, i.e., of black and white higher education. Specifically, these states were directed to eliminate duplicate program offerings between proximate black and white institutions; to close duplicate institutions in the same vicinities; to merge HBCUs and other colleges and universities; to establish highly desirable graduate and professional programs at HBCUs; and to desegregate faculty and staff systemwide (Joint Center for Political and Economic Studies, 1993, 11).

As the Joint Center's Committee on Policy for Racial Justice provides, after 20 years of administrative and legal developments emanating from this case, there have been some enhancement of traditionally black institutions; some integration of students, faculty, and staff; and governance is more inclusive. However, student and faculty desegregation has occurred more rapidly at HBCUs; relatively fewer blacks have successfully made it into the traditionally white "flagship" institutions (Joint Center for Political and Economic Studies, 1993).

In the more recent *Fordice* decision, the high court has called on Mississippi to exercise an affirmative obligation to eradicate all traces of segregation in its state system of higher education. While making no reference to the *Adams* directives, "The Court flatly rejected the contention that Mississippi had a constitutional duty to upgrade the historically black institutions." Rather, it remanded to the lower courts the decision as to whether "an increase in funding is necessary to achieve full dismantlement" (Joint Center for Political and Economic Studies, 1993, 13).

Given previous state actions in Mississippi, Tennessee, and Louisiana, there is well-founded apprehension among blacks in higher education that, left to their own devices, policymakers will find that the only appropriate action will be to merge certain HBCUs with majority institutions or to close them completely. To some, the former is almost as devastating as the latter. It means integration, not just of people, but also of principles and causes wherein African Americans will undoubtably be left with the short end of the stick.

Although there is nonbinding consensus among most all U.S. colleges and universities on the sentiment of equal education opportunity, as Morris (1979) in his classic work, *Elusive Equality*, notes of HBCUs, "Their specific concern with black students has never permitted them the luxury of indifference to equal opportunity for all." As a result, HBCUs do well by black students. Given the generally poor recruitment, retention, and articulation records of many majority colleges and universities in educating African-American students, to rely solely on these institutions is pure folly. History suggests that minority institutions will rise to this most recent challenge and successfully negotiate maintenance of their institutions, albeit within an alien system. It is nonetheless disheartening to realize that HBCUs enter their bicentennial years grappling with some of the same issues of survival and growth that they did decades ago. It is even more troubling that the same issues are pertinent today.

HBCU FINANCIAL STRENGTH: MAKING DO

"Ideally, the viability of any educational institution should be based on its ability to provide a quality education with adequate resources" (Garibaldi, 1991, 104). As HBCUs attempt to meet the academic needs of their student bodies, they are also confronted with similar external pressures, particularly financial ones. Consistent with their majority/white counterparts, public HBCUs ". . . have weathered multiple, often abrupt, cuts in funding that have forced layoffs and other cutbacks at a time when enrollment and applications have been rising" (El-Khawas, 1993, 3). While private HBCUs report minor funding increases similar to their majority counterparts, they still struggle to maintain quality programs and high enrollments.

The typically less than advantaged background of HBCU students suggests that the HBCU charge is more challenging than that for white/majority institutions. The UNCF reports that its 43 private colleges have dramatically increased the proportion of their operating funds allocated to student aid from 12 percent in 1985-86 to 20 percent at present. Further, in 1991-92, the $4,848 average cost of tuition and fees at UNCF colleges was less than half the $10,017 average charged by private colleges nationally (Fordyce and Kirschner, 1993, viii).

The most recent data available indicate that private and public HBCUs spend about the same proportion of their funds on instruction as do other institutions. However, not surprisingly, public HBCUs spend a higher proportion of their funds on student services and instructional support and on scholarships and fellowships than do other public institutions. Private HBCUs also spend considerable portions of their budgets on student aid. In general, HBCUs also spend a greater proportion of their revenues on improving deteriorating physical plants than do other institutions, which speaks to the cumulative impact of decades of neglect necessitated by disproportionate funding (Hoffman, Snyder, and Sonnenberg, 1992). Maintaining a balance between student financial needs and attending to aging physical plants in order to accommodate new program needs and opportunities are just a few of the challenges facing these institutions in the 1990s.

Historically black colleges and institutions garner financial support from sources similar to other IHEs (see Figure 1). However, public HBCUs secure a smaller proportion of their revenue from endowments, private gifts, grants, and contracts. Private HBCUs rely less on tuition than other private institutions but at roughly the same levels as public HBCUs. While public HBCUs rely on auxiliary services, they do not garner the same level of revenue from items such as film rentals, scientific and literary publications, testing services, or university presses as do other public institutions (Hoffman, Snyder, and Sonnenberg, 1992). One indicator of financial stability is an institution's endowment. The value of the endowment per student at UNCF institutions, $8,117, was only about one-quarter the $30,856 average found at all private four-year colleges in 1990-91 (Fordyce and Kirschner, 1993, viii).

Figure 1. Current-fund revenue of historically black colleges and universities, by source of funds and control of institution: 1988-89

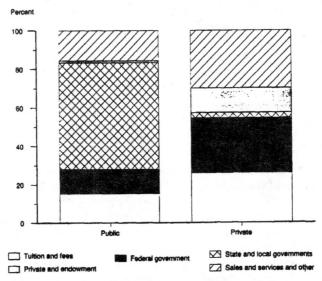

Source: U.S. Department of Education, National Center for Education Statistics, Integrated Postsecondary Education Data System (IPEDS), "Finance" survey.

The financial progress and well-being of HBCUs is directly attributable to the opportunities that they have been afforded, the clients that they serve, and the values that they embrace. They frequently pay a premium for the values that they hold and have a more difficult time than others becoming established in the areas where other institutions garner additional income, prestige, and support, e.g., technology and research. Simply put, most HBCUs seek to educate those in greatest need, i.e., African-American students entering college for the first time at the undergraduate level. Within the higher education community, institutions that issue advanced degrees are in the best position to receive major grants and contracts from government and industry. These institutions in turn attract noted professionals as they are able to pay more competitive salaries than HBCU faculty who are paid approximately 80 percent of the average faculty at postsecondary institutions (Hoffman, Snyder, and Sonnenberg, 1992). These faculty in turn attract students who are often more privileged and less likely to need financial and other support services.

Of all the HBCUs, only 21 universities issue advance professional degrees, e.g., pharmacy, law, and—with one exception, Howard University—these institutions are limited to offering the highest level degrees in two to three areas.

Table 1
Advanced Degree Granting
Historically Black Colleges and Universities

Alabama A&M U.	Clark Atlanta U.
Drew Graduate Medical	Florida A&M U.
Grambling U.	Hampton U.
Howard U.	Jackson State U.
Meharry Medical College	Morehouse College of Medicine
Morgan State U.	North Carolina A&T U.
North Carolina Central U.	South Carolina State U.
Southern U.	Tuskegee Institute
Tennessee State U.	Texas Southern U.
U. of Maryland–Eastern Shore	Virginia Union U.
Xavier U. (LA)	

Sources: "Institutional and Presidential Profiles of the Nation's Historically and Predominantly Black Colleges and Universities," National Association for Equal Opportunity in Higher Education, Vol. XIV, March-April, 1993, and Devarics, C., "Congress Settles HBCU Graduate Funding Issue," *Black Issues in Higher Education,* Vol. 10, No. 18 (November 4, 1993), p. 8.

It should be noted that the limitations on programs and degree level offerings are not self-imposed. The authority to establish graduate and professional programs in public institutions lies with the state, and it is not, or has not been, in the best interest of certain programs to be authorized when and where they will compete, potentially successfully, with neighboring majority institutions for valuable enrollment, grant, and contract revenues.

Within the past three decades, two ambitious government programs have been designed, at least in theory, to increase the institutional capacity of HBCUs to compete effectively for grants and contracts. Specifically, Title III of the Higher Education Amendments of 1965 was authorized to award funds to under-financed colleges which were traditionally isolated from the mainstream of higher education for improvement of their faculty and administration, development of new curricula, student services, etc. (Hill, 1984). As Blakey (1983) notes, the original criteria for eligibility were not race specific, and the absence of clear criteria for identifying the target schools or intended beneficiaries made it particularly difficult to substantiate the claim that the program was originally intended for HBCUs. These institutions were eventually written into the program in 1986; however, this did not occur until after other majority and two-year colleges were able to secure successfully funds from the Title III program.

There is no doubt that Title III funds enhance and continue to assist HBCUs. In fact, the Clinton administration's recently approved 1994 budget request for Title III was 2.7 percent above the 1993 appropriation level, making significantly more funds available to graduate level HBCUs than in the past. However, the lack of any sizable increases in the previous three years, in addition to newly authorized activities in the areas of telecommunications, teacher education, fundraising, and community outreach, as well as set-aside funds for Hispanic-serving institutions, makes Title III dollars far more competitive for HBCUs than before (Payne and Smith, 1993).

One federal effort that has not met its original goals is the White House Initiative (WHI) on Historically Black Colleges and Universities. Operating by executive orders issued by every president since the Carter administration in 1980, this effort was designed to encourage federal agencies to grant a certain percentage of their contract dollars to HBCUs. Each of Carter's successors has tailored and signed executive orders, appointed commissions to advise and report on the initiatives, and organized newsworthy conferences and events. However, the impact of each initiative has been less than impressive. Penalties for noncompliance are nonexistent, and incentives are absent. The result is short term and high visibility for the institutions and the respective administration, but very limited resources for enhancing the infrastructures of the institutions to be more competitive for available contract funds.

For instance, in 1990, the most recent report year data are available, HBCUs received only 5 percent of the $18 billion in federal funding for all institutions of higher education. Approximately 65 percent of this money came from the U.S. Department of Education, with nearly $182 million to Howard University through special congressional authority, and $94.5 million through the Title III program. By and large, the greatest federal funding allocation came from various student financial aid programs. Less than half (43 percent) of federal appropriations was in discretionary awards. In that year, seven of the 27 designated agencies made 30 percent of the federal contribution (Fiscal Year 1990 Annual Federal Performance Report, 1991).

Table 2 provides clear evidence of the disparities in federal contract awards. The HBCU share of FY 1990 funding for agencies awarding $500 million or more to postsecondary institutions ranges from 1.2 percent to 9.3 percent: only 1.2 percent from the National Science Foundation; 1.5 percent from Health and Human Services; 2.5 percent from the Department of Energy; 2.9 percent from NASA; 3.6 percent from the Department of Defense; 8.5 percent from the Education Department; and 9.3 percent from the Department of Agriculture.

A close look at the relationship of HBCUs and their missions with certain of these agencies suggests an even more dismal picture. For instance, Headstart and several other federal programs that by design impact significant numbers of African-American children and families are administered by the Department of Health and Human Services (HHS). It is noteworthy that while HHS accounts for more than half of all research and development (R&D) funds obligated to all postsecondary institutions ($4.9 billion), only 1 percent of these funds was awarded to HBCUs. Further, in the R&D category, which accounts for over 50 percent of all higher education contributions, HBCUs received the smallest share (Stedman, 1993).

Although there is reasonable optimism within the HBCU community that the Clinton initiative will be more robust than those orchestrated by previous Republican administrations, the pace has been slow and the key problem areas of incentives and sanctions are still unresolved. Some HBCU administrators are encouraged by the most recent executive order in that it helps to establish goals for each federal agency and, more importantly, provides the Office of Management and Budget—a federal fiscal agency—with oversight responsibility. Clearly, much more needs to be done, as indicated by the title of the most recent but yet to be released report of the WHI Board, "Not Gaining Ground, But Falling Back: The Condition and Status of Historically Black Colleges and Universities and the Higher Education of African Americans" (Hawkins, 1993).

HBCU LEADERSHIP: MAKING THE GRADE?

As with any type of institution, the leadership sets the tone, pace, and direction. HBCU administrators are no exception. Although Jones (1984) contends HBCU presidents' administrative styles parallel those of others, the presidents of these institutions have been criticized frequently for being more

TABLE 2
Distribution of FY 1990 Obligations by Selected Federal Agencies to Historically Black Colleges and Universities, and Other Higher Education Institutions
(dollars in millions)

	Research and Development	Evaluation	Training	Facilities and Equipment	Fellowships	Tuition Assistance	Other	Total
Department of Agriculture								
HBCUs	9.0%	6.6%	4.5%	17.9%	45.8%	20.9%	0.0%	9.3%
Other IHEs	91.0%	93.4%	95.5%	82.1%	54.2%	79.1%	0.0%	90.7%
Total	$338.7	$368.1	$5.7	$55.5	$14.4	$6.9	$0	$789.2
Department of Commerce								
HBCUs	0.5%	3.2%	8.5%	0.5%	18.4%	9.9%	100.0%	4.5%
Other IHEs	99.5%	96.8%	91.5%	99.5%	81.6%	90.1%	0.0%	95.5%
Total	$5.8	$0.2	$8.2	$15.1	$1.9	$0.2	$0.2	$31.5
Department of Defense								
HBCUs	1.2%	61.1%	5.7%	93.5%	14.3%	5.1%	100.0%	3.6%
Other IHEs	98.8%	38.9%	94.3%	6.5%	85.7%	94.9%	0.0%	96.4%
Total	$1,124.4	$2.1	$55.7	$20.6	$17.4	$191.2	$1.2	$1,412.5
Department of Education								
HBCUs	2.2%	0.0%	14.3%	18.5%	5.6%	4.2%	100.0%	8.5%
Other IHEs	97.8%	0.0%	85.7%	94.4%	95.8%	95.8%	0.0%	91.5%
Total	$266.4	$0	$298.7	$32.0	$34.0	$5,961.6	$277.8	$6,871.3

	Research and Development	Evaluation	Training	Facilities and Equipment	Fellowships	Tuition Assistance	Other	Total
Department of Health and Human Services								
HBCUs	1.0%	19.3%	1.2%	0.5%	8.8%	3.7%	100.0%	1.5%
Other IHEs	99.0%	80.7%	98.8%	99.5%	91.2%	96.3%	0.0%	98.5%
Total	$4,864.7	$0.2	$244.9	$60.0	$265.0	$211.1	$2.8	$5,648.6
Department of Housing and Urban Development								
HBCUs	100.0%	0.0%	94.2%	0.0%	13.1%	0.0%	0.0%	38.0%
Other IHEs	0.0%	0.0%	5.8%	0.0%	86.9%	0.0%	0.0%	62.0%
Total	$0.2	$0	$1.6	$0	$4.1	$0	$0	$5.9
Department of Interior								
HBCUs	7.0%	100.0%	19.2%	100.0%	39.0%	100.0%	100.0%	17.1%
Other IHEs	93.0%	0.0%	80.8%	0.0%	61.0%	0.0%	0.0%	82.9%
Total	20.0	$0.4	$5.0	$0.2	$6.0	$0.02	$0.07	$31.7
Department of Energy								
HBCUs	1.7%	0.0%	100.0%	0.6%	18.3%	28.6%	62.4%	2.5%
Other IHEs	98.30%	0.0%	0.0%	99.4%	81.7%	71.4%	37.6%	97.5%
Total	$478.2	$0	$0.6	$116.9	$3.4	$18.1	$0.5	$617.8
Department of Justice								
HBCUs	100.0%	0.0%	0.0%	0.0%	100.0%	0.0%	0.0%	100.0%
Other IHEs	0.0%	0.0%	0.0%	0.0%	0.0%	0.0%	0.0%	0.0%
Total	—	$0.02	$0	$0	$0	$0.3	$0	$0

	Research and Development	Evaluation	Training	Facilities and Equipment	Fellowships	Tuition Assistance	Other	Total
Department of Labor								
HBCUs	5.9%	0.0%	22.3%	0.0%	27.9%	50.0%	0.0%	20.5%
Other IHEs	94.1%	0.0%	77.7%	100.0%	72.1%	50.0%	0.0%	79.5%
Total	$1.0	$0	$13.4	$0.6	$0.2	$.01	$0	$15.2
Department of State								
HBCUs	0.0%	0.0%	0.0%	0.0%	0.0%	13.3%	0.0%	13.3%
Other IHEs	0.0%	0.0%	0.0%	0.0%	0.0%	86.7%	0.0%	86.7%
Total	$0	$0	$0	$0	$0	$1.2	$0	$1.2
Department of Transportation								
HBCUs	6.3%	0.0%	25.0%	0.2%	6.2%	4.9%	6.5%	9.8%
Other IHEs	93.7%	100.0%	75.0%	99.8%	93.8%	95.1%	93.5%	90.2%
Total	$14.5	$0.6	$7.3	$1.0	$7.1	$3.5	$0.3	$34.3
Department of Treasury								
HBCUs	0.0%	0.0%	100.0%	0.0%	94.9%	1000.0%	0.0%	97.8%
Other IHEs	0.0%	0.0%	0.0%	0.0%	5.1%	0.0%	0.0%	2.2%
Total	$0	$0	$0.03	$0	$0.7	$0.9	$0	$1.6
Department of Veterans Affairs								
HBCUs	0.0%	0.0%	1.0%	0.0%	90.3%	0.5%	0.0%	1.0%
Other IHEs	0.0%	0.0%	99.0%	0.0%	9.7%	99.5%	0.0%	99.0%
Total	$0	$00	$165.3	$0	$0.02	$8.8	$0	$174.1

	Research and Development	Evaluation	Training	Facilities and Equipment	Fellowships	Tuition Assistance	Other	Total
Agency for International Development								
HBCUs	10.1%	0.0%	0.0%	0.0%	0.0%	24.0%	0.0%	14.0%
Other IHEs	89.9%	0.0%	0.0%	0.0%	0.0%	76.0%	0.0%	86.0%
Total	$105.5	$0	$0	$0	$0	$41.3	$0	$146.8
Appalachian Regional Commission								
HBCUs	0.0%	0.0%	0.0%	0.0%	0.0%	0.0%	0.0%	0.0%
Other IHEs	0.0%	0.0%	0.0%	0.0%	0.0%	0.0%	0.0%	0.0%
Total	$0	$0	$0	$0	$0	$0	$0	$0
Central Intelligence Agency								
HBCUs	16.10%	0.0%	0.0%	60.0%	81.1%	100.0%	0.0%	52.8%
Other IHEs	83.9%	0.0%	0.0%	40.0%	18.9%	0.0%	0.0%	47.2%
Total	$2.2	$0	$0	$0.5	$0.3	$1.5	$0	$4.5
Environmental Protection Agency								
HBCUs	1.2%	0.0%	0.0%	100.0%	100.0%	100.0%	0.0%	4.8%
Other IHEs	98.8%	0.0%	0.0%	0.0%	0.0%	0.0%	0.0%	95.2%
Total	$86.0	$0	$0	$0.2	$2.4	$0.7	$0	$89.2
Equal Employment Opportunity Commission								
HBCUs	0.0%	61.1%	0.0%	0.0%	0.0%	100.0%	0.0%	100.0%
Other IHEs	0.0%	38.9%	0.0%	0.0%	0.0%	0.0%	0.0%	0.0%
Total	$0	$2.1	$0	$0	$0	$0.4	$0	$0.4

	Research and Development	Evaluation	Training	Facilities and Equipment	Fellowships	Tuition Assistance	Other	Total
National Aeronautics and Space Administration								
HBCUs	2.1%	0.0%	15.4%	100.0%	100.0%	2.9%	0.0%	2.9%
Other IHEs	97.9%	0.0%	84.6%	0.0%	0.0%	97.1%	0.0%	97.1%
Total	$470.7	$0	$22.3	$0.3	$0.7	$18.6	$0	$512.6
National Credit Union Administration								
HBCUs	0.0%	0.0%	0.0%	0.0%	0.0%	0.0%	0.0%	0.0%
Other IHEs	0.0%	0.0%	0.0%	0.0%	0.0%	0.0%	0.0%	0.0%
Total	$0	$0	$0	$0	$0	$0	$0	$0
National Endowment for the Arts								
HBCUs	0.2%	0.0%	0.0%	0.0%	0.0%	0.0%	0.0%	0.2%
Other IHEs	99.8%	0.0%	0.0%	0.0%	0.0%	0.0%	0.0%	99.8%
Total	$3.6	$0	$0	$0	$0	$0	$0	$3.6
National Endowment for the Humanities								
HBCUs	2.3%	0.0%	0.0%	6.8%	0.6%	0.0%	0.0%	2.5%
Other IHEs	97.7%	0.0%	0.0%	93.2%	99.4%	0.0%	0.0%	97.5%
Total	$35.7	$0	$0	$7.5	$15.3	$0	$0	$58.6
National Science Foundation								
HBCUs	0.7%	0.0%	5.9%	0.0%	0.1%	0.0%	0.0%	1.2%
Other IHEs	99.3%	0.0%	94.1%	0.0%	99.9%	0.0%	0.0%	98.8%
Total	$1,321.5	$0	$129.2	$0	$29.8	$0	$0	$1,480.4

	Research and Development	Evaluation	Training	Facilities and Equipment	Fellowships	Tuition Assistance	Other	Total
Nuclear Regulatory Commission								
HBCUs	6.8%	0.0%	0.0%	0.0%	12.5%	0.0%	0.0%	6.9%
Other IHEs	93.2%	0.0%	0.0%	0.0%	87.5%	0.0%	0.0%	93.1%
Total	$4.5	$0	$0	$0	$0.08	$0	$0	$4.5
Small Business Administration								
HBCUs	0.0%	0.0%	100.0%	0.0%	100.0%	0.0%	0.0%	100.0%
Other IHEs	0.0%	0.0%	0.0%	0.0%	0.0%	0.0%	0.0%	0.0%
Total	$0	$0	$1.6	$0	$0.03	$0	$0	$1.7
United States Information Agency								
HBCUs	0.0%	0.0%	0.0%	0.0%	5.3%	0.0%	0.0%	5.3%
Other IHEs	0.0%	0.0%	0.0%	0.0%	94.7%	0.0%	0.0%	94.7%
Total	$0	$0	$0	$0	$2.6	$0	$0	$2.6
All Reporting Agencies								
HBCUs	1.5%	7.0%	7.5%	12.2%	10.6%	4.5%	99.8%	5.0%
Other IHEs	98.5%	93.0%	92.5%	87.8%	89.4%	95.5%	0.2%	95.0%
Total	$9,143.7	$371.5	$959.5	$311.1	$405.7	$6,466.0	$282.9	$17,940.4

Source: *Fiscal Year 1990 Annual Federal Performance Report on Executive Agency Actions to Assist Historically Black Colleges and Universities.* Washington, DC: White House Initiative on Historically Black Colleges and Universities.

autocratic than is appropriate and necessary. Dasher-Alston's (1993, 4) remarks may be instructive on this issue: "For every leadership role (formal and informal), there are commensurate motivations of the subordinate on which the leader is dependent. Women and minority males who assume positions of leadership are hindered not only by societal expectations regarding the propriety of who should lead but also by the lack of access to the attendant sanctions and rewards necessary to adequately compensate and motivate others."

There was a time when the black college president was the most academically prepared individual on campus and thereby felt authorized to bypass issues of academic freedom and faculty rights. This is no longer the case, and HBCU leadership, as well as their peers in white/majority institutions, represent the full range of governance styles.

Although HBCU and other leaders' administrative challenges and governance styles are similar, there are differences between African-American presidents generally and all presidents. Specifically, black presidents are more likely to:

- have an earned doctorate (87 v. 78 percent)
- have earned their highest degree in education (57 v. 43 percent)
- have been an external candidate for the position (80 v. 72 percent)
- report to a chancellor (35 v. 22 percent) rather than to a governing board (62 v. 75 percent)
- have identified themselves as Protestant (79 v. 56 percent)
- have spouses who are employed (69 v. 50 percent) and who work full-time (84 v. 66 percent)
- have participated in the following outside advisory boards: community service (77 v. 67 percent) and educational organizations (65 v. 53 percent)

Significantly, there are also differences between African-American college presidents generally and those at HBCUs. Specifically, HBCU presidents are more likely to:

- be men (93 v. 77 percent)
- be members of religious orders (18 v. 4 percent)
- work at independent baccalaureate colleges (35 v. 5 percent)
- report to a governing board (77 v. 42 percent) rather than to a chancellor (22 v. 53 percent) (Ross, Green, and Henderson 1993).

Nationally, 88 percent of college presidents are male. Women's greatest representation is in two-year public (11 percent) and in four-year private institutions (10 percent). As Tables 3 and 4 indicate, HBCU female representation in the presidential ranks is poor. There are 26 African-American female chancellors or presidents of any postsecondary institutions in the nation: the majority (54 percent) are in two-year public colleges; nine are in four-year public universities; and three are in private colleges. Only half (13) of these women lead historically or traditionally black institutions, and in five (19 percent), minority enrollment is at least 25 percent (Featherman, 1993). Although leadership access opportunities for women are few, African-American women aspiring to leadership roles have greater opportunity in HBCUs than in majority/white institutions.

Table 3
Women University CEOs, by Race and Sector

Sector	All Women		African-American Women	
	Number	Percent	Number	Percent
2-year private	30	9	-	-
2-year public	107	31	14	54
4-year private	154	44	3	12
4-year public	56	16	9	35

Source: Featherman, S. "Gender and Caste in Higher Education Leadership: Women's Voices in Setting the Agenda for Higher Education" (1993).

Table 4
African-American Presidents
at HBCUs and Other Institutions by Sex: 1990

Sex	HBCUs		Other Institutions	
	Number	Percent	Number	Percent
Women	5	6.6	13	22.8
Men	71	93.4	44	77.2
TOTAL	76	100.0	57	100.0

Source: Ross, Green, and Henderson. *The American College President: 1993 Edition* (Washington, DC: American Council on Education, 1993), p. 26.

While it is difficult to discern whether greater gender balance will make a difference in the policies and approaches of HBCUs, research on gender issues suggests that it will. Vandevender and Kemp (1993, 5), in reporting on gender distinctions in leadership style, state: "Women focus on the ecology of leadership. . . . They relate decisions to their larger effect on the family, the educational system, the environment, even world peace." Male leaders are typically portrayed as competitive and focused on single issues. Although the differences between male and female leaders are often blurred, one cannot help but wonder whether more gender diversity in higher education leadership generally, and in HBCUs specifically, would make a difference in policy and program development. As Wilcox and Epps (1992, v) posit, "Leadership in higher education continues to be under intense pressure to respond to societal issues resulting from trends in demographics and enrollment and economic and social forces that bring both possible disruption and opportunity." Given the increasing number of college-educated (Carter and Wilson, 1992) and experienced African-American women, greater participation of women in HBCU leadership positions should be viewed as an opportunity.

HBCU MISSIONS AND GOALS: MEETING THE NEED

Similar to their white counterparts, the original missions of HBCUs are clear and directed toward the advancement of a select group as well as the greater society. Changing educational standards and access, greater mobility, technological advances, and economic imperatives require that higher education institutions broaden their missions to accommodate the new order. For instance, most "normal schools" established to train teachers for particular vicinities or regions have become part of complex university systems, offering a full range of disciplines and serving students from around the globe. The parameters of HBCUs have expanded as well; however, given their establishment during a period of segregation and deprivation, HBCUs' missions are clearly framed around the needs of the black population of this nation.

Nevertheless, it seems that HBCUs are often penalized for prioritizing the needs of their students, as their needs often vary from those of the mainstream population. In HBCUs, there is an expectation and often a premium for good, quality teaching and for community involvement. Although some HBCU leaders have attempted to encourage greater scholarship, the "publish or perish" ethos—though integral to any academic institution—does not necessarily drive the agenda of HBCUs or their faculty (Wiley, 1993a).

As Morris (1979) posits in discussing a higher education desegregation case, there seems to be a conceptual disagreement regarding HBCU goals and the role they fill in society. On the one hand, they are viewed as being just like all other colleges and universities, except for their histories of unique service to blacks under conditions in which black students and faculty have had no other educational choices. On the other hand, the historical conditions are similarly emphasized, but there is a rarely articulated view that HBCUs are a product of choice among African Americans and not simply a by-product of a no-choice situation. Given the HBCU enrollment increases of recent years, the latter view is clearly the more appropriate.

What the African-American community needs specifically and society needs generally from HBCUs does not appear to have changed dramatically over time. For instance, improved and increased technology has been the focus of recent conferences examining HBCUs, such as the 1991 White House Initiative (WHI) on Historically Black Colleges and Universities, as well as a frequent theme for the National Association for Equal Opportunity in Higher Education (NAFEO). Madelon Delany Stent (1984), among others, noted the same issues as compellingly nearly a decade ago.

The call for more blacks in natural sciences, in engineering, and in graduate education is a theme that also has prevailed for more than two decades. As Stent noted in 1984, "In the mid-1970s and early 1980s, many international scholars and IHEs were involved in projects to assess the potential for the control of technology and its direction toward the attainment of social goals. Black U.S. academics were hardly ever involved in these international conferences" (p. 115). There is little evidence that in 1993 things have changed in this domain. While there are several programs that focus on international and particularly non-European studies, there is no school or college within a historically black university to prime this potential. C. Payne Lucas (1993), president of the highly regarded Africare organization, in speaking to a group of HBCU presidents recently, noted the compelling need for HBCU involvement. In his view, given the rapidly changing geopolitical climate, global knowledge exchange is imperative, particularly between HBCUs and the nations of Africa.

Several scholars (Hughes, 1992; Williams, 1984; Morris, 1979) noted the inappropriateness of comparing HBCUs with majority institutions, particularly when missions and goals were considered. As John B. Williams stated, "Much of the historical research presents the view that black colleges attempt to achieve the same goals as other colleges in the United States, and they endorse the same social and cultural values" (p. 193). The result has been a presentation of black institutions as simply having failed to achieve the cultural goals of predominantly white major research universities. "One would not expect the development of black colleges and universities to parallel or necessarily mimic that of predominantly white colleges; not because the black colleges have failed to achieve cultural parity, but because their goal was to create a fundamentally different college culture" (p. 194).

An ambitious programmatic mission does not necessarily secure an institution's place within academia or society. As Foster (1987) noted in speaking about small private HBCUs, "An unusual mission, a historic past, a generous benefactor, or a loyal and financially sacrificial faculty—all of these factors can help any institution survive for a while. However, a day of reckoning cannot be avoided indefinitely" (p. 141).

HBCUs: RECONSIDERING THE MISSION

The tenacity of HBCUs to achieve all that they have accomplished is a testament to "strength in numbers." African Americans frequently point to other racial/ethnic/cultural groups' apparent loyalty with a mix of admiration/disdain. "They" stick together and get ahead. Yet, clearly without similar loyalty, HBCUs would not be in existence today. The black community has and likely always will support its churches and its colleges. The extent to which it is financially able to do this is another matter.

The idea that HBCUs should or would serve other underserved groups in addition to their own is threatening to many, but perceived as a strategic act by others. Threatening, in that once acknowledged as a viable partner, other minority groups, e.g., Hispanics, have the potential to confiscate all that has been acquired, physically and spiritually, by these institutions. On the other hand, a deliberate effort to court or collaborate with other communities on the surface gives the outward perception of generosity and fair play. It also, in theory, opens the window of opportunity for additional support from new and different sources. At least two HBCUs have begun to foster convenient program initiatives with Native Americans. However, since, the advantages of coalition politics have yet to be realized in other areas, whether more and similar efforts with HBCUs and other groups emerge remains to be seen.

To some it may seem ludicrous to consider the needs of other underrepresented and disenfranchised groups when the African-American community is so needy. However, there is a demographic imperative that all institutions become more globally knowledgeable and communicative (Wiley, 1993b). This is not to suggest that HBCUs begin to dismiss those African Americans that are key to their mission, but it does indicate that those students should be advantaged in this competitive, multicultural society to engage and learn in other than white and black terms.

In some respects, HBCUs are more prepared to do this than other colleges and universities. When directed or encouraged to better understand diversity, faculty and students in well-established majority/white institutions typically arrange study tours for places such as Europe or Australia. Rarely do these individuals look to the wealth of cultural diversity in their own vicinity.

Due to limited resources that will not allow extensive/foreign travel and because neighboring communities are invariably segregated, HBCU faculty, staff, and students are often more familiar with individuals from other cultures, languages, and mores than their nonminority counterparts. There appears to be a premium on the horizon for fine-tuning these experiences and knowledge in the academy towards the advancement of domestic as well as international tranquility.

The ability to operate effectively from within is in some way an indicator of the ability to work outside of an institution. In arguing for the establishment of consortia among HBCUs, Hughes (1992) identified a number of factors mitigating against such a high level of cooperation: social disorganization and cultural and psychological discontinuity in the African-American community; the lack of consensus on the direction of Black America; and vestiges of segregation-era, survival-oriented, cultural complexes. Implicit

146

n the work of Hughes and Verharen (1993) is the need for a shared value system between and among African Americans and their institutions before they share or expand their missions.

There are a number of misconceptions that deter advancement of HBCUs from outside the institutions. One lies in the approach to policy analyses related to such institutions. Morris (1979) noted, "A difficulty so often found in policy analyses of black higher education is the assumption that racial isolation and related experiences 'cause' further racial isolation. It is a fallacy of correlation analysis to assume that things occurring together are mutually interdependent" (p. 181). Hughes (1992) posed an interesting question in this regard. "If, over a period of nearly 400 years, African Americans as a whole have not been socialized within a continuous set of shared beliefs and expectations in either African-American culture or culture in general, can it be reasonably expected that the majority of African Americans will be capable of effectively functioning in either culture?"

Smith (1984) also cited deterrents to collaboration among HBCUs. He wrote, ". . . interdisciplinary alliances may be difficult to establish because of traditional jealousies, competition, and rivalries that often exist among departments. To give effective service, the colleges and universities must make a commitment that supersedes their often parochial and provincial notions of discipline, integrity, and autonomy" (p. 36). During a period of shrinking budgets and demands for quality as well as accountability, historically black colleges and universities can ill afford to work in isolation from one another.

CONCLUSION: THE INTERDEPENDENCE OF HBCUs AND THE COMMUNITY

There has always been a strong relationship between HBCUs and the black community. According to Hill (1984), "The status of the black population greatly influenced the development of the black colleges, just as the black colleges had a great impact on the progress made by the black population in improving their status in the United States" (p. xii).

As early as 1896, Atlanta University began to convene annual conferences to document, discuss, and find resolutions for the problems faced by blacks in the cities of the South. Graduates of Atlanta University, Fisk, Lincoln, Spelman, Howard, Meharry, and other HBCUs conducted surveys and studies for 11 years. The purpose as noted by then President Horace Bumstead in the proceedings was "the solution of the Negro problems." In his view, ". . . certainly one great step toward the solution is the independent study of the question by Negroes themselves and spontaneous efforts at reform" (Du Bois, 1968, 45).

Specifically, this group tackled a number of pressing issues of the times which were virtually no different than those that plague the current U.S.

147

black population and that typify the annual programs and agendas of today' most prominent national black organizations. Under the editorship of W.E.B Du Bois, the Atlanta conferences issued reports on the following topics:

- Mortality of Negroes in Cities (1896)
- Social and Physical Conditions of Negroes in Cities (1897)
- Some Efforts of American Negroes for Their Own Social Bettermen (1898)
- The Negro in Business ((1899)
- The College-Bred Negro (1900)
- The Negro Common School (1901)
- The Negro Artisan (1902)
- The Negro Church (1903)
- Some Notes on Negro Crime (1904)
- A Select Bibliography of the Negro American (1905)
- The Health and Physique of the Negro American (1906)

By way of example, the National Urban League's *State of Black America* within the past seven years, has included chapters on the same or simila topics of import decades ago: "Crime in the Black Community"; "Urba Infrastructure: Social, Environmental, and Health Risks to African Ameri cans"; "African-American Business Development"; "Health and Status o Black Americans"; and "Knowing the Black Church."

The so-called "Atlanta Papers" were used by the government and commu nities to substantiate and validate critical issues to African Americans i much the same way that *The State of Black America* is used today. While i would require volumes to explain why these issues still plague us nearly century later, it does seem fair to ask: to what extent did HBCUs continue t contribute to resolution? Certainly their greatest contribution has been i providing safe haven for students to grow and to develop. Historically blacl colleges' unique contribution is in ". . . the overall orientation of thes institutions toward developing in their students a capacity to deal with racia and nonracial barriers in society —society as it is, rather than as it might be (Morris, 1979, 201).

It would be very difficult to identify an HBCU that has not recentl addressed, for the benefit of the greater community, at least one of thes critical issues through institutes, seminars, and symposia. And contrary t decades ago, HBCUs have garnered adequate support to offer academi programs in virtually all of these areas, with their greatest value being tha they are offered from the black perspective and for the ultimate benefit o African Americans. Even with these contributions, much more can b accomplished, given the support of the community.

HBCUs clearly have had a strong commitment to their surrounding an greater communities, yet many still operate in semi-isolation. It is likely tha an urban planning student can write a term paper on the local housing projec

nd that a teacher education student has had field experience in the neighbor-
ng school. It is less likely, however, that the local residents know what goes
n within the university gates. It is this one-way communication system that
nay deter greater advances on societal issues. Long-term and tangible
rojects that require regular work and communication with the university and
ne community serve several purposes. They better inform the university
ommunity of actual needs and knowledge; they provide real and vital
ervices to the community; and they provide a greater sense of empowerment
o the residents. By virtue of their diverse individual memberships from the
cademy as well as from the community, organizations such as the National
Jrban League are in an excellent position to prime the potential of histori-
ally black colleges and universities for the benefit of the African-American
ommunity as well as of the nation (Phillip, 1993, and Quality Education for
Minorities, 1993).

Finally, there are limitations in advancement for all institutions; however,
or HBCUs and their development into the next century, these issues include:
imited financial resources to create enabling infrastructures on campus;
imitations on program and course offerings; resistance to engage communi-
ies other than their own; lack of collaboration between and among institu-
ions; and the lack of gender diversity in leadership.

• • •

*The author greatly appreciates the informed critiques of this work by
William A. Blakey, Attorney-at-Law, Clohan and Dean; Antoine M. Garibaldi,
Vice President for Academic Affairs, Xavier University (LA); and N. Joyce
Payne, Director, Office for the Advancement of Public Black Colleges/Na-
tional Association of State Universities and Land Grant Colleges. All com-
ments and opinions are those of the author.*

REFERENCES

merican Association of Colleges for Teacher Education (AACTE). 1993. *Teacher Education
Pipeline: School, College, and Department of Education Enrollments by Race and Ethnicity.*
Washington, DC: AACTE.

lake, E. 1991. "Is higher education desegregation a remedy for segregation but not educational
inequality?: A study of *Ayers v. Mabus* desegregation case." *Journal of Negro Education*
60:4, Fall, pp. 538-565.

lakey, W.A. 1983. "Black Colleges and Universities: Desegregation, Disintegration, or
Equity?" *ISEP Monitor* 7:1-2, June, pp. 11-30.

arter, D. and R. Wilson. 1992. *Minorities in Higher Education: 1992 Status Report.*
Washington, DC: American Council on Education.

he Committee for Racial Justice. 1993. "The Inclusive University: A New Environment for
Higher Education." Washington, DC: Joint Center for Political and Economic Studies.

Dasher-Alston, R. 1993. "Challenging Traditional Perceptions of Leadership: Black Women Administrators in Higher Education." Paper presented at the conference, **Reconciling Gender Issues in Higher Education**, sponsored by the University of Vermont and the National Association for Women in Higher Education. Burlington, VT, October 4, 1993.

Devarics, C. 1993. "HBCUs may win more graduate, professional funds." *Black Issues in Higher Education* 10:10 (July 15), pp. 16-20.

Devarics, C. 1993. "Congress Settles HBCU Graduate Funding Issue." *Black Issues in Higher Education* 10:18 (November 4), p. 8.

Du Bois, W.E.B., ed. 1968. *Atlanta University Publications Volumes 1 and 2.* New York: Octagon Books.

El-Khawas E., 1993. *Campus Trends 1993.* Washington, DC: American Council on Education.

Featherman, S. 1993. "Gender and Caste in Higher Education Leadership: Women's Voices in Setting the Agenda for Higher Education." Paper presented at the conference, **Reconciling Gender Issues in Higher Education**, sponsored by the University of Vermont and the National Association for Women in Education. Burlington, VT, October 4, 1993.

Fiscal Year 1990 Annual Federal Performance Report on Executive Agency Actions to Assist Historically Black Colleges and Universities. 1991. Washington, DC: White House Initiative on Historically Black Colleges and Universities.

Fordyce, H.R. and A.H. Kirschner. 1993. *1992 Statistical Report.* New York: United Negro College Fund.

Foster, L.H. 1987. "Hazards in black higher education: Institutional management." *Journal of Negro Education* 56:2, pp. 137-144.

Garibaldi, A.M. 1984. "Black colleges: An overview," in Garibaldi (ed.), *Black Colleges and Universities: Challenges for the Future.* New York: Praeger, pp. 3-9.

Garibaldi, A.M. 1991. "The role of historically black colleges in facilitating resilience among African-American students." *Education and Urban Society* 24:1, pp. 103-112.

Green, M.F. 1988. *The American College President: A Contemporary Profile.* Washington, DC: American Council on Education, p. 4.

Hawkins, B.D. 1993. "Making black colleges a priority." *Black Issues in Higher Education* 10:18 (November 4), pp. 11-13.

Hill, S.T. 1984. *The Traditionally Black Institutions of Higher Education, 1860 to 1982.* Washington, DC: National Center for Education Statistics/U.S. Government Printing Office.

Hoffman, C.M., T.D. Snyder, and B. Sonnenberg. 1992. *Historically Black Colleges and Universities, 1976-90.* Washington: National Center for Education Statistics.

Hughes, C.E. 1992. "A case for the formation of strategically focused consortia among HBCUs." *Journal of Negro Education* 61:4, pp. 539-553.

Institutional and Presidential Profiles of the Nation's Historically and Predominantly Black Colleges and Universities. 1993. Washington, DC: National Association for Equal Opportunity in Higher Education. Volume XIV (March/April 1993).

Jones, S. 1984. "Adapting governance, leadership styles, and management to a changing environment," in Garibaldi (ed.), *Black Colleges and Universities: Challenges for the Future.* New York: Praeger, pp. 268-286.

Lucas, C.P. 1993. Remarks to members of the Commission for the Advancement of Public Black Colleges of the National Association of State Universities and Land-Grant Colleges. November 10, 1993.

orris L. 1979. *Elusive Equality: The Status of Black Americans in Higher Education.* Washington, DC: Institute for the Study of Educational Policy, Howard University.

.yne, N.J. and B. Smith. 1993. "Memorandum on Title III, Institutional Aid." Washington, DC: Office for the Advancement of Public Black Colleges/National Association of State Universities and Land-Grant Colleges and National Association for Equal Opportunity in Higher Education, June 21, 1993.

iillip, M. 1993. "QEM: A message to America's minority colleges: Help reverse the cycle of poor housing and poor grades." *Black Issues in Higher Education* 10:7 (June 3), pp. 17-19.

iality Education for Minorities. 1993. *Opening Unlocked Doors: A National Agenda for Ensuring Quality Education for Children and Youth in Low-Income Public Housing and Other Low-Income Resident Communities.* Washington, DC: QEM Network.

iss, M., M.F. Green, and C. Henderson. 1993. *The American College President: 1993 Edition.* Washington, DC: American Council on Education, pp. 25-26.

nith, C.V. 1984. "Community Services and Development in Historically Black Colleges and Universities," in Garibaldi (ed.), *Black Colleges and Universities: Challenges for the Future.* New York: Praeger, pp. 29-47.

edman, J.B. 1993. "Memorandum on Federal Agencies' FY 1990 Funding of Historically Black Colleges and Universities and Other Higher Education Institutions." Washington, DC: Congressional Research Service, April 6, 1993.

ent, M.D. 1984. "Black college involvement in international and cross-cultural education," in Garibaldi (ed.), *Black Colleges and Universities: Challenges for the Future.* New York: Praeger, pp. 93-115.

indevender, J.K. and M. Kemp. 1993. "New Faces, New Realities: Academic Leadership and Gender in a Time of Dramatic Change." Paper presented at the conference, **Reconciling Gender Issues in Higher Education,** sponsored by the University of Vermont and the National Association for Women in Higher Education. Burlington, VT, October 4, 1993.

erharen, C.C. 1993. "A core curriculum at historically black colleges and universities: An immodest proposal." *Journal of Negro Education* 62:2.

ilcox, J.R. and S. L. Epps. 1992. *The Leadership Compass: Values and Ethics in Higher Education.* Washington DC: ASHE-ERIC Higher Education Report No.1.

iley, E. 1993a. "Re-emphasizing teaching: The best lesson for large, traditionally white universities may be found at small black colleges." *Black Issues in Higher Education* 10:11 (July 29), pp. 9-11.

iley, E. 1993b. "Diplomacy, Scholarship and a Global Perspective: Ambassador Donald F. McHenry." *Black Issues in Higher Education* 10:5 (May 6), pp. 18-23.

illiams, J.B. 1984. "Public Policy and Black College Development: An Agenda for Research," in Garibaldi (ed.), *Black Colleges and Universities: Challenges for the Future.* New York: Praeger, pp. 178-198.

Serving the People:
African-American Leadership and
the Challenge of Empowerment

Ronald Walters, Ph.D.

INTRODUCTION: A DIALOGUE AMONG BLACK LEADERS

As a part of the annual series of week-long events sponsored by the Congressional Black Caucus (CBC) on September 16, there was a National Town Hall Meeting on "Race in America: The Political Perspective" which featured such speakers as Congressman Kweisi Mfume (D-MD), Chair of the CBC; Dr. Benjamin Chavis, Executive Director of the NAACP; Minister Louis Farrakhan, head of the Nation of Islam; Congresswoman Maxine Waters (D-CA); and the Rev. Jesse Jackson, President of the National Rainbow Coalition and Statehood Senator for the District of Columbia. The session has been easily the most discussed of any because of the drama evoked by the tension among the leaders, but also because their collective presentations surfaced many of the problems of black leadership in America today.[1]

This forum was an attempt by the Congressional Black Caucus to refocus the general crisis of the African-American community upon the issue of racism as the major impediment to its forward progress and to reaffirm the responsibilities of race leaders. It was evident from the summary comments of all the speakers that the racial conflict remains indeed a critical dynamic, both in the problems faced by the black community and in the nature of cooperation among its leaders.

Thus, the assembled group of leaders addressed first and foremost the issue of *unity* and the question of whether or not the relationship among black leaders should take precedence over and yield to challenge from outside of the black community. Minister Farrakhan had been excluded from a speaking role in the mass demonstration to commemorate the 1963 March on Washington, which had taken place on August 28, because of objections to his presence from Jewish leaders.[2] At the CBC forum, Dr. Chavis said that this decision had been wrong and vowed to work together with the Nation of Islam in the future in an "alliance." Likewise, Rep. Mfume said that the CBC had struck an "alliance" with the Nation of Islam, and Rev. Jackson called for "unity without uniformity"—a slogan that had in the past been the standard formula for operational unity among various segments of the black leadership. Exactly what was meant by an "alliance" was not made explicit, and they pledged to work it out in subsequent private meetings.

Second, because of the issue raised by Minister Farrakhan, this Town Hall Meeting acted as a forum for political *accountability*. It was clear that there existed a strong undercurrent of expectation among those in the audience which suggested that, in fact, black leaders should coalesce, that it had indeed been wrong not to acknowledge Minister Farrakhan as an authentic black leader, and that the quality-of-life issues were so urgent that black leaders needed to pool whatever resources they possessed in order to address them. This was important testimony to the fact that the audience still considered that black leaders were material to their well-being, but that they wanted them to address increasingly their immediate problems.

The leaders addressed issues such as the role played by the CBC in the budget process, the necessity to work with youth and gangs to stop the violence and crime, the necessity for economic development funding, opposition to the *Shaw v. Reno* decision of the U.S. Supreme Court on redistricting, inequitable drug sentencing guidelines, and foreign policy issues such as Haiti and Somalia. However, the strongly positive response to Rep. Waters' call for self-determination, based on individual accountability among the 2,000 in attendance, was significant recognition of the desire for autonomy in the style and substance of the positions of these leaders. It reaffirmed that whatever the problems of black people, they were the dominant aspect of the solution.

Third, there appeared to be a consensus among all concerned about the comments of Minister Farrakhan that unity among black leaders was possible so long as there was no *intervention from forces outside the black community*. Therefore, running through the dialogue and response from the audience was a deep alienation and sensitivity to the influence of outsiders, and especially the media, upon black leaders.[3] To this extent, the leaders were reticent to discuss publicly problems, for example, which had divided Minister Farrakhan and Rev. Jesse Jackson in the past, for fear that they would be exploited by the media. This position implied that there exists—or should exist—a preserve of black autonomy as an important factor in maintaining the legitimacy not only of black leadership but also of the common ethos of the black community in general.

Many elements of the discussion referred to above have been validated empirically in studies of black leadership. The most recent study of the attitude of African Americans toward civil rights organizations was published by *The Detroit News and Free Press* in February 1992.[4] From this national study, we find the following results:

Table 1
Survey: "Who Speaks for Black America?"
Selected Results

Question	Percent
White people have too much influence on the policies of the NAACP, National Urban League, SCLC, and CORE.	55 agree
Federal and local governments pay attention to what the NAACP, the National Urban League, SCLC, and CORE have to say.	57 agree
The NAACP, National Urban League, SCLC, and CORE are useful to blacks.	86 agree
The overall situation of black Americans can be improved only if every black person works hard to get ahead on his/her own.	78 agree
What type of job are the NAACP, the National Urban League, SCLC, and CORE doing in building unity in the black community?	55 poor

How important to you is the involvement of the civil rights organizations in (the following issues):

Affirmative Action	Education	Unemployment	Crime	Poor
73%	89%	82%	84%	84%

Source: Poll, "Who Speaks for Black America," *The Detroit News and Free Press*, p. A9.

While the results of the above study validate the extent to which black Americans still express overwhelming support for civil rights organizations, they also manifest the desire for substantial change in their style and substance. Contrary to many assertions in the media, blacks believe that civil rights organizations are still necessary and that they are legitimate to the extent that the federal government does pay attention to their demands. The desire for unity among black leaders is strong to the extent that most blacks think the job done so far has not been sufficient and that the influence of whites constitutes an impediment. And while most blacks believe strongly in self-determination as the basic ingredient in their progress, they still expect government assistance in making progress on a series of high priority issues such as education, unemployment, crime, and poverty, like other taxpaying citizens. And although affirmative action was not quite as highly valued as other issues in this survey, support for it was still significant. The study is concerned with a narrow category of black leadership and civil rights organizations; nevertheless, the findings might be suggestive of their feeling towards black leadership in general.

Paradigm of Empowerment

Put simply, the above study, validated by the audience responses to the September 1993 CBC Forum, is demonstrative of the challenge that black leadership faces in the process of the "empowerment" of the black community. Therefore, I would like to discuss some of the significant elements of that challenge, but to do so within the context of the national and local arenas in which black leadership operates. Before addressing this subject, however, it will be necessary to offer a few theoretical comments.

To begin with, all objective discussions of power involve the ability of an individual or group to utilize resources in a manner which makes it possible to achieve certain objectives in a given situation. Professor James MacGregor Burns says that in the variety of definitions about leadership, one of the most compelling reasons why people submit to the authority of certain other individuals or groups to lead them is the overriding issue of the *purpose* involved for coming together in an organized form.[5] He suggests that "power and leadership are measured by the degree of production of intended effects."[6] Since leaders use the support provided them by others as a power resource with which to achieve certain ends (produce intended effects), ultimately, the discussion of leadership is a discussion about the rationale for that support, its magnitude, and the responsible use of the legitimacy it provides.

Leadership is intrinsic to the comprehensive process of empowerment as an instrument to acquire and manage influence. The importance of such leadership is that it moderates and accumulates community power resources, not only for the purpose of *external power projection* into the major political arena but also more fundamentally for the sociocultural organization of community life itself. The primary function of religious leaders is religious, economic leaders—business, governmental leaders—public policy, but to the extent that some individuals from each of these categories cohere into a leadership class for certain purposes, it is to direct community affairs by participation in the agenda-setting and decision-making process. The point should not be missed, therefore, that the community is the primary level in the process of empowerment, since it is the origin of the legitimacy of its leaders and the recipient of their efforts in a reciprocal flow of power, legitimacy, and authority.

As such, leadership reflects the community from which it emerges, and the African-American community is a relatively coherent cultural group, seeking to develop and control community resources and external resources in a manner which creates the influence that enables the achievement of both collective and individual objectives. This suggests a paradigm of several factors which can be utilized to discuss the broad issue of the challenges of black leadership in the process of empowerment: *community leadership, national system influence, strategies,* and *operational unity and effectiveness.*

The concept of black "empowerment" often begins with a recognition that effective access to given political arenas, such as legislatures, is important. However, access per se, in the form of having won seats on city councils or in state, county, or national legislatures, is not, in itself, empowerment. If anything, elected or appointed office is a form of potential "instrumental power" depending upon how it is utilized. Empowerment entails utilizing these assets to obtain actually the items which enable the community to perform at an optimum level for its members. Thus, it is possible to say that the process of "empowerment" enables the community through the exercise of its instrumental resources (elected and appointed officials, community leaders, financial and political power, demonstrations, etc.) to acquire and manage the requisite influence (have more power) that would facilitate its ability to obtain the items necessary to its survival and development. Therefore, "empowerment" is the process at which the possession of an enriching form of power by the community is the result of the cycle.

Community Leadership

Since the community is the basic level where resources are managed which has an effect on all other levels, to the extent that community power is diminished by the lack of effective leadership and the absence of resources, it will be impossible to organize the community or to project its power into the larger political arena with any degree of success. And with weak or misdirected control over elected leaders, the process of accountability to community interests suffers.

In another work, I observed that the "frame reference" of the original community structure had been broken or severely damaged by a number of factors and that the most urgent agenda of leadership was to reconstruct that frame of reference, since it had been the key to *group* progress.[7] The condition of the national "black community" as reflected in its cumulative status has felt the impact of the massive shift of federal resources away from localities and the consequent serious effect upon problems of development.

The impact of the Reagan budget cuts, beginning in 1981, on the rapid deterioration of the inner city could be found in a devastating critique by Michael K. Brown who concluded that ". . . as long as the budget cuts continue to be concentrated in social welfare programs, blacks will suffer accordingly, [and] there is little doubt that the much-discussed economic gains blacks have made in relation to whites over the last two decades will diminish as these cutbacks take place."[8]

In 1986, an analysis by the Center on Budget and Policy Priorities indicated that the Reagan administration had further cut low-income programs—upon which a significant portion of the black community was dependent—by $8 billion dollars.[9] Then, a national overview of the problem analyzed in 1986 by the Center revealed that by 1988, the problem had grown even more severe.[10] In that same year, the 1988 Commission on the Cities released its report and found that the resulting concentration of poverty had fostered "rapid social deterioration [in inner-city neighborhoods] with sharp increases in social dislocation and the massive breakdown of social institutions in ghetto areas."

The report indicated that this pattern of deepening poverty had led to the "quiet riots" of unemployment, poverty, social disorganization, segregation, family disintegration, housing and school deterioration, and crime.[11] By the early 1990s, it was easily seen that a pattern of resource withdrawal had occurred, involving individuals who had moved to the suburbs and the private sector, which had shifted thousands of jobs either to the suburbs or overseas.[12] The result was that by 1993, cities were greatly impoverished such that the annual survey of the National League of Cities indicated that cities had received no support, since city revenues were in a period of no-growth and as such, cities balanced their budgets by reducing services and raising taxes.[13]

The major effect of the massive resource withdrawal has been to enhance the "quiet riots" since the resulting infrastructure of the typical inner community has not been strong enough to sustain progress toward development on their own resources. The resulting social conditions of homelessness, poverty, failing education systems, drug abuse, teenage pregnancy, crime, and widespread youth violence are corroding the quality of life in the inner city and beyond. These conditions have not only resulted in a permanent "underclass," as described by Professor William J. Wilson, but have also promoted a pattern of youthful crime and violence that has taken many forms and which has placed an urgent demand upon all leaders at all levels. So serious is the emergency this has caused that communities such as Baltimore and Washington, DC, have found black leaders calling for the use of the National Guard.[14] And in the wake of the social explosion of April 1992 in Los Angeles, touched off by the Rodney King court decision—the magnitude of which, most careful analysts agree, was fueled by urban neglect, decay, and lack of opportunity—there has been an acknowledgment of the need to begin the task of reconstructing the inner city.

This task has placed great demands upon the existing leadership. From Liberty City in Miami, where the Talcocy Economic Development Corporation was created, to the Homewood area near Pittsburgh, where Homewood/ Brushton Revitalization Corporation is working, and to organizations such as "REBUILD LA," there have been some creative responses to the urban crisis. Nevertheless, Paul Grogan, head of the Local Initiative Support Corporation

(LISC) of New York City, has said: "We're all groping in this country for a new urban strategy at a time when it's clear the old strategy is broken."[15]

This has challenged leaders to employ more complex tools of urban development, such as those which enhance the function of Community Development Corporations, to challenge locally based financial institutions (ACORN/ NAACP) for capital; and to leverage urban programs such as Youth Build to combat high levels of youth unemployment, delinquency, and violence. It has mobilized gang leaders to take responsibility for fostering urban violence and for calling on other national and local leaders to be responsive to their needs.[16] All of this has caused a transition in inner-city leadership from attempting to break into the urban bureaucracy of the 1960s and administer cities and programs such as Model Cities to developing creative survival strategies in the absence of resources that were formerly available.

National System Influence

Great strides have been made by blacks in obtaining the franchise and in the product of that process which has been the growth in the number of black elected officials at every level of government. With the re-emergence of the Congressional Black Caucus as a political force in the Congress, based upon its possession of 40 votes, three standing committee chairmanships, and 17 subcommittee chairmanships, this impression is even more solidified. The total number of elected officials has reached 7,532 (as of March 1993), and the number of appointed officials has likewise grown. There are five black Cabinet Secretaries in the Clinton administration, and the pace of appointments could eclipse the record of the Carter administration.[17]

The above data show that elected and appointed officials have grown in their size and importance as a category of black leadership. Consequently, they have grown in the status accorded to them among the kinds of black leaders within the community. With the growth of institutional and professional leaders, it is tempting to suggest that civil rights leaders and community organizers have suffered a relative decline in their status.[18] In fact, some have even declared them superfluous, and the tactics they initiated, such as protest demonstrations and other forms of civic pressure and grass-roots community involvement, are often considered to be outdated.

However, a Gallup Poll taken in the summer of 1993 found that Rev. Jesse Jackson, a civil rights leader, was considered by far to be the most important national black leader in a survey of national black opinion.[19] But perhaps the real basis of Rev. Jackson's support is that his activities have involved elements of both civil rights and elected leaders in his rise to national prominence.

Table 2
Most Influential Black Leader

Leader	Blacks	Whites
Jesse Jackson	39	35
Colin Powell	3	4
Clarence Thomas	0	1
Benjamin Chavis	3	1
Ron Brown	1	1
Louis Farrakhan	3	0
Douglas Wilder	1	1
Carol Moseley-Braun	1	0
Athletes	0	1
Entertainers	0	1
Other Public Officials	4	1
Miscellaneous	10	5
None/no leader	8	6
No opinion	27	43

Source: CNN/*USA Today*/Gallup Poll, August 1993.

The poll cited above also confirmed the finding in the *Detroit News* survey reflecting strong loyalty by the black public to traditional civil rights organizations. But the poll found that, *as a category*, athletes and entertainers were the "most influential" black leaders (see Table 3); there may be some substantiation of the widely held view that "public regardingness" (media, notoriety, etc.) helps to shape who comes to be considered a "black leader."

Table 3
Most Influential Black Leaders
Very Influential

Black Members of Congress	45%
Black Mayors	45%
Black Businesspersons	44%
Black Ministers and Clergy	50%
Black Athletes	64%
Black Entertainers	53%

Source: CNN/*USA Today*/Gallup Poll, August 1993.

A common corollary to the popular notion of the primacy of elected and appointed office is the presumption that, by definition, membership in a major political institution is more powerful than a role in community leadership. However, *this is also a questionable assumption*. In fact, two case studies of public policy, passed by the Congress of the United States in the mid-1980s and signed into law by a hostile president, indicate that it was the combination of citizen mobilization *and* public policy actors that was responsible for these victories.

For example, the 1986 Anti-Apartheid Act which cut off American investment and trade in South Africa was a product of massive demonstrations at the South African Embassy and its consulates around the country and the fortunate presence of black legislators who managed the outcome of the policy process in the House of Representatives. The presence of black officials alone was not enough, since they had previously proposed legislation to cut off economic relations with South Africa, but it was not passed until the action of blacks ignited a national protest which President Reagan could not ignore.

A similar scenario was the case of the Martin Luther King, Jr., Holiday Bill. For several years, Congressman John Conyers (D-MI) had proposed such legislation, but it was not until it became a popular national cause through high visibility demonstrations on the Mall in Washington, DC, that it was addressed seriously by the Congress and the president and signed into law in 1985.

Another case study involving national black mobilization was the massive demonstration intended to influence public policy on August 27, 1993, commemorating the 1963 March on Washington for "Jobs, Peace, and Justice." This march/demonstration was widely held to have been less effective than the 1963 March because it took place outside the context of any wider mobilization of the black community and because its message was unfocused, largely through an effort to attract the largest supportive and diverse set of compatible policy interests and social groups.

Yet, perhaps overlooked was the fact that the effectiveness of the CBC in the wake of this demonstration helped to obtain $10 billion in the budget package. For example, the CBC had an acknowledged influence on keeping in the Act the $3.5 billion "Empowerment Zones" (commonly known as Enterprise Zones); expanding the Earned Income Tax Credit $3 billion over the Senate figure to $21 billion; keeping $2.5 billion in Food Stamps phased out in the Senate version; and securing $1 billion for Family Preservation.[20] Without a mobilization, they had not been as successful with the stimulus package, which contained $17 billion of economic resources—much of which was directed at the cities, even though it passed the House of Representatives by six votes. Perhaps the March had only marginal effect, but the fact that it served as a stage for policy accountability for the CBC may have helped to enable it to work successfully with the Clinton administration.[21] For despite the CBC's decline of an overture by President Clinton to meet with them in the wake of his rejection of Professor Lani Guinier's nomination, a meeting subsequently occurred, and administration officials were not only present at the events surrounding the March, but also Attorney General Janet Reno marched in the demonstration itself. Thus, it was inevitable that administration officials were socialized to the demands of the March to the extent that they also viewed it as a moment of policy accountability.

The above case studies were illustrative of the exercise of political influence in a way that is applicable at all levels of government. The method is the union between citizens and elected officials in a given action which acknowledges that *with an aware, mobilized constituency, elected officials often have the leverage to accomplish far more than through the singular power of their office alone.* Therefore, black leaders are challenged to not only share the responsibilities but also the status of leadership with community leaders by devising common forums and strategies of action.

Strategies

At the CBC forum of black leaders previously cited, Rev. Jesse Jackson suggested that "some combination of registration, legislation, demonstration, and litigation" will be necessary to move issues forward as the major political strategies. If this is accepted, then voting, public policy formation, civic pressure, and court suits are the major political strategies through which the black community mobilizes its power to levy influence upon institutions and issues in the political system. What follows is an illustration of selected cases in each category.

Voting: As the two campaigns for Jesse Jackson illustrated, the issue increasingly involved in using voting to obtain political resources is not only the encouragement of strong turnout and voting so that a suitable representative can be elected to office; it is also the fact that such support creates strategic leverage for leaders in the political process.[22] Jackson was not elected to office, but support for his candidacy enabled him to deliver a clear expression of the progressive agenda directly to the American public rather than indirectly; the general mobilization for his candidacy caused some to be elected at other levels of government; and the legitimacy of his campaign enabled him to bargain to include progressive items on the agenda of the Democratic Party. Increasingly, strategic voting should provide leaders with even more flexibility to leverage issues.

Public Policy: Leaders are involved in a process of what has been called "agenda setting" when they seek to establish priorities for community or national consideration.[23] Perhaps the greatest public policy consensus among black leadership is with respect to the importance of jobs. In fact, the 1993 March on Washington decried the high level of unemployment and launched a strong challenge to the North American Free Trade Agreement, widely held to reduce eventually high-wage jobs in the United States by putting low-wage workers in the United States in competition with low-wage workers in Mexico. March leaders said: "We demand that the basic standards of American and international law be upheld, both in our country and by those with whom we trade. These rights include a minimum age for the employment of children and acceptable conditions of work with respect to wages, hours, working conditions, and occupational safety and health for every worker."[24]

Civic Pressure: In Miami, Florida, leaders of the black community initiated an economic boycott of tourism when the city rescinded a key to the city for South African leader Nelson Mandela, who had spoken out in support of Cuban leader Fidel Castro on his 1990 visit to the United States. The boycott was continued for three years, during which it cost Miami more than $20 million in direct tourism from the cancellation of an estimated 24 meetings involving 46,000 delegates. The leaders of the protest negotiated a 20-point agenda for change that contained demands for greater representation of blacks in the tourism industry, a black-owned convention-quality hotel on Miami Beach, 125 visitor industry scholarships for blacks, and single-member voting districts for Miami, Dade County, and the school board, among other concerns. The boycott was ended on May 12, 1993, when the agreement, which will be monitored by Miami Partners for Progress, was signed between black leaders and city officials. One observer said of the agreement: "Their ambitious blueprint for change . . . will test not only the commitment of the local business community, but also the credibility of the handful of boycott leaders who acted on behalf of the black community."[25]

Litigation: The next major litigation battle over the legitimacy of the Voting Rights Act was precipitated by the *Shaw v. Reno* decision of the Supreme Court in the spring of 1993. The five-to-four decision, supported by Justices William Rehnquist, Antonin Scalia, Anthony Kennedy, and Clarence Thomas, was delivered by Justice Sandra Day O'Connor, who deprecated districts based solely on race and that dismissed so-called traditional standards of redistricting such as "compactness" and "contiguity." The Court stated that the five white plaintiffs were allowed to raise questions of "equal protection" since the 12th Congressional District of North Carolina, which precipitated the case, was "so irrational on its face that it can be understood only as an effort to segregate voters into separate voting districts because of their race, and that the separation lacks sufficient justification."[26]

The district, represented by African American Mel Watt, was created by the application of Section 5 of the 1982 Amendments to the Voting Rights Act, and this action, by implication, challenges the legitimacy of that section. If not overturned, it could also challenge some of the other 52 majority black and Hispanic congressional districts and at this writing, the Fourth District of Rep. Cleo Fields (D-LA) had already been challenged. The stakes here are that the size of the Congressional Black Caucus, black state legislative delegations, and blacks representing other jurisdictions are under attack with this ruling; it will take a significant political effort in support of litigation and perhaps eventually legislation to reverse this challenge.

If there is any shift that is endemic to the focus of such strategies outlined above, it is the fact that in the long struggle for racial equality—which essentially positioned black civil rights leaders against the system—that integration as the standard of race advancement should be refocused toward the internal problems of development faced by the community where they exist. It is a logic which says, for example, that in a 90 to 95 percent black school district, the strategies for achieving quality education should not continue to emphasize busing and school integration at the expense of acquiring quality resources and performance for that system the way it exists.[27]

The Challenge of Operational Unity

The issue of leadership divisiveness often turns around the question of which one or which category best reflects the interests of the black community. In fact, such conflict has been promoted by opinion leaders, politicians, and others who have been uncomfortable with the liberal cast of thought as the dominant ideology of the black leadership group. For example, in December of 1980, a meeting was held in San Francisco, arranged by Dr. Thomas Sowell and funded by a foundation associated with the subsequently appointed Attorney General, Edwin Meese. After two days of discussion by various black intellectuals and politicians, Meese characterized the participants as having discussed the value of a "new corps of trans-ethnic political leaders. . . . You also talked about the diversification of black leadership. I think it is tremendously important for people who come from similar backgrounds to be able to have different ideas about how to solve their problems."[28] This initiative was followed by Reagan's rejection of meetings between his administration and black leaders with traditional constituencies and the attempt to put far more conservative black leaders forward as spokespersons for the national black community. When liberal leaders were invited to testify on issues of importance to the black community, conservative blacks were also invited; when black leaders representing hundreds of thousands of members were invited to appear on media forums, conservative spokespersons representing a narrow category of interests were invited to oppose them. The illusion created by such staged conflict was that the major black leaders were "out of touch" with the followers and that the followers actually desired a far more conservative approach to public policy.[29]

Although it is clear that there exists a set of traditionally conservative attitudes within the black community, the conservative movement may also have made some inroads into mainstream black opinion. For example, despite the previous strongly held set of attitudes toward the role of government in assisting blacks, a recent survey found that black respondents considered it "most important" (24 percent), "very important" (23 percent), or "somewhat important" (25 percent) that "Government programs have held blacks down by making them dependent," as opposed to those who considered this "not very important" (20 percent) or were "not sure" (8 percent).[30]

164

In any case, the issue here is whether or not the views of the masses of blacks differ significantly from those of black leaders as alleged by analysts from the ideological right.[31] The findings from a survey of black and white, Democratic and Republican Convention delegates, compared to the general public, revealed that there was significant difference by party on the issues of term limits, public school choice, health insurance, government services, and defense spending. Race was more important as the reason for party differentiation generally, and it was decisive specifically where the issue of affirmative action was concerned.[32]

Although the effort to de-legitimize traditional black leaders was largely unsuccessful, the residue of this strategy has been rationalized in the name of tolerating "diversity." Cultural diversity is a fact of existence for any large group; however, when that group engages in competition within the political system to attain its basic objectives, the *utmost political unity* is required. Unity, then, is a primary political resource for success.

One outgrowth of the differences which have emerged within the black community, as was illustrated by the CBC forum, is that there are still important residual conflicts among black leaders which have little to do with differences among the issues. Very often the source of such differences relates to role differentiation and leadership style; for the success of "operational unity," an appreciation of the different roles leaders play is necessary both for leaders and followers alike. The following diagram might be useful in illustrating this point. It asserts that political legitimacy of a leader is based upon the origin of his or her resources and that this is a major factor, if not the decisive key, to his or her political behavior.

Table 4
Leadership Legitimacy

BC Legitimacy	External Legitimacy	Leadership Behavior
Yes	Yes	Consensus
Yes	No	Community
No	Yes	External
No	No	Auto-selected

The above typology is meant to suggest that the *consensus* leader is effective at acquiring resources both within and outside of the black community (BC) and as such is in a maximum position to exercise leadership. The leader who has *internal* legitimacy/resources from the black community alone can be very effective in leading it, but has limitations with respect to the extension of the influence of the community into the dominant political system. The leader who primarily utilizes *external* resources/legitimacy can be most effective outside the black community and often is called upon to represent it within that arena. However, there will always be a question of legitimacy raised from within the black community in this regard. Finally, the individual who has no significant sanction either within the black community or external is *auto-selected* and can usually be only marginally effective in very limited leadership situations, since his or her resource base does not permit legitimate representation.

Leadership/organization resources are important because they determine the extent to which intervention into the organizational affairs of the black community is possible and therefore, whether the "zone of autonomy" which the leaders attempted to construct within the context of the forum discussion above is actually possible.[33]

Thus, leaders will often have different roles based on the origin of their resources, but they will also have such differences based on the nature of the organizations they lead, whether religious or secular, political or economic, national or local, and so on. To this extent, it should be acknowledged that there has historically been an attempt to create a rational leadership structure comprised primarily of organizational representatives at the national level. For example, there have been such organizations as:

- *The Black Leadership Forum*: a loose organization of 13 to 15 members which meets intermittently in private to discuss approaches to issues of interest to the black community.
- *The Congressional Black Caucus*: an association of 40 members of Congress—39 members of the House of Representatives and one member of the Senate.
- *The National Black Caucus of Local Elected Officials*: an organization of elected officials at the local level, such as city council, school board, county officials, and judges.
- *The National Conference of Black Mayors*: national organization of mayors of cities of all sizes.
- *The National Conference of Black State Legislators*: an organization of members of state legislatures.

This illustrative listing must be augmented by single-occupation organizations such as the religious organizations like the National Baptist Convention; professional organizations such as the National Medical Association; and business organizations such as the President's Council (of banking leaders). A previous attempt to involve single-occupation leaders into a broad organization known as the National Black Leadership Roundtable was initiated for a period between 1981 and 1991 as a part of the Political Participation Brain Trust of the Congressional Black Caucus. It is no longer in existence but was a useful model to coordinate leadership issues.

Collective leadership is important to the task of agenda-building on behalf of the black community, and although the civil rights organizations have had the most experience with this process because of their history of collaboration, this dynamic needs to be adapted to a wider variety of leaders.

Thus, in the CBC forum cited above, the talk of getting into a "back room" to which they could repair and discuss sensitive issues was symbolic of the necessity for an institutionalized process of collective leadership.

Perhaps at this point it is necessary to enumerate, without benefit of extensive discussion, those minimal issues which might facilitate the achievement of an effective unity among black leaders both operationally and structurally. Effectiveness is presumed to be the ability of the leadership class to coalesce their resources in order to direct them to initiatives that result in the empowerment of the black community. Therefore, regardless of the resource base, there is the cross-cutting need for national organizations to:

1. define and elaborate a style of leadership consultation that allows for both problem-solving and accountability to the wider black community;

2. give mutual respect to the diversity of roles among black leaders and the individual requirement of their organizations, but give primacy to the maintenance of collective leadership among blacks above outside commitments;

3. achieve a technical capability that would allow them to both service national memberships effectively and communicate with each other, such as the enhancement of managerial skills and use of telecommunications for rapid information sharing and mobilization;

4. be responsive to the main currents of black opinion, but seek to enrich it with creative and diverse ideas;

5. provide accurate analytical information to the public on the condition of the black community and the aspirations of its people;

6. be aggressive in the process of agenda-building in light of the considerable odds generally weighted against black leadership in whatever forum.

CONCLUSION

Despite the lifestyle tolerance of diversity, individualism, and the emerging variety of African-American cultures, what Martin Luther King, Jr., said in 1967 is still as important today: "Our nettlesome task is to discover how to organize our strength into compelling power so that government cannot elude our demands."[34] However, it is ever more urgent that the focus of our attention not only be addressed to government but also directly to the original communities which many African Americans have left but where most still live. There, the deteriorating quality of life necessitates the development of strategies employing to a maximum degree the energy and skills of those who have left as much as those who remain.

This is a substantial challenge to the black middle class which has historically borne the brunt of the leadership responsibility. One understands the strains and tensions of those who pursue the opportunity rightfully won by dint of their own persistent struggle and sacrifice into new areas of residential and professional life on the one hand, and the countervailing direction in which their efforts must also be directed toward shoring up the old places which gave and still give meaning to that opportunity. This is perhaps one of the greatest of all questions, whether or not the black middle class will still see this task of reconstructing the black community as its primary responsibility or that of someone else. In other words, will they begin to operate out of their own class interest or continue the tradition of doing for the preservation of the race?

Finally, as argued here, to the extent that leadership is a process of consent which flows from the masses to legitimate, authoritative organizations and individuals, it involves not only the middle class but also all classes. And here, the struggle to obtain a consent that is not distorted by the disabilities of black life is the greatest challenge. Shall we call in the National Guard as a middle-class act in the name of preserving the peace for all, when the lower class will likely suffer most from the occupation? Given the magnitude and complexity of the problems, what is a responsible act of leadership? Authentic leaders must be grounded enough in the history and culture of our people to know, or to know how to find, the answer to such questions.

ENDNOTES

[1] D. L. Kinch, "March Leaders Seek Unity With Farrakhan," *The Washington Afro-American,* September 25, 1993, p. 1.

[2] A letter of complaint from Rabbi David Saperstein of the Religious Action Center of Reform Judaism, to the major sponsors of the March, chiding them for not consulting Jewish leaders, indicating that if Minister Farrakhan spoke, they would not participate. See *The Washington Afro-American,* September 6, 1993, p. 1.

[3] Indeed, a few days later, a *New York Times* editorial charged that Rep. Mfume, who had thus far made a creditable showing in his leadership of the CBC, had been "had" with his pledge of an alliance with Minister Farrakhan. "The Black Caucus Gets Mugged," Editorial, *The New York Times,* September 25, 1993, p. A22.

[4] This poll was performed by the Gordon S. Black Corp. from a survey questionnaire designed by Dr. James Jackson, Director of the Program of Research on Black Americans in the Survey Research Center at the University of Michigan. The survey contained a sample of 1,211 black adults, was conducted in the winter of 1991-92, and contained a 2.8 percent margin of error. Janice Hayes and Ellyn Ferguson, "Who Speaks for Black America?," *The Detroit News and Free Press,* February 23, 1992, p. A9.

[5] James MacGregor Burns, *Leadership* (New York: Harper and Row, 1978), p. 19.

[6] *Ibid.,* p. 22.

[7] Ronald Walters, "Imperatives of Black Leadership: Policy Mobilization and Community Development," *Urban League Review,* Vol. 9, No. 1, Summer 1985, pp. 20-41. Special issue, "Reflections on Black Leadership," Ronald Walters and Robert Smith, eds.

[8] Michael K. Brown, "Gutting the Great Society: Black Economic Progress and the Budget Cuts," *Urban League Review,* Vol. 7, Winter 1982/83, pp. 11-24.

[9] "Administration Budget Contains Large Cuts in Programs for the Poor" (Washington, DC: Center on Budget and Policy Priorities, 1986).

168

[10]"Holes in the Safety Nets: Poverty Programs and Policies in the States" (Washington, DC: Center on Budget and Policy Priorities," 1988).

[11]Fred. R. Harris and Roger Wilkins, "The Kerner Report Updated: Report of the 1988 Commission on the Cities—Race and Poverty in the United States Today," National Conference: "The Kerner Report Twenty Years Later," Washington, DC, March 1, 1988.

[12]Ronald Walters, "Targeting Resources to Central Cities: A Strategy for Redeveloping the Black Community," *The Black Scholar,* Vol. 23, No. 1, Winter/Spring, 1993, pp. 2-10.

[13]Michael Hinds, "The Cities Are Scraping By, But At a Cost," *The New York Times,* July 9, 1993, p. A8.

[14]Mayor Sharon Pratt Kelly's call for the limited use of the National Guard in Washington, DC, has touched off a debate at this writing. Reuben Castanada and Keith Harriston, *The Washington Post,* September 30, 1993, p. 1.

[15]Cited in Rob Gurwitt, "Neighborhoods and The Urban Crisis," *Governing,* Vol. 5, September 1992, p. 57

[16]See "A Time to Heal, A Time to Build," *Sojourners,* Vol. 22, No. 7, Special Issue on the Gang Summit, August 1993.

[17]JCPES Political Trendletter, "Number of Black Elected Officials in the United States, by State and Office, January 1992," *Focus,* March 1993.

[18]See Professor Robert Smith, *Black Leadership: A Survey of Theory and Research* (Washington, DC: Institute for Urban Affairs and Research, Howard University, 1984), pp. 35-48.

[19]"Civil Rights and Gender," CNN/*USA Today*/Gallup Poll, August 23-25, 1993, p. 6.

[20]Press Conference, "Role of the CBC in the Budget Reconciliation," Congressional Black Caucus, August 1993.

[21]Professor Manning Marable, "Along the Color Line," *Commentary,* September 1993.

[22]Ronald Walters, *Black Presidential Politics in America* (Albany, NY: SUNY Press, 1988), pp. 110-138.

[23]See Roger W. Cobb and Charles D. Elder, *Participation in American Life: Dynamics of Agenda-Building* (Baltimore: Johns Hopkins University Press, 1983).

[24]"Jobs, Peace, and Justice" Coordinators' Guide (Washington, DC: The New Coalition of Conscience, 1993). p. 3.

[25]Tony Pugh, "Biracial Blueprint for Change Boycott Ends with Pact, Promises," *The Miami Herald,* May 13, 1993, p. 1A.

[26]Dave Kaplan, "Constitutional Doubt Is Thrown on Bizarre-Shaped Districts," *Congressional Quarterly,* July 3, 1993, p. 1762.

[27]This sentiment is strong in areas governed by desegregation consent decrees of long standing where, as citizens in Prince George's County, MD, and San Francisco, CA, argued, the original goals of desegregation have either been met or are unattainable because of continued out-migration by whites, but the goals of quality education have not been attained for minorities. Rex Bossert, "Wider Desegregation Action Sought," *Daily Journal,* Oakland, CA, March 9, 1993, p. 1.

[28]*The Fairmont Papers: Black Alternatives Conference, December 1980* (San Francisco: Institute for Contemporary Studies, 1981), p. 160.

[29]The press has long appeared to be interested in the possibility that the liberal interests represented by black leaders in politics and public policy were not congruent with the views of black people generally. See, for example, "Black Leaders Out of Step With Their People?," *U.S. News and World Report,* April 7, 1980, pp. 68-70.

169

[30]"Highlights From An Anti-Defamation League Survey On Racial Attitudes," Anti-Defamation League, June 1993, p. 14. Survey of 400 blacks and 400 Jews performed October 22-26, 1992, by Martila & Kiley, Boston, MA. In addition, a study of blacks' opinions performed by Fabrizio, McLaughlin and Associates for The Christian Coalition appeared to indicate that blacks shared many of the attitudes of white conservatives on issues such as approval of school prayer, government strengthening traditional values, school choice, English as the U.S. official language, the death penalty, workfare for welfare recipients, solving the federal deficit by cutting spending rather than raising taxes, and disapproval of homosexuality. (500 black respondents, confidence interval of 95 percent, error rate of 4.4 percent, published September 9, 1993.)

[31]An example is Linda Lichter, "Who Speaks for Black America," *Public Opinion,* August-September, 1985, pp. 41-44, 58.

[32]David Bositis, "McCloskey Revisited: Issue Conflict and Consensus Among African American Party Leaders and Followers," Joint Center for Political and Economic Studies, Washington, DC, paper prepared for delivery at the Annual Meeting of the American Political Science Association, Washington, DC, September 2-5, 1993.

[33]For example, with respect to the issue of unity pledged by leaders on the CBC forum with Minister Farrakhan, in addition to *The New York Times* editorial, which denounced this action as a mistake, Rep. Mfume responded to a series of requests for meetings by prominent Jewish organizations. In the statement issued after one meeting with the ADL leadership on September 28, Mfume indicated in effect that the CBC had to be allowed to work with anyone in their communities who could help bring progress and that, in that process, there would be some respectful disagreement with others of their allies, but that they should understand that it should not be a barrier to their mutual support of other mutual interests. Some members of the CBC were critical of the announcement of an "alliance" with Minister Farrakhan as well.

[34]Martin Luther King, Jr., *Where Do We Go From Here: Chaos or Community?* (Boston: Beacon Press, 1967), p. 137.

Silent Suffering:
The Plight of Rural Black America

Shirley J. Jones, D.S.W.

INTRODUCTION

This paper describes the geographical location of rural blacks in America, notes the history of rural blacks speaking out about the economic and social structures that fostered their oppression, describes the transitions that have occurred in many rural areas since 1980, and examines the socioeconomic problems that have resulted from these transitions. It also laments the lack of national concern about rural families and their communities. Further, it identifies the changes in advocacy since 1980 and points to the need for the black community to unite as it did during the civil rights era. Alliances and coalition-building are seen as means to develop strategies for economic and community development.[1]

This paper focuses primarily on the southern region of the United States because of the large percentage (54.7 percent) of rural residents who live there, the number of rural blacks who live there (26.3 percent), and the fact that more than half of all rural poor live in the South.[2] This region has the potential to serve as a model for alliances and coalition-building. Research indicates that progress is evident, even though poverty and racism remain in the region. Many blacks are moving to the South due to its potential and because race relations are now less hostile.[3] Indeed, rural blacks live in predominantly white areas such as the Northeast region of the United States. Their small numbers and limited Census information provide barriers to addressing their concerns.

GEOGRAPHY AND HISTORY

As a result of slavery, America's rural black population was rooted in the South. Alabama, Arkansas, Arizona, Georgia, Louisiana, Mississippi, New Mexico, North Carolina, North Dakota, South Carolina, South Dakota, and Texas are home to a majority of rural people of color as shown in Diagram 1. Eight states—Alabama, Louisiana, Mississippi, Georgia, North and South Carolina, Texas, and Virginia—account for 78 percent of all rural blacks. Several of these states were once noted for beating, lynching, and denying blacks many of their basic rights.[4]

Nonmetro minority counties, 1990

Specified minority or ethnic group is 50% or more of the population

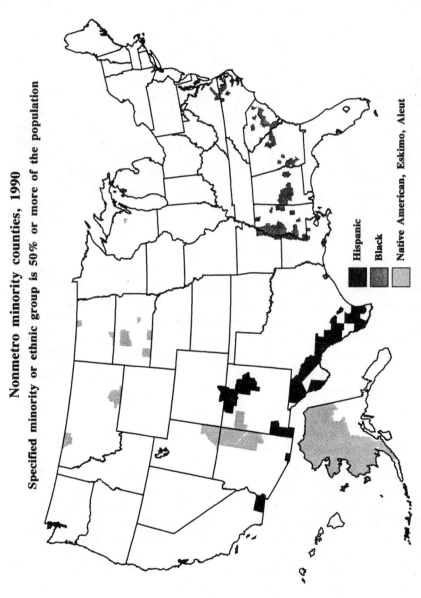

Hispanic

Black

Native American, Eskimo, Aleut

Source: U.S. Department of Agriculture, Economic Research Service, Agriculture and Rural Economy Division, October

Blacks have historically spoken out about their oppressive conditions. Sojourner Truth, Frederick Douglass, Harriet Tubman, and Ida Wells Barnett are but a few involved in the early protest movements against the unequal treatment of blacks in America.[5]

During the civil rights movement of 1954-65, rural blacks significantly contributed by challenging the political systems that did not encourage their participation and by questioning the socioeconomic structure that mired them in poverty. For example, many rural black communities were testing grounds for securing the rights of all people. Fannie Lou Hamer, a sharecropper and civil rights activist from Mississippi, helped to form the Mississippi Freedom Democratic Party, challenging the regular state Democratic Party to represent all the people of Mississippi.[6] The "Little Rock Nine" students, surrounded by police officers, federal troops, and jeering mobs of angry whites, broke down racial barriers at an all-white high school in Arkansas. James Meredith secured admission to the University of Mississippi; Medgar Evers, Harry T. Moore, and Martin Luther King, Jr., among other heroes, paid the ultimate price to bring about change.[7]

Injustices such as the brutal murders of three civil rights workers (Andrew Goodman, James Chaney, and Michael Schwerner) in rural Mississippi were documented. The use of dogs, water hoses, and bombings to silence the movement appeared on national and international television. This media attention helped to encourage government intervention and heighten public outrage. The federal government's response to the outcries and demands from the black community resulted in laws and policies for change.

TRANSITIONS

Many of the socioeconomic gains of the civil rights movement were diminished during the Reagan and Bush administrations, which used strategies to heighten the fears of whites. Blacks were blamed for causing the economic and social problems of the time. President Bush's veto of the 1990 Civil Rights Act and his appointment of conservatives to the U.S. Supreme Court did not support a climate in which blacks felt they could speak out and make demands.[8]

It appears that the values and beliefs of the Reagan and Bush administrations also influenced the media, which shifted from being supportive to being critical of blacks. Malveaux states that, "Media have played a major role in shaping perceptions of welfare, affirmative action, black economic status, and the role of blacks in society on the part of both black and white Americans. For a very brief and shining moment, we were portrayed as moral giants. . . . Now, we are depicted as moral midgets, rapists, murderers, and welfare cheats and . . . [a]t the same time, because the media glorify athletes and entertainers, many of whom are African American, there is a public perception of African-American privilege, not disparity."[9]

Since the civil rights era ended, the government has paid less and less attention to the needs of blacks, who were portrayed more and more negatively by both the Reagan and Bush administrations. Furthermore, rural blacks are suffering more economically: from 1959 to 1986, they showed improved economic status; however, as of 1986, their real income declined and poverty increased.[10]

The decline in income and increase in poverty are due in part to the fact that rural areas are no longer completely dependent on farming, mining, or forestry; they rely, instead, on manufacturing and service industries, many of which pay low wages. Today, retirement communities, government, and business sectors contribute more to rural employment than does agriculture. However, this industrial transformation has not increased the income of rural residents; it has resulted in displaced and unemployed workers.[11] Now, mental health problems such as depression and suicide have increased among rural families.

During the 1980s, the concentration of higher-skilled and higher-paying employment in urban areas expanded the earning differential between urban and rural workers and encouraged the out-migration of highly educated and trained rural residents. Between 1983 and 1985, almost half of all rural counties lost population. Most of this loss was in the Great Plains, the Western corn belt, the lower Great Lakes region, and parts of the South.[12]

Diagram 2 shows the loss of population since 1986. What is noticeable is that the South is not losing its rural population in significant numbers. Between 1950 and 1960, large numbers of blacks migrated from the South to seek refuge from lynching and inequalities in education, housing, and employment. A case in point is the more than 315,000 blacks who migrated from Mississippi between 1950 and 1960.[13] However, reverse migration is now occurring: "Since 1980, more than 100,000 more blacks have moved into the South than have left."[14] This is a historic change, suggesting that the South may become a model of how to handle race relations for the betterment of all. Another plus for the South: Mississippi is the home state of U.S. Secretary of Agriculture Mike Espy.

A further review of rural populations shows a significant change in the regional distribution of the farm population. In 1950, a majority (51.6 percent) of the farm population resided in the South; by 1988, more than 50 percent of the farm population was located in the Midwest, and only 29.6 percent was in the South.[15] Diagram 3 shows the farming-dependent population in 1986; it provides an indication that Midwestern states may influence agriculture policy and programming during the 1990s.

174

States Losing Nonmetro Population and Rapid Loss Counties, 1982–1987

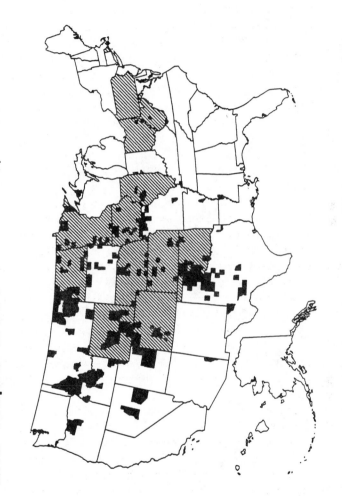

States losing over 7.5% of nonmetro population

Counties losing over 7.5% of population

Source: U.S. Department of Agriculture, Economic Research Service.

175

Farming-Dependent Counties in Nonmetro Areas, 1986

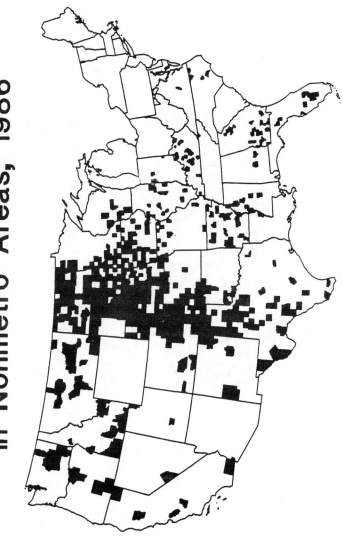

Source: U.S. Department of Agriculture, Economic Research Service.

LACK OF PUBLIC AWARENESS

Little attention has been paid to the impact of the economic transition on rural America and its implications for the black community. Ninety-seven percent of all poor blacks live in the southern region, characterized by persistently low incomes and poverty.[16] Compared with their urban counterparts and with rural whites, rural blacks have considerably lower median incomes and higher poverty rates. Table 1 shows the median family income and family poverty rates by race and rural states from 1959 to 1986. These statistics document the economic loss by blacks during the Reagan administration and show the wide gaps between urban and rural income and poverty. Porter emphasizes these gaps by stating, "Despite the popular perception of concentrated black poverty in the nation's cities, more than two-fifths (44.1 percent) of nonmetro blacks were poor in 1987, compared to one-third (33.3 percent) of blacks living in central cities."[17]

Diagram 4 documents that in 1986, the low per capita income and persistent low-income counties were centered in southern states. The location of this problem strongly suggests that rural blacks must take the leadership in the 1990s by sharing this information with the general public and decision-makers. Such information is crucial to forming policies and programs that bode well for the overall self-sufficiency of residents in this region.

Table 1
Median Family Income and Family Poverty Rates
by Race and Rural Status, 1959-1986
(In Constant 1986 Dollars)

Year	Black Rural	Black Urban	White Rural	White Urban
1959	$ 6,131	$14,034	$17,710	$24,052
1969	11,469	20,122	23,873	32,496
1979	14,964	19,276	25,948	33,152
1986	13,182	18,950	24,310	34,556

Family Poverty Rate

Year	Black Rural	Black Urban	White Rural	White Urban
1959	71.9%	36.3%	23.0%	9.4%
1969	38.1	20.2	9.8	4.6
1979	26.0	20.3	6.9	4.2
1986	31.0	23.0	9.6	4.7

Source: Porter, 1989.

Low Per Capita Income States, 1986 and Persistent Low Income Counties

State nonmetro per capita incomes below $11,300

Counties in the lowest 20% of nonmetrocounties since 1950.

Source: U.S. Department of Agriculture, Economic Research Service.

Table 2 shows that all but one of the states—New Mexico—with the 220 highest poverty-level counties in 1986 were centered in the South. In other regions, the states with the highest poverty-level counties include South Dakota with 10, and Missouri and North Dakota with two each.

Table 2
States with the 220 Highest Poverty-Level Counties*

States	Number of Counties
Mississippi	35
Georgia	32
Kentucky	24
Louisiana	16
Alabama	14
Arkansas	12
Tennessee	11
South Carolina	8
New Mexico	6
North Carolina	4
Florida	4

*Highest poverty-level indicators include percentage in poverty (100 percent of federal poverty level), percentage of elderly (over 65) in poverty, percentage of children (5 and under) in poverty, and percentage of persons in deep poverty (75 percent of federal poverty level), using 1980 statistics.

Source: Gwyn, Douglas, Edward, and Durford, *A Geography of American Poverty: U.S. Strategy Assessment for the Meals for Millions/Freedom from Hunger Foundation,* 1986.

Even though a large percentage of rural residents are poor, many of them do not receive public assistance and related support. The 1987 *Current Population Survey* (CPS) data show that about 54 percent of poor rural black families receive some public assistance, as compared with 64 percent of their urban counterparts.[18] Many of these rural families are not eligible for Aid For Dependent Children (AFDC) because, compared to their urban counterparts, they are more likely to have at least one working family member. Lack of information, accessibility, and trust of government intervention; the stigmatization of welfare programs; and the sense of pride are other reasons that help account for many rural blacks not receiving public assistance and other social services, even though they may be eligible. Programs such as JOBS (Family Support Act) and the Job Training Partnership Act (JTPA) have been urban-focused, failing to address the special needs of rural residents, including job development and transportation.

Since 1970, there has been little sustained and coherent political articulation of the plight of rural blacks (the Rodney King case and the violence in the cities have sparked some discussions regarding the plight of urban blacks). Some of the silence by rural blacks may relate to a sense of false comfort that often occurs when other groups are facing similar problems. For example, it can be argued that unemployment, poverty, homelessness, out-migration, and the lack of accessible and affordable social services and housing are universal problems in America and therefore are not specific to rural blacks. However, a review of Table 1 shows marked inequities in terms of income and family poverty by race and location. Census data reinforce the resource inequities between blacks and whites, thereby suggesting that racism and discrimination still exist.

Jan S. Tin, using 1991 statistics, reports that rural blacks have a median income of $15,870, while whites have a median income of $28,320. Rural blacks and whites also differ substantially in other characteristics. Black households are larger but are less likely to be married-couple families than white households. White householders are more likely than their black counterparts to complete four or more years of college. Black householders are less likely to occupy single-family units and more likely to live in crowded homes than white householders. Black householders are far more likely than whites to live in units with severe plumbing, inadequate heating, and upkeep problems. The median value of homes occupied by blacks is $39,710—only 59 percent of the $67,840 median value of white households.[19]

President Clinton's universal approach to policy and programming has the potential to further silence blacks who are concerned about their socioeconomic plight in this country. While the goal of Clinton's approach is to be location- and race-neutral, it still influences where and how socioeconomic change should occur, and what options and choices are available to communities. Rural blacks cannot be complacent about their problems; they must be aware of their options and choices on how best to solve them. They must be as politically astute as they were during the civil rights movement, identifying, assessing, and prioritizing their needs and making them known to federal, state, and local decisionmakers.

To illustrate the need for blacks to become more political, Graph 1 highlights the employment/job growth from 1969 to 1987. It shows the role of the private services sector, which has always been open to blacks in terms of employment/job potential, notwithstanding the fact that most blacks had jobs in the lower-paying areas. The graph indicates that agriculture, which has enabled more rural blacks to become entrepreneurs, is on the decline. This clearly suggests that the black community needs to reassess employment/job growth potential and strategies for economic development.

The government sector, while small, is an area that blacks should not overlook. As of 1990, more than two-thirds of all black elected officials in this country (67.5 percent) were located in the South.[20] The increasing number of blacks migrating to this area has implications for economic and

180

Diagram 5

Graph 1

Nonmetro job growth 1979-87

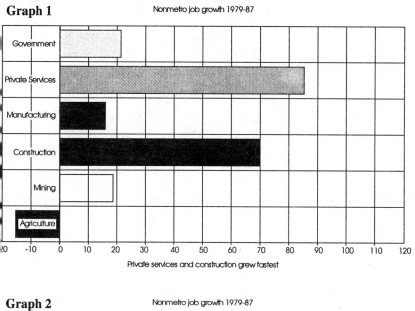

Private services and construction grew fastest

Graph 2

Nonmetro job growth 1979-87

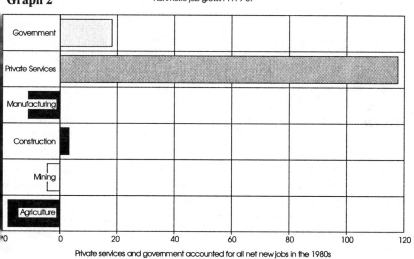

Private services and government accounted for all net new jobs in the 1980s

Source: Reid, N. & Frederick, M. (1990) *Rural America Economic Performance 1989*, U.S. Department of Agriculture, Economic Research Service.

181

community development, in that the South can provide a model for racial alliances and coalitions across the nation. Whites in many southern states support blacks in their efforts to win elective offices; Mike Espy's election to Congress—the first African American from Mississippi to do so this century—is a case in point. This support is leading to a better quality of life for all residents of the South.

At the 23rd Annual Legislative Weekend of the Congressional Black Caucus September 15-19, in Washington, DC, representatives from all regions of America testified about the problems and needs of rural blacks. The Land Loss Fund, Inc., estimated that there will be only 1.7 million farms and 2.7 million farmers in the United States by the year 2000. Blacks are losing land at the rate of 9,000 acres per week. At this pace, there will be no black-owned land by the year 2000. Many blacks and their heirs will be unprepared to combat the loss of their land due to lack of information, education, tax payments, as well as economic and social injustice.

For example, a recent field visit to the Sea Islands off the coast of Georgia highlighted the loss of black-owned land and the influence of this loss on the culture and the environment. The building of golf courses, hotels, and restaurants in these coastal areas has destroyed cultural landmarks. The pollution from marinas has not only closed shellfish beds but also endangers the health of children and families. This pollution is not unique to the Sea Islands because hazardous waste incinerators and metal recycling plants have been proposed for locations within a 20-mile radius in northeastern North Carolina. A report by the Land Loss Fund, Inc., of Tillery, NC, notes that these proposed plants will pose health risks through air, water, and soil pollution. Because many of these plants are being planned for communities which include at least 90 percent black residents, the Fund has cited this action as "environmental racism." Bullard concurs that waste facility sites are not chosen by chance in rural or urban areas. Recommendations for and actual sites are, for the most part, in communities least likely to express opposition—older, poor, and minority communities. These recommendations and decisions often include cooperation between government and industry officials.[21]

Rural blacks must be concerned with land loss in the 1990s. This is not just a land issue but also a power issue. "Black farm operators in particular are losing their land to agencies of the federal government, discriminatory bankers and creditors, unscrupulous lawyers and speculators, landfills, and the concentration of agriculture in fewer and fewer hands. As a result, this historic source of African-American economic and political power is being brutally, permanently, and systematically destroyed. The farm bills of the 1980s and 1990s, touted as salvation for black farmers, have failed to rectify past discrimination. For example, one 1987 act set aside monies for 'socially disadvantaged' farmers who could apply under the very same regulations that were already in effect. One of these regulations requires farmers to show five ears of positive cash flow. But this is impossible for farmers who have suffered under discriminatory lending policies all their lives."[22]

Agriculture Secretary Mike Espy and Bob Nash, Undersecretary of Agriculture for Small Community and Rural Development, conducted the forum, "Rural America: Changes, Challenges, and Opportunities" on October 8, 1993. Such a forum allows hope for rural blacks to voice their concerns and to prompt action. In order to assess the results of such meetings, they will have to be evaluated and monitored by those concerned with rural issues, such as the Land Loss Fund, Inc., which will have to lead in this area.

Another issue which rural black organizations must address is the lack of a precise, standard, federal and state definition of the term "rural." This problem erects barriers to rural participation in certain federal and state programs.[23] A case in point is Congress's directive to the Health Care Financing Administration to use the Office of Management and Budget's (OMB) metropolitan statistical area (MSA) designation to categorize hospitals as urban or rural for purposes of reimbursement under Medicare and to use the Census Bureau's Non-Urbanized Area designation to certify health facilities under the Rural Health Clinics Act.[24]

A uniform definition of "rural" is essential, particularly in the area of health, since federal and state funding are crucial when addressing the health needs of rural blacks. Poor rural residents are more likely to be unhealthy than their urban counterparts, and they disproportionately lack health insurance coverage. Summer states that, "For rural residents, particularly those who live in sparsely populated areas, geographic barriers to receiving health care services are significant. Often the population base in rural areas is simply not large enough to support the type of medical facilities and practitioners available to residents of more densely populated areas."[25] It should be noted that a larger percentage of blacks (20.6 percent) living in nonmetro areas, as compared with their black counterparts (14.4 percent) living in metro areas, reported their health as fair or poor.[26] These statistics point to the disproportionate number of rural blacks who have health problems and limited service.

Aaron Shirley, Project Director of Jackson-Hinds Comprehensive Health Center in Jackson, Mississippi, emphasizes the need for increased coordination among service delivery agencies.[27] A precise, standard definition of "rural" could assist with this coordination. Reducing the number of agency forms is also essential to improving health care delivery to rural areas.

This chapter has referred to the lack of attention paid to rural America, especially to blacks residing in rural areas. Therefore, another priority concern of the black community must be the absence of national and state statistics related to rural areas. Existing government statistics and media coverage focus primarily on urban, not rural, issues. Many rural communities have neither the funds nor the qualified staff to spotlight and solve their problems, nor do they want to change their existing public image—families and communities as strong and self-reliant entities. But the absence of information given to legislators, other decisionmakers, and the general public about the many problems facing rural America serves as a barrier to forming policies and programs which would begin to correct rural problems. The result is further inequity in services and resources necessary to support these families and their communities.

RECOMMENDATIONS

Today, as during the civil rights era, rural blacks can play a major role in helping all blacks develop a sense of community. The re-migration of black to the South will enable rural and urban leadership to work together. In the 1950s and 1960s, it was understood by urban blacks that they could not "overcome" if their rural counterparts were also suffering. We must, therefore, return to this partnership in the 1990s. This decade has displayed a lack of hope, meaning, and love, encouraged by cutbacks of federal funds, market forces, market "moralities," and the crisis in leadership.[28] "Like all Americans, African Americans are influenced greatly by images of comfort, convenience, machismo, femininity, violence, and sexual stimulation that bombard consumers. These seductive images contribute to the predominance of the market-inspired way of life over all others, and thereby edge out nonmarket values—love, care, service to others—handed down by preceding generations."[29]

Rural black communities cannot be silent about the social crises (such as suicides among young black males and black-on-black crime) which disproportionately affect their urban counterparts and which will soon reach their own doorsteps. Nor can they remain silent about those market-driven strategies that are stealing their land and therefore their culture and power. Rural blacks' appreciation of the work ethic, self-help, and self-esteem must be reemphasized, reinforced, and shared with their urban relatives.

Rural and urban black leadership must be identified and supported. For example, Mike Espy's and Bob Nash's efforts to meet with grass-roots rural residents should be applauded in general and emulated in particular. Espy and Nash must work with grass-roots organizations like the Coastal Georgia Area Community Action Authority, Inc., in Brunswick, GA, which has comprehensive community-based program in both rural and urban areas. The Penn Center, Inc., is another grass-roots program which Espy and Nash can use as a model for change. Penn Center, Inc., represents coastal islands and links the loss of culture with the loss of land. This organization has embarked on a three-pronged approach for change: (1) workshops and one-on-one counseling for individual landowners; (2) identification of and training for community leaders; and (3) advocacy for land retention, cultural preservation, and environmental protection.[30]

Besides renewing their bonds with urban blacks, rural black Americans must cultivate and form political alliances with other racial and ethnic groups. Gray points out that, while relations with other groups may involve conflict, African Americans will better serve their own interests by pursuing shared, cooperative leadership and political activity with other key groups.[31] These partnerships are complex yet beneficial; they are often formed because of crisis or mandate. However, partnerships are also formed based on networking, interest, and need.[32] Self-help is one of the major facilitators of public-private partnerships because grass-roots organizations have coaxed and cajoled this type of investment.[33] Partnerships are important vehicles for economic development; rural blacks must facilitate more of these partnerships during the 1990s.

Because both rural and urban black communities need economic productivity, an investment program should be adopted addressing the specific needs of both urban and rural residents.

The National Urban League's Marshall Plan is just such a program for economic growth. The plan is characterized by investments that include human resource initiatives (people) as well as physical infrastructure initiatives (facilities). Highlights of the plan:

- address both long-term economic productivity goals and short-term improvements in social well-being;
- maximize returns by concentrating on areas of greatest need;
- involve sustained, programmed collaborations on the part of government, the private sector, and nonprofit organizations;
- operate under rigorous accountability systems for monitoring, assessing, and adjusting results over time.[34]

Proposed alliances and coalitions should be composed of people representing all levels of the community. Their members must identify and assess strategies to address many of the issues discussed in this chapter. An effective plan must focus on the needs of rural blacks and yet provide ideas for fostering the worth, dignity, and promotion of the strengths of all.

The geography and history of rural blacks in America suggest that the South has the potential, as it did during the civil rights movement, to help facilitate change. It is imperative that leaders in rural black America develop a coherent plan to identify and prioritize needs and publicly voice their concerns in the 1990s.

Hesitancy to speak out about rural issues and failure to develop a plan of action will only continue the systematic discrimination and oppression of rural and urban black communities alike. If change does not take place, then we will be faced with two Americas—one urban and prosperous; the other rural, poor, and disproportionately black.

The author extends special thanks to the New York State African-American Institute, State University of New York; Calvin Beale, U.S. Department of Agriculture; and Dianne Harley and Sam Johnson, U.S. Census Bureau, for their help with the research on the geographical location of rural blacks.

The author acknowledges with appreciation the key informants who confirmed the notion of silent suffering of black rural Americans—Jesse Banks, Leonard Dawson, Wilbur Hawkins, and Rosemary Sullivan.

REFERENCES

Brown, D., Reid, N., Bluestone, H., McGranahan, D., and S. Mazie, eds. 1988. *Rural Economic Development in the 1980s: Prospects for the Future.* Washington, DC: U. S. Department of Agriculture, Economic Research Service, Agriculture and Rural Economy Division.

Encyclopedia Americana. 1990. Volumes 1-30. Danbury, CT: Grolier, Inc.

Flora, C., and Christenson, J. 1991. "Critical Times for Rural America: The Challenge for Rural Policy in the 1990s." In *Rural Policies for the 1990s*, eds. C. Flora and J. Christenson. Boulder, CO: Westview Press.

Flora, J., Flora, C., and Houdek, E. 1991. *Rural Communities, Legacy and Change.* Boulder, CO: Westview Press.

Gwyn, Douglas, Edward, and Durford. 1986. *A Geography of American Poverty: U.S. Strategy Assessment for the Meals for Millions/Freedom from Hunger Foundation.* Davis, CA: Meals for Millions.

Haskins, J. and Biondi, J. 1993. *The Historic Black South.* New York: Hipposcrene Books.

Hayden, W. 1989. "Black Families: Forgotten People in Appalachia." Invited paper presented at the annual conference of the National Association of Social Workers, San Francisco, CA, October 11, 1989.

New York African American Institute. 1991. *The State of African American New Yorkers: A Statistical Profile 1991.* Institute Document 91-12.

Rasmussin, W., and Bowers, D. 1988. "Rural America in the Twentieth Century." In *Rural America in Transition*, eds., M. Drabenstott and L. Gibson. Kansas City, MO: The Federal Reserve Bank of Kansas City, Research Division.

U.S. Departments of Agriculture and Commerce. 1988. *Rural and Rural Farm Population.* Washington, DC: U.S. Government Printing Office.

ENDNOTES

[1]The term "black" is used interchangeably with the political term, "African American." The Census Bureau's designation of "nonmetro," as an area outside of metropolitan statistical areas, is used interchangeably with the term "rural."

[2]Lief Jensen, "The Doubly Jeopardized: Non-Metropolitan Blacks and Mexicans," in C. Flora and J. Christenson, eds., *Rural Policies for the 1990s* (Boulder, CO: Westview Press, 1991), pp. 181-193; and Juan Williams, *Eyes on the Prize: America's Civil Rights Years, 1954-1965* (New York: Penguin, 1988).

[3]T. Bonnett, *Strategies for Rural Competitiveness: Policy Options for State Governments* (Washington, DC: Council of Governors' Policy Advisors, 1993).

[4]*Ibid.;* Edyth L. Ross, *Black Heritage in Social Welfare, 1860-1930* (Metuchen, NJ: The Scarecrow Press, Inc., 1978).

[5]*Ibid.*

[6]*Ibid.*

[7]Juan Williams, *Eyes on the Prize: America's Civil Rights Years, 1954-1965* (New York: Penguin, 1988), and Wynetta Devore, "The African-American Community in 1990: The Search for a Practice Method," in F. and J. Erlich, eds., *Community Organization in a Diverse Society* (Boston: Allyn and Bacon, 1992), pp. 67-89.

[8]Julianne M. Malveaux, "The Party Imperative: Civil Rights, Economic Justice, and the New American Dilemma," in Billy J. Tidwell, ed., *The State of Black America 1992* (Washington, DC: National Urban League, Inc., 1992), pp. 281-303.

[9]*Ibid.*, p. 282.

[10]Shirley J. Jones, "Campaign Watch—Rural America: The Domestic Agenda." Paper presented at the State University of New York, Albany, NY, April 22, 1992.

[11]Norman Reid, "Education and Rural Development: A Review of Recent Evidence." Paper presented at the Annual Conference of the American Educational Research Association, Boston, MA, April 17, 1990.

[12]"Race and the South," *U.S. News & World Report,* July 23, 1990, pp. 22-30; Williams, *op. cit.*

[13]*Ibid.*

[14]L. Dacquel and D. Dahmann, *Residents of Farms and Rural Areas* (Washington, DC: U.S. Department of Commerce, Bureau of the Census, 1993).

[15]*Ibid.*

[16]Katherine Porter, *Poverty in Rural America: A National Overview* (Washington, DC: Center on Budget and Policy Priorities, 1989).

[17]*Ibid.*

[18]Jan S. Tin, *Housing Characteristics of Rural Households: 1991* (Washington, DC: U.S. Department of Housing and Urban Development; U.S. Department of Commerce, Bureau of the Census, 1993), pp. 28-29.

[19]*U.S. News and World Report, op. cit.*

[20]*Ibid.*, pp. 23-24.

[21]The Land Loss Fund, Inc., report presented at the 23rd Annual Legislative Weekend of the Congressional Black Caucus, Washington, DC, September 15-19, 1993; Robert D. Bullard, "Urban Infrastructure: Social, Environmental, and Health Risks to African Americans," in Billy J. Tidwell, ed., *The State of Black America 1992* (Washington, DC: National Urban League, Inc., 1992).

[22]*Ibid.*

[23]Shirley J. Jones, "Rural Families at Risk: Implications for Social and Economic Development." Keynote presentation at the National Rural Families Conference, Kansas State University, Manhattan, KS, September 26, 1991.

[24]Maria Hewitt, "Defining 'Rural' Areas: Impact on Health Care Policy and Research," in Shirley Jones, ed., *Sociocultural and Service Issues in Working with Rural Clients* (Albany, NY: Rockefeller College Press, 1993).

[25]L. Summer, *Limited Access: Health Care for the Rural Poor* (Washington, DC: Center on Budget and Policy Priorities, 1991), p. xiii.

[26]Jensen, *op. cit.*

[27]Aaron Shirley, "Education and Nutrition," *Journal of Health Care for the Poor and Underserved* 2:1, Summer 1991, pp. 87-94.

[28]Cornel West, *Race Matters* (Boston: Beacon Press, 1993).

[29]*Ibid.*

[30]Emory S. Campbell, remarks presented at the 23rd Annual Legislative Weekend of the Congressional Black Caucus, Washington, DC, September 17, 1993.

[31]Sandra Gray, "Public-Private Partnerships: Prospects for America . . . Promise for African Americans," in Billy J. Tidwell, ed., *The State of Black America 1992* (Washington, DC: National Urban League, Inc., 1992), pp. 231-247.

[32]Shirley J. Jones, "Sociocultural Service Issues: Implications for Support to Rural Families." Speech presented at the 18th National Institution on Social Work and Human Services in Rural Areas, Oxford College, Oxford, GA, July 28, 1993.

[33]*Ibid.*

[34]Billy J. Tidwell, "Serving the National Interest: A Marshall Plan for America," in Billy J. Tidwell, ed., *The State of Black America 1992* (Washington, DC: National Urban League, Inc., 1992), pp. 11-30.

ORGANIZING AFRICAN-AMERICAN SELF-DEVELOPMENT: THE ROLE OF COMMUNITY-BASED ORGANIZATIONS

Joan Wallace-Benjamin, Ph.D.

INTRODUCTION

African-American communities across this nation stand on the threshold of decision-making about what they will be, how they will survive, and how they will sustain themselves. For a variety of reasons, both internal and external, the life conditions of African-American citizens, particularly their children, are worse today than they were in the 1940s and 1950s. Poverty, inadequate education, housing, health care, drug and alcohol abuse, and AIDS have increased in severity and abundance within the African-American community and other communities of color. There is no question that the **development** of the African-American community at an individual and institutional level is currently the major challenge for African Americans committed to and concerned about the long-term health, welfare, and security of an entire group of America's people. As John E. Jacob, president, National Urban League, so eloquently stated in his 1993 National Urban League Conference keynote address:

> The "No Blacks Allowed" signs have come down, but the presumption that African Americans are unable to compete finds its way deep into the hearts of basic institutions. It is a major barrier to developing a world-class work force and a decent society. . . . The single most important task for the African-American community today is self-development. We must create 21st century communities that nurture 21st century citizens.[1]

The changing political, economic, and social landscape of the latter part of this century and into the new century will require that community-based organizations participate in the process of African-American self-development in ways that heretofore may not have been fully required of them. The institutional base created by both the older, more established organizations of

189

a community and by the more recent organizations developed to respond to changing needs is itself a resource for 21st century community change that offers hope and possibility for the African-American community. A challenge to the ability of community organizations to participate in the process of African-American self-development will be the rebuilding of a strong, stable institutional base within communities. Unfortunately, in communities across the country, the erosion of a strong institutional base has resulted in organizations fragmented, financially insecure, diffuse in their mission and goals, and fighting for survival. Unstable institutions contribute to an unstable community. Unstable communities are unable to develop within themselves the informal service network of families, friends, and neighbors in whom members of the community can depend. When the formal and informal service networks are working in sync, fragmentation of services and isolation are avoided. Ultimately, the community is able to use the resources it has to take care of itself.

THE ISSUE OF SELF-DEVELOPMENT

The major enemy of black survival in America has been the "threat of nihilism" which Cornel West defines as the loss of hope and the absence of meaning:

> The genius of our black foremothers and forefathers was to create powerful buffers to ward off the nihilistic threat, to equip black folk with cultural armor to beat back the demons of hopelessness, meaninglessness, and lovelessness. These buffers consisted of cultural structures of meaning and feeling that created and sustained communities; this armor constituted ways of life and struggle that embodied values of service and sacrifice, love and care, discipline and excellence. In other words, traditions for black surviving and thriving under usually adverse New World conditions were major barriers against the nihilistic threat.[2]

Unfortunately, every day the human service community faces increasing numbers of children and their families who are overwhelmed by hopelessness, meaninglessness, and lovelessness. Families, unlike their foremothers and forefathers, are unable right now to provide the needed buffers and armor that enable them to survive and thrive under extremely difficult circumstances. This reality may mean that all community-based organizations (not just those providing social services) will have to be about the business of facilitating community self-development so that, in the long term, our families will again be in the position to buffer and armor themselves.

How should the process of self-development begin anew, and why is it important to the African-American community? It begins with a change in belief about what is possible. It begins with a belief in our ability to compete, to be the best, the smartest. It means, as John E. Jacob says, that we have to "liberate our thinking and understand we must rely on ourselves."[3] It means that we must instill in our children, their parents, and ourselves the same winning attitude about education and learning that we as a people take for granted in the world of athletics. It means that our community organizations must model a new set of the highest standards and expectations for themselves. Well-run, professional, efficient, clean, appropriately quiet, on-time, and respectful environments must be the normative standard. We have been sold by American society, and now sell ourselves, a destructive "bill of goods" about who we are as African Americans. Any time we believe and hear articulated in our community by our own children that being smart in school, serious about intellectual pursuit, well spoken; or by our adults that being efficient, on time, or professionally dressed on the job is "white" or "bourgeoisie," we have allowed ourselves to fall into the cleverest of traps that could be created to immobilize any group of people.

We have allowed the educational, economic, employment, and residential diversity among us as African Americans to pull us apart instead of to bring us together. The social class gap within the African-American community must be understood, discussed, and a strategy developed to overcome its destructive effects on our ability to do what we must for our collective well being. We must recreate the psychological ties that African Americans have to the black community: that the African-American community is anywhere African Americans live.

Community organizations, as they deliver services, must again instill in themselves and their people the traditional value of excellence in everything they do. In the 25 years since the civil rights movement, we have allowed this community ethic to slowly seep away. By doing so we have weakened our defenses against the pernicious external forces that have always existed and diminished the number of people in our population with the skills or, in some instances, even the interest, in problem-solving new strategies appropriate to these times.

In delivering services, we have not maintained currency on human development pedagogy and techniques for effectively serving people. We must ensure that the people who come to work within the human service setting have a commitment to both organizational and personal development and that we provide staff with the support they need to meet the psychological, emotional, and social challenges that come with the service to our people in a changing world. Unfortunately, the nonprofit human service sector has been poorly represented by some within it who see it as the place to come to exert minimal effort and not work very hard. This attitude has been reinforced by a society that fails to value the importance of, the hard work involved in, or the skill-sets needed to serve human needs. This same society has failed to allocate sufficient resources—federal, state, or local—to do the job that needs to be done. Dr. Hubert Jones, Dean Emeritus, Boston University School of Social Work, says that, "The public sector fails to meet the minimal expectations and legitimate demands of the black community. This outrageous neglect undermines the capability of black social institutions to carry out the cultural, educational, religious, social support, and community development work which are their primary responsibility."[4]

As we move into the second half of this decade, African-American community organizations must come together in a collaborative mode, not just in the actual delivery of services but also around some hard and fundamental discussion about what the standards and expectations of the community and its institutions will be. What are the values they share that inform the way they serve? What are the outcomes they will hold themselves accountable for? For example, every African-American community is concerned about the issue of adolescent pregnancy. Service providers, parents, teachers, clergy, and others would agree that the unabated continuance of adolescent pregnancy is destroying the positive life chances for thousands of young children being born to children and locking them forever into poverty. However, is there agreement in that community about what the solution is? Is the solution more services to young pregnant and parenting teens, enabling them to care for their children at home and at school? Is the solution a return to the past when community sanction and disapproval was greater and perhaps served as a deterrent to certain behavior? The ability of a community to provide positive life chances for all of its children is ultimately the answer. But what do we do, in the short term, about the escalating incidence of adolescent pregnancy while we develop our communities to where they need to be? These kinds of questions are not only about adolescent pregnancy but also about the range of problems troubling our communities which need to be asked in honest and serious ways by a broad representation of community stakeholders. "More important to the successful development of youth than the impact of any single institution is the continuity and congruence of all the various institutions in their lives. Value confusion occurs when the social institutions youth relate to present conflicting values and expectations." [5]

Dr. James Jennings, Acting Director of the William Monroe Trotter Institute, University of Massachusetts, Boston, writes that given that blacks are both racially and politically exploited, there are three responses human service providers can utilize to assist people in black communities. These responses prepare clients to challenge the social and value contexts under which they receive human services:

1. raising racial, and therefore, political consciousness of the clients of human service programs.

2. countering the negative images and messages about blacks emanating from the media.

3. community-controlled self-help, which is most critical.[6]

Jennings and others agree that racial consciousness and group pride help to create an environment in which African Americans can empower themselves. The ability of human service providers to incorporate history, culture, and racial consciousness into the educational and social components of service delivery increases the effectiveness of those services and creates the kind of supportive environment that improves the receptivity to and internalization of the help being offered. History, culture, and consciousness also empower and enable the service recipient to take responsibility for his/her role in improving the quality of life, particularly when this consciousness includes the expectation of political participation. Jennings goes on to say that "Racial consciousness is a way of instilling confidence and motivation in youth; but it also allows the black community greater insight in demanding and gaining greater accountability and effectiveness from institutions delivering human services."[7] The individual consciousness of members of the black community is necessary but not sufficient. The community must also build into its infrastructure reliable mechanisms to ensure accountability. Once a set of standards and expectations are established by the African-American community, how do you ensure that local organizations do what they are in business to do? How does the success of their outcomes get measured, who measures it, and how are rewards or sanctions on organizational behavior and performance given? A process for the appropriate "division of labor" among the human service institutional base is an important part of the discussion and first step.

The history and culture of the African-American community is a rich, strong, and powerful legacy for today's youth and the youth of generations past. As community-based organizations play an all-important role in the infusion of history, culture, and consciousness into their programs, it must be emphasized that the history is replete with examples of Africans and African Americans as intelligent, capable, "can do" people who value the excellence of an endeavor. Was not the civil rights movement, launched on behalf of and by African Americans, an example of the "can do" ability of an intelligent, capable people? The leadership of that movement at all levels believed that they could change the outcomes for African Americans over time, and they did. Their strategy was tactical and based on data. It was realistic and utilized the intelligence of every able-bodied member of the community wanting to act. It created opportunity and access for large numbers of African Americans who were able to enter classrooms and board rooms across the country. It opened lunch counters, schools, and neighborhoods to African Americans and other disenfranchised Americans. It created an African-American middle class.

Our current condition as a community is not the result of a failed movement; it is partly a result of the fact that, in realizing gains had been won, we failed to shift from the protest mode of the 1960s into the institutional development mode that is required today. We failed to manage fully what had been gained; to take advantage of the new level of access and resource acquisition that came as a result of the movement.

African-American children of the 21st century, if they are to compete and succeed, must have restored to them by the adults of their community the confidence and belief in their intellectual (not just athletic, musical, and creative) capability. That, as Dr. Jeffrey Howard of the Efficacy Institute clarifies for us, "smart is not something that you are, smart is something that you can get."[8] The adults themselves must come to believe this if they are to help our children believe it. The society in which we live does not support this notion for any of its people, particularly its African American and other people of color. There are few, if any institutions, including our own community institutions, that truly believe that black people can learn **anything**. We have allowed the historical abuse that we have received as a people from this nation to convince us that we cannot be the best and the brightest. Many of our youth and a number of our adults believe, inside where it counts, that were there no barriers at all, they still would not be capable of competing at the highest intellectual level. This belief is destructive to the 21st century survival of African Americans on an individual and institutional level because:

1. it renders us at an extreme disadvantage in the economic reality of the year 2000. Given the highly technological requirements of education and employment in the 21st century and the virtual restructuring of the United States and world economies as we know them, as a community we have not developed the external and internal strategies needed to ensure that our children be taught at 21st century standards. These strategies include making public education do what it needs to do for our children; and it means seeing to it that the community structures itself to make sure that all of its children "can do" what is required.

2. it allows us to accept mediocrity in the way our community institutions operate, the way our children speak and behave, and the way we as adults treat one another.

The Efficacy Institute, an African-American, nonprofit educational service organization, in Lexington, Massachusetts, involved in promoting the overall development of children of color, has identified Efficacy 21st Century Educational Objectives to which all children must measure up by the end of high school if they are to compete and succeed in the 21st century.

- Master calculus (or any substitute form of mathematics certified by mathematicians as equivalent) at the advanced placement level.
- Achieve fluency in at least one language in addition to English.
- Demonstrate a capacity to write a literate, well structured, well researched, 25-page essay on any topic deemed important by teachers and interesting to the student.

- Demonstrate a capacity to live by strict high ethical standards.[9]

The fourth objective was added at the 1992 National Urban League Conference by its president and chief executive officer, John E. Jacob. Certainly, the fourth objective is achievable right now within our community organizations to begin setting the pace for what will be the organizational requirements throughout this century and into the next.

Local community organizations must be the translators of history and culture using it to develop service pedagogy that is current and responsive to the rapidly changing circumstances of the children and families they serve. The development of pedagogy must include an internal process of fact finding and research; knowledge of current, relevant literature; assessment of trends; rigorous experimentation; and strategic planning. This was the role of the National Urban League in 1910, responding to the need for a pedagogy to train African-American social workers to work with the various challenges African-American migrants faced as they moved into urban America. Community-based organizations must also be committed not only to the development of the people they serve but also to the development of the people that work within the organization who are, in most cases, members of the community. The ability to build individual strength and capacity to survive is enhanced and made possible by the strength of the institutional base in place to facilitate that process. Organizational policies and practices must be reflective of the belief in and attitude toward the community that says all people can learn, and learning is a life-long process for children as well as for adults; intelligence is not innate and fixed at birth but is itself subject to being developed. There is a learnable, teachable process of development[10] that organizations can incorporate into their daily business operations and support mechanisms for their staff.

Organizations must be part of the strategy development process that identifies what is required of the adults in the community if they are to assist their children in achieving the previously defined 21st century achievement standards. A function of time may prevent all of the community's adults from achieving the 21st century educational objectives themselves. However, what characteristics and qualities must the adults have which will enable them to provide the support young people need to reach the academic and character standards for the 21st century? The following qualities will be needed:
- openness to new ideas
- ability to think globally
- personal sacrifice
- continuous learning and development
- high ethical standards
- entrepreneurship
- commitment to cooperation and collaboration with colleagues, friends and neighbors

- ability to write and speak English
- a focus on something greater than self
- a control of ego
- more principled interactions with others
- membership/active participation in the activities, goals, and mission of local community organizations.

Such qualities will create an environment in which our children can grow, learn, and reach the next century.

A final and critical role in the process of African-American self-development for local community organizations is the practice of community organization and mobilization around the previously discussed issues of community wellness and stability. Dr. Hubert Jones says that "the sustained mobilization of consumers, constituents, and residents at large is not a major operational priority of black service institutions. . . . Because service institutions fail to devote resources to the consistent mobilization of consumers and constituents, institutional leaders and politicians cannot acquire the people clout they need to be effective in political advocacy. Thus, they are unable to play their part in the struggle for resources and services the black community has a right to expect."[11] Community organization and mobilization must become a priority for local communities. Advocacy around specific health care, employment, day care, and other issues is key. Also critical are organization and mobilization around what our communities will be; what they stand for; and what the community holds as its standards and expectations for itself.

THE STATUS OF AFRICAN AMERICANS IN BOSTON

Not unlike other large urban centers, the city of Boston, with its relatively small African-American population (see Table 1), is faced with increased educational, employment and training, career development, and other service needs.

Table 1
Summary Results from Boston Foundation Study,
In the Midst of Plenty, **and Official Poverty Estimates**

	Results from *In the Midst of Plenty*			Official Results	
	Total Population	(125%) Total Poor	(125%) Poverty Rate	Official Total Poor	Official Poverty Rate
Boston	387,700	71,500	18.4%	53,452	13.8%
Blacks	91,700	20,900	22.8%	17,219	18.8%
Hispanics	35,000	16,000	45.7%	12,524	35.8%
Whites	214,700	16,100	7.5%	11,483	5.3%
Others	46,300	18,500	40.0%	N/A	N/A

Sources: The Boston Foundation, *In the Midst of Plenty*. A Program of the Boston Persistent Poverty Project, 1989. Calculations for "Official Results" based on data fron U.S. Census Bureau: *Current Population Reports*, "Money, Income, and Poverty Status in the United States, 1987," Series P-60, No. 161.

• The state unemployment rate for African Americans in the first quarter of 1992 was 16.6 percent. In the second quarter, it rose to 23 percent. The national unemployment rate for all African Americans in 1991 was 16.5 percent.[12]

• 24 percent of Boston's African Americans are considered at or below the poverty level. One-third of that population is under the age of 18. More than 35 percent of African-American children under the age of six live in poverty in Boston.[13]

• 191 African-American youths have been killed in Boston since 1985 as a result of violence.

• At the end of the year, the number of African Americans in the communities of Roxbury and Dorchester receiving Aid to Families with Dependent Children increased to 5,240, from 851 in 1991.[14]

• Out of 57,274 students in the Boston public school system, 48 percent are African American (approximately 27,492 children). The dropout rate for this population is a staggering 33.5 percent (approximately 9,210 children).[15]

• In the decade between 1982 and 1992, the number of out-of-wedlock births to black women rose from 49 percent to 67 percent as compared with Hispanic women at 27 percent in 1992, and white women at 17 percent in 1992.[16]

Boston's African-American community has a number of multi-service and specialized service organizations working to meet the tremendous needs of the men, women, and children living in the community. Many of these approaches are some of the most innovative in the nation.

In the next section, two examples of community mobilization and organization in progress will be discussed. In Boston and communities across the country, black people of like mind and spirit are grappling with these issues and learning as they go. The belief in learning and development as a lifelong process will enable us as a people not to give up and to acknowledge that we are smart enough and capable enough to figure out the answers to our questions, no matter how challenging they seem. Today's problems, placed in the perspective of our struggle, are no more impossible to solve than in our past. Our communities need a new way to envision what is required and what each of us will need to bring to the discussion.

THE TEN DEMANDMENTS

After the Rodney King verdict in May 1992, the Urban League of Eastern Massachusetts, in collaboration with the Boston Chapter of the NAACP, developed an action-oriented response designed to channel the justifiable rage felt in Boston and cities across the country. Because of the historical collaboration between the Urban League and the NAACP, we were able to organize and mobilize Boston's African-American community and others around the necessity for a plan and its implementation. We wanted our response to be nonviolent; we wanted it to be specific; and we wanted it to be action oriented.

The plan we developed was called the Ten Demandments, which are interrelated and internally reinforcing. Each works well if the others work well. They also acknowledge that successfully addressing the quality of life issues, characterized by these Demandments, for all Americans requires ownership of the problems by everyone. The Demandments addressed the areas of educational improvement and adequate funding, the equitable distribution of financial resources, employment, training and job opportunity, health and day care access, police community relations, representation in the media, and voter registration. The Boston media were asked to respect in its coverage the interrelatedness of the Demandments one with the other. They were asked to communicate that, while the community was prepared to take responsibility for those things they believed they could begin to control, the problems that needed to be addressed were not of their creation alone. The myriad of complex problems in Boston had not been perpetuated by the African-American community alone and were not the community's alone to correct. The Ten Demandments were an articulation of the social contract that must exist among the elected, business, and community leadership of a city.

The Ten Demandments evolved from a number of existing community initiatives already in progress and built on the hard work and untiring efforts

198

in the areas of housing, day care, health care, economic development, etc.

What is so powerful and relevant about the Ten Demandments to the issue of self-development is that they represent a community consensus process as a way to organize on our own behalf. They represent a framework of priorities and issues in which all who participated in their drafting and ratification had a role and could use those roles to organize and mobilize already existing activity around the issues.

Demandment Victories

To date, the majority of the Ten Demandments have been met. A committee structure was created, co-chaired by members of the community who had been working on these issues personally and/or organizationally. Their charge was to get each Demandment met. While we knew that the nature of the issues addressed by the Demandments could result in numerous related activities, we focused on the achievement of the Demandment first. We believed that it was important to experience success with and for the community as a way to sustain momentum in the process of community mobilization. With the exception of the Media and Day Care Demandments, all others have been met or have significant activity ongoing toward achievement.

COMMUNITY MOBILIZATION AND EMPOWERMENT

The first Demandment—Declaration of War on Apathy and Irresponsibility—is the community's Demandment to itself. It is also, we believe, the most difficult to achieve easily, is the one requiring the most time, and is the one the success of which speaks to the question of self-development. Inner-city black communities face all of the issues articulated in the first Demandment, which is why it is applicable not only to the work going on in Boston's African-American community but also to other cities. Many communities are struggling with ways to begin holding themselves accountable and responsible for making changes in outcomes for the children and families in the community. The Demandment states:

Demandment: Declaration of War on Apathy and Irresponsibility

That, as leaders, our job is to carry out the collective will of this community **with** you, not **for** you. We must commit to each other to hold each other accountable. We have to be honest enough to say what isn't right isn't right. Responsibility to and for each other is absolutely critical.

Therefore, we demand of ourselves that:

- Our churches open their doors to **all** our youths, **all** our community residents, and **all** people in need.

We take responsibility as individuals and as a community for:

- Reinstating and enforcing a community norm that says that the sale and use of drugs are wrong, illegal, destructive, and will not be tolerated.
- Committing more energy to preventing adolescent pregnancy and parenthood than accommodating after it happens.
- Holding ourselves and our neighbors accountable when we know criminal activity is going on.
- Keeping our streets, yards, and places of business clean, even in the face of faulty and uneven city services.
- Taking responsibility for education of our children in the home and promoting the concept of the extended family of friends and relatives traditional to our culture.
- The legal, financial, and moral obligation for fathering children.
- Respecting the difference in background, class, appearance, political affiliation, and place of residence, among ourselves. There is strength and power in the diversity within our own community.

The Urban League of Eastern Massachusetts chose to begin the process of operationalizing Demandment #1 by offering to the community a new way of thinking about itself—a new paradigm. The Urban League of Eastern Massachusetts, at the time of the Rodney King verdict, was working in collaboration with the Efficacy Institute to use its framework for human development to transform the policies, practices, and service delivery structure within the Urban League.

That framework, designed for use in public schools with young people, destroys the assumptions about intelligence that guide American educational practices (innate ability paradigm) and offers a new paradigm which looks at intelligence as a process that can be organized and managed by adults for their children and by adults for themselves. Dr. Jeffrey Howard, the Institute's president, writes: "It is a small jump from the idea that intelligence and character are distributed unequally among individuals to the conclusion that they may be distributed unequally among different population groups, too. In the atmosphere generated by the innate ability paradigm on the one hand, and racism on the other, African-American children (and adults) are routinely subjected to very negative expectations about their intellectual capabilities. There is a rumor of inferiority about black people—a major legacy of American racism—that follows black children to school, especially racially integrated schools."[17] This rumor follows African-American adults into work (and our community organizations) as well. He continues: "The academic difficulties displayed by many black people, children, and adults are rooted in the fears and self-doubts engendered by the constant projection of strong negative stereotypes about black intellectual capabilities. . . . The embarrassment and self-doubt that are the inevitable by-products of exposure to this kind of public spectacle generate, in many people, a sequence of avoidance, evasion, and general unwillingness to commit to intellectual engagement."[18]

After the Rodney King verdict and the Ten Demandments, the Urban League sought funding from the Boston Foundation, the city's largest community foundation, to offer training in this new paradigm-thinking to 70 members of the African-American leadership community, including the executives of local community organizations, African-American small businesses, and African-American clergy. Having seen the "liberating" effects of exposing the Urban League staff to a new belief system about their capabilities, we believed that a beginning way to facilitate self-development for the African-American community was to transform the belief/attitude structure of the institutional base of the community. New thinking reflected in revised organizational policies and practices, a new confidence in the community's ability to figure out how to solve its problems, and a commitment to mobilize the greater community around a new set of internal expectations and standards were the places to start. We knew this approach would not change conditions quickly, nor would it be simple. Internal change is the most difficult to realize. The training also challenges so many deeply rooted beliefs held by African Americans and the resultant lack of confidence they feel in their ability to change their circumstances.

Those African-American organizations and individuals who have participated have found tremendous value in the training they received; a number of them are participating in the ongoing process of achieving the first Demandment.

The ultimate desire of all involved in the Ten Demandment process and those who have been looking for ways to improve the conditions of African Americans in Boston is to create a community that can ensure a future for its children in perpetuity. The Efficacy Institute has been working for the past 20 years in schools to achieve the development of African-American children and other children of color. The Urban League of Eastern Massachusetts has been working for the past 75 years to be a catalyst for change and development of the African-American community. Both organizations have had similar goals that they realize can be met only if their goals and the goals of others converge around a strategy for how to do it. Both organizations know that children only develop when the adults responsible for them (parents, teachers, community service workers) know how to support that process; and the institutions (schools, community-based organizations, churches) of the community are able to organize and mobilize themselves around achieving specific outcomes of success, health, and well-being for those children. A well-defined and structured interplay between the individuals of a community and its institutional base must be in place for individual and community self-development to take place.

The Urban League of Eastern Massachusetts and the Efficacy Institute are in collaboration to develop Boston's African-American children and other children of color to 21st century standards of achievement and character. Dr. Howard introduced this process in his article "The Third Movement: Developing Black Children for the 21st Century."[19] Though this is a long-term organizational commitment by both organizations, a year-long planning process that began in May 1993, is in place to accomplish the following two activities:

- coordinate key community institutions and stakeholders (The Coordinating Council) to understand and commit that changes in attitude and belief are fundamental to the kind of community-wide transformation needed to develop African-American children and the community for the demands of the future; and begin the process of agreement on what the standards and expectations of Boston's African-American community should be.
- operationalize the theory, methodology, and organizational policies and practices, using The Efficacy Institute's framework, in three community-based youth development organizations in Boston's African-American community. It will be critical throughout this first year to demonstrate that measurable change and improvement can be made in the delivery of services to African-American children through a community-based venue; that, in fact, organizational transformation can have a desired effect on the way children are treated, spoken to, supported, and nurtured within a community setting and can be replicated by others.

The Coordinating Council membership has been identified and has already begun to meet. The three community-based demonstration sites have begun the Efficacy training process and have identified five performance outcomes to be met within these community sites by the spring of 1994. All three demonstration sites agree that an over-arching goal for all of them is to create an environment that enforces/supports the concept of excellence at all levels. Through the application of the new conceptual framework taught, the targeted outcomes to be achieved are:

1. increased academic performance for the children they serve
2. increased parental involvement and support
3. improved staff management of children and increased staff professional behavior
4. increased skills in conflict resolution and behavior management among children
5. reinforcement and teaching of cultural pride and identity.

Boston's African-American community is poised for change, and there are activities in progress that we can look to and learn from.

John E. Jacob again reminds us that, "There is a huge reservoir of institutional strength in the African-American community that can be organized to help communities develop their potential. Those institutions can strengthen our businesses . . . build housing . . . enforce respect for our women . . . drive out the drug dealers and the muggers . . . and inspire our children to aim high and to perform at the highest levels. That is what community organization is all about . . . bringing those institutions together to focus tightly on developing world-class communities. And through that organized community, we can mobilize individuals for action. We've got to put the burden on each and every member of the community to do right, to act right, and to help each other."[20]

CONCLUSION

At a recent Urban League of Eastern Massachusetts staff retreat, Bruce Taylor, the director of the Urban League's Positive Futures Program (one of two male responsibility/youth development programs), shared a framework of his for working with the 60 boys in his program. In many ways, his framework characterizes the substance of the discussion in this paper. He outlined it in these three words:

BE . . . DO . . . HAVE

The key to organizing African-American self-development will require that, as a community, we define and reach consensus on what we want all of us to **BE**; what we want our community to **BE**. It is then the responsibility of the community's adults and the community's institutions to outline what we must **DO** to become what we want to be. And if the members of our community, young and old, **DO** what is expected, we must **DO** everything within our control (and develop strategy for those things currently out of our control) to ensure that our children and their families **HAVE** what they need to lead a life of quality in which we can all be proud. [21]

ENDNOTES

[1]John E. Jacob, Keynote Address, National Urban League Annual Conference, Washington, DC, August 1, 1993, pp. 2, 9.

[2]Cornel West, *Race Matters* (Boston: Beacon Press, 1993), p. 15.

[3]Jacob, *op. cit.*, p. 11.

[4]Hubert Jones, "The Status of Institutions in Boston's Black Community," *The Emerging Black Community of Boston,* Institute for the Study of Black Culture, University of Massachusetts, 1985, p. 271.

[5]Clearinghouse on Urban Education Digest, "Meeting Youth Needs with Community Programs," Number 86, December, 1992, p. 1.

[6]James Jennings, ed. "Blacks, Politics and the Human Service Crisis," *Race, Politics, and Economic Development* (Verso Press, 1992), p. 96.

[7]*Ibid.*, p. 97.

[8]Jeffrey Howard, "The Third Movement: Developing Black Children for the 21st Century," in Billy J. Tidwell, ed., *The State of Black America 1993* (New York: National Urban League, Inc., 1993), pp. 11-34.

[9]*Ibid.*, p. 18.

[10]*Ibid.*

[11]Jones, *op. cit.*, pp. 298, 306.

[12]The Massachusetts Department of Labor, 1993.

[13]The Boston Foundation, *In the Midst of Plenty*, A Program Paper of the Boston Persistent Poverty Project, 1989.

[14]Cited by Massachusetts Welfare Department, 1993.

[15]Cited by Office of Research and Evaluation, Boston Public Schools, 1993.

[16]Cited by the Massachusetts Department of Health, 1993.

[17]Howard, *op. cit.*

[18]*Ibid.*

[19]Howard, *op. cit.*

[20]Jacob, *op. cit.*, pp. 12-13.

[21]This framework was developed by Bruce Taylor, Director, Urban League of Eastern Massachusetts' Positive Futures Program, 1993.

REFERENCES

Bandura, A. 1982. "Self-Efficacy: Toward a Unifying Theory of Behavioral Change," *Psychological Review* 84, 191-215.

Boston Foundation. 1989. *In the Midst of Plenty.* A program paper of the Boston Persistent Poverty Project.

Hayden, Robert. 1992. "An Historical Overview of Poverty Among Blacks in Boston: 1850-1990," *Perspectives on Poverty in Boston's Black Community.* The Boston Persistent Poverty Project. The Boston Foundation.

Howard, Jeffrey. 1993. "The Third Movement: Developing Black Children for the 21st Century," in (ed.) Billy J. Tidwell, *The State of Black America 1993.* New York: National Urban League, Inc.

Jennings, James, ed. 1992. *Perspectives on Poverty in Boston's Black Community.* The Boston Persistent Poverty Project, The Boston Foundation.

_____. 1992. *Race, Politics, and Economic Development.* Verso Press.

Jones, Hubert. 1985. "The Status of Institutions in Boston's Black Community," *The Emerging Black Community of Boston.* Institute for the Study of Black Culture, University of Massachusetts, Boston.

Norman, Alex J. 1977. "Mutual Aid: A Key to Survival for Black Americans." *Black Scholar.* December.

Raspberry, William. 1993. "High Standards for Black Children," *The Washington Post,* August 6.

Schwartz, Wendy, ed. 1992. "Helping Young Urban Parents Educate Themselves and Their Children." *Clearinghouse on Urban Education Digest*. Number 85.

_____. 1992. "Meeting Youth Needs With Community Programs," *Clearinghouse on Urban Education Digest*. Number 86.

Sewell, Carl. 1977. "The Impact of External Funding Policies on the Development of Black Community Organizations." *Black Scholar*. December.

U.S. Commerce Department. Bureau of the Census. 1989. *Current Population Reports*, "Money, Income, and Poverty Status in the United States, 1987." Series P-60, No. 161.

Weiss, Nancy. 1974. *The National Urban League, 1910-1940*. New York: Oxford University Press.

Recommendations

Nineteen ninety-three was a significant year on the domestic policy front—for both the nation and the African-American community itself. Of course, it is axiomatic that the condition of African Americans is vitally dependent upon the overall condition of the nation. However, it is also true that development of the African-American community contributes to the well-being of the larger society. Thus, promoting African-American self-development should be treated as a matter of national interest and a principal criterion by which to evaluate the merits of contemporary public policies.

This perspective—the assertion of mutual dependency between the "state of Black America" and the general welfare—makes it clear that the National Urban League's concept of African-American self-development is neither isolationist nor adversarial. To the contrary, the idea is grounded in the proposition that the efforts of African Americans themselves to improve their conditions are broadly beneficial.

Of course, the degree to which the self-development thrust serves the mutual interests of the African-American community and the nation *in practice* is contingent upon a number of factors, not the least of which is the quality of African-American leadership. Ron Walters expounds upon this prerequisite in "Serving the People: African-American Leadership and the Challenge of Empowerment." Also, the judicious use of existing institutional and personal resources within the African-American communities is paramount. In his paper, "Mission to Mandate: Self-Development Through the Black Church," W. Franklyn Richardson assesses the role of religious organizations in these terms. Likewise, Harry Edwards's chapter, "Playoffs and Payoffs: The African-American Athlete as an Institutional Resource," examines the resource question as it relates to the expanding pool of professional African-American athletes.

And public policy is also a crucial part of the equation. Hence, the positive potential of African-American self-development is more likely to be realized when these efforts are undergirded by strong public policy support.

These observations comprise important context as we provide quick updates on some of the policy recommendations included in *The State of Black America 1993* and then proceed to present the National Urban League's proposals for the coming year.

SELECTED 1993 UPDATES

In the 1993 report, the National Urban League proposed a comprehensive policy agenda toward the mutually dependent goals of "completing the unfinished business of racial justice and preparing the nation to meet the formidable challenges of the 21st century." The selective updating that follows is limited to recommendations around which definitive and positive policy action occurred.

Recommendation: Enact legislation establishing the National Urban League's Marshall Plan for America as the cornerstone of a comprehensive strategy to increase the nation's economic productivity and competitiveness.
Policy Update: Introduction of President Clinton's economic plan, which contains human resource and physical infrastructure initiatives similar to those called for in the Marshall Plan. Major differences remain in the amount of investment proposed and provisions for targeting groups and areas most in need.

Recommendation: Reauthorize Chapter I of the 1965 Elementary and Secondary Education Act at a level of funding more commensurate with the need.
Policy Update: Congressional approval of $216 million increased funding for Chapter I over FY 1993 amount. However, the increased funding still falls well short of the need.

Recommendation: Adopt comprehensive health care reform that provides coverage for all Americans.
Policy Update: Administration's universal health care reform legislation developed and introduced.

Recommendation: Reintroduce and pass the Family and Medical Leave Act.
Policy Update: "Family and Medical Leave Act of 1993" signed into public law.

Recommendation: Enact national voter registration legislation to break down barriers to exercising the franchise.
Policy Update: "National Voter Registration Act of 1993" signed into public law.

Recommendation: Pass the "Brady Bill" to better regulate the acquisition of handguns.
Policy Update: "Brady Bill" enacted into public law.

MAJOR RECOMMENDATIONS FOR 1994

In offering our recommendations for 1994, we cannot overemphasize the importance of partnership among the administration and the Congress and the community-based organizations that are dedicated to fostering African-American self-development. Again, the National Urban League is firmly convinced that stronger efforts toward self-development within the African-American community are essential to its well-being and to the nation's ability to produce and prosper for everyone's benefit. Both Lenneal Henderson in his essay, "African Americans in the Urban Milieu: Conditions, Trends, and Development Needs," and Joan Wallace-Benjamin in her case study, "Organizing African-American Self-Development: The Role of Community-Based Organizations," elucidate the potential. Payoff from the potential is optimized by the existence of public policies that are supportive and reinforcing. The proposals below speak to some key areas of concern in this regard.

EDUCATION

Improved basic education for African Americans remains a dominant priority. This observation is especially relevant to the educational problems that beset African Americans who reside in the nation's urban centers. However, as Shirley Jones observes in the paper, "Silent Suffering: The Plight of Rural Black America," more attention to the educational needs of African Americans in rural areas is imperative, also. Nor is the concern limited to elementary and secondary education. Thus, Mary Dilworth cogently advocates, in "Historically Black Colleges and Universities: Taking Care of Home," strengthening the capacity of HBCUs in the higher education of African Americans. In any case, there is much that must be done. Pursuant to the requirements, the National Urban League recommends:

- That efforts to expand the Head Start program to serve all eligible children be intensified and that the program be made available on a full-time, year-round basis.
- That more aggressive measures be taken to promote equity in school financing, which require that the U.S. Department of Education assume a much more active role in ensuring that federal support for public education reach the school districts that are most in need of assistance.
- That Chapter I of the Elementary and Secondary Act be reauthorized at a funding level that enables this critical education legislation to fulfill its mandate on behalf of economically disadvantaged students.
  That Title III of the Higher Education Amendments of 1965 be reauthorized at the level of funding necessary to sustain and strengthen HBCUs as institutional resources in African-American communities.

WORK-FORCE PREPARATION

The National Urban League recognizes that the productivity of the American work force will be decisive in strengthening the nation's competitive position in the world economy and in improving our standard of living. Thus, in 1994, the administration and the Congress must pursue improved work-force preparation with a renewed sense of urgency and purpose, particularly with respect to the neglected human resource development needs of African Americans and other disadvantaged segments of the population. To this end, we recommend:

- That a national work-force development strategy that provides every individual the opportunity to participate in high-wage, high-skill employment be designed and implemented.
- That the work-force preparation initiatives be adequately targeted to groups that are most in need.
- That the "School-to-Work Opportunities Act," having passed the House, be approved by the Senate.

HEALTH

A healthy mind and body are indispensable to realizing personal potential. By the same token, a healthy citizenry fundamentally determines the well-being of the nation and its capacity to perform. These truisms affirm the saliency of universal health care, as an alarmingly large proportion of the American population lacks access to quality medical services. This condition constitutes a national liability that we can no longer afford. Thus, the National Urban League recommends:

- That the initiative toward universal health care be pursued vigorously and brought to fruition without undue delay.
- That the health care reform initiative stress improved access to care by increasing the availability of doctors, clinics, and hospitals in economically disadvantaged communities.
- That the health care reform initiative be structured and financed in a way that ensures equity of benefits between the poor and the affluent.

CIVIL RIGHTS

Contrary to popular belief, this nation still has a long way to go in the area of civil rights. Even allowing for the tremendous progress that has been achieved over the long-term, the National Urban League remains firmly committed to the cause of racial justice and will continue to press the case in those areas where it is still lacking. In this spirit, we recommend:

- That the 1989 U.S. Supreme Court decision in *City of Richmond v. Croson* which attacked the validity of minority set-aside programs, be reversed.
- That the Equal Remedies Act, which has been put forward to eliminate cap

on damages awarded for employment discrimination under Title VII of the 1964 Civil Rights Act, be passed.

That legislation be implemented to counteract the U.S. Supreme Court decision in *St. Mary's Honor Center v. Hicks* and to shift the burden of proof in employment discrimination cases back to the employer.

CRIME AND CRIMINAL JUSTICE

The National Urban League is encouraged by the concerted efforts underway in local communities around the country to check the disturbing incidence of crime and violence. These conditions are severe constraints on African-American community development, in addition to the personal pain and hardship they cause. The recently passed "Brady Bill" gives much-needed support to local initiatives against crime. However, additional measures to control the instruments of violence are warranted. At the same time, we must continue to eradicate racial inequities in the operation of the criminal justice system. Accordingly, we recommend:

That strong legislation be enacted to control the production, sale, and use of semiautomatic assault weapons.

That the Racial Justice Act, aimed at eliminating racial bias in imposition of the death penalty, be passed.

COMMUNITY ECONOMIC DEVELOPMENT

There is broad agreement that economic development is key to the overall advancement and well-being of the African-American community. Among others, the paper by Marcus Alexis and Geraldine Henderson, "The Economic Base of African-American Communities: A Study of Consumption Patterns," echoes this thesis. Similarly, William Bradford's assessment in "Dollars for Deeds: Some Prospects and Prescriptions for African-American Financial Institutions" leaves little doubt about the strategic importance of financial institutions as vehicles for African-American self-development. Here, we recommend:

That the infrastructure initiatives included in our proposed Marshall Plan for America be adopted as integral parts of a multifaceted national economic development strategy that gives special attention to communities that are most distressed.

That legislation be enacted to abolish insurance "redlining" and to ensure access to coverage on a nondiscriminatory basis.

That legislation be enacted providing for the establishment of a network of "community development banks" in economically disadvantaged communities.

APPENDIX

Fast Facts:
Comparative Views of
African-American Status and Progress

Dionne J. Jones, Ph.D.
with
Greg Harrison of the Research Department
National Urban League, Inc.

Profiles of the status of African Americans are more instructive when the group's current position on given indicators of collective well-being is compared with their position on these same indicators at some earlier point in time. Such cross-time comparisons provide measures of change that should be taken into account in evaluating the needs of the African-American community and developing policy and program initiatives around them.

Additional empirical insight can be gained by applying this comparative approach to particular age subgroups of the population. Thus, one would compare the condition of African Americans in a given age range at one point in time with the condition that characterized their counterparts at some earlier point.

The following presentation makes use of this "life cycle" perspective on the status of African Americans. As we move toward the new century, this life-cycle approach will be increasingly important to understanding and improving the state of Black America.

The presentation is not intended to be comprehensive. However, the selected status indicators reflect issues that command widespread concern. Also, while the precise age ranges vary across indicators, the two groups of general interest are comprised of persons who might be considered "young adults" and "mature adults." Data for corresponding white groups are included, and there are separate tables for males and females. Finally, the comparison time frames cover the period from the early '80s to the early '90s.

213

Table 1
Real Median Income by Race and Selected Age Cohorts:
1983 and 1992

	1983		1992	
Age Cohort	African American	White	African American	White
25-29 Years	$19,100*	$24,064	$18,672 (-2.2%)**	$22,940 (-4.7%)
35-44 Years	23,992	31,073	23,322 (-2.8%)	30,973 (-0.3%)
Total Population	20,775	27,267	21,609 (+4.0%)	27,325 (+0.2%)

*Income in 1992 dollars for year-round, full-time workers.
**Figures in parentheses show percent change during the period.

Source: Calculated by the National Urban League from U.S. Bureau of the Census, Current Population Reports, Series P60-146, *Money Income of Households, Families, and Persons in the United States: 198.* Washington, DC, U.S. Government Printing Office, 1985, Table 46 and unpublished Bureau of the Census data.

- Between 1983 and 1992, African Americans ages 25 to 29 years and 35 44 years showed a decrease in their median income of 2.2 percent and 2. percent respectively, despite an overall 4 percent **increase** among the tota African-American population.

- In spite of the overall increase of 4 percent during the period, Africa Americans averaged just 80 percent of the income of whites in 199 ($21,609 v. $27,325).

Table 2
Female Real Median Income by Race and Selected Age Cohorts:
1983 and 1992

| | 1983 | | 1992 | |
Age Cohort	African American	White	African American	White
5-29 Years	$17,883*	$20,414	$18,757 (+4.9%)	$21,510 (+5.4%)
5-44 Years	21,289	22,531	21,751 (+2.7%)	24,674 (+9.5%)
Total Population	18,312	20,675	20,299 (+10.9%)	22,423 (+8.5%)

ncome in 1992 dollars for year-round, full-time workers.

ource: Calculated by the National Urban League from U.S. Bureau of the Census, Current Population Reports, Series P60-146, *Money Income of Households, Families, and Persons in the United States: 1983, Table 46,* and Series P60-184, *Money Income of Households, Families, and Persons in the United States: 1992,* Table 26, Washington, DC, U.S. Government Printing Office, 1985 and 1993.

Like the larger female population, African-American females in the selected subgroups saw their income increase between 1983 and 1992.

The income gain for the African-American subgroups was smaller than that of their white counterparts, while African-American females as a whole posted a larger percentage increase than white females.

Table 3
Male Real Median Income by Race and Selected Age Cohorts:
1983 and 1992

| | 1983 | | 1992 | |
Age Cohort	African American	White	African American	White
25-29 Years	$20,428*	$27,206	$18,591 (-9.0%)	$24,505 (-9.9%)
35-44 Years	28,729	37,092	25,753 (-10.4%)	35,942 (-3.1%)
Total Population	23,116	32,559	22,942 (-0.8%)	31,737 (-2.5%)

*Income in 1992 dollars for year-round, full-time workers.

Source: Calculated by the National Urban League from U.S. Bureau of the Census, Current Population Reports, Series P60-146, *Money Income of Households, Families, and Persons in the United States: 1983,* Table 46, and Series P60-184, *Money Income of Households, Families, and Persons in the United States: 1992,* Table 26, Washington DC, U.S. Government Printing Office, 1985 and 1993.

- While the average income of the total African-American male population was virtually unchanged during the reference period, the subgroups experienced steep declines.

- Compared to their white counterparts, 35- to 44-year-old African-American males were especially hard hit.

Table 4
**Percent of Persons Below Poverty Level by Race and Selected Age Cohorts:
1982 and 1992**

	1982		1992	
Age Cohort	**African American**	**White**	**African American**	**White**
18-24 Years	35.4	12.3	31.7 (-10.5%)	15.3 (+24.4%)
35-44 Years	25.9	9.2	23.3 (-10.0%)	7.8 (-15.2%)
Total Population	35.6	12.0	33.3 (-6.5%)	11.6 (-3.3%)

Source: Calculated by the National Urban League from U.S. Bureau of the Census, Current Population Reports, Series P60-144, *Characteristics of the Population Below the Poverty Level: 1982*, Table 1, and Series P60-185, *Poverty in the United States: 1992,* Table 1, Washington, DC, U.S. Government Printing Office, 1984 and 1992.

• Between 1982 and 1992, the percentage of African Americans living below poverty decreased more among the two age cohorts than among the total African-American population.

• Among 18- to 24-year-olds, the poverty rate for African Americans decreased, while rising substantially for whites in this age group.

Table 5
**Percent of Females Below Poverty Level by Race and Selected Age
Cohorts:
1982 and 1992**

Age Cohort	1982		1992	
	African American	White	African American	White
18-24 Years	41.0	13.9	38.5 (-6.1%)	18.2 (+30.9%)
35-44 Years	33.7	10.4	27.3 (-19.0%)	8.7 (-16.3%)
Total Population	39.3	13.2	36.8 (-6.4%)	13.0 (-1.5%)

Source: Calculated by the National Urban League from U.S. Bureau of the
Census, Current Population Reports, Series P60-144, *Characteristics
of the Population Below the Poverty Level: 1982,* Table 1, and Series
P60-185, *Poverty in the United States: 1992,* Table 1, Washington,
DC, U.S. Government Printing Office, 1984 and 1992.

• The poverty rate for all African-American women was lower in 1992 than in
1982, with the rate for "mature adults" showing a particularly sharp drop.

• Although the poverty rate for African-American women in the 35- to 44-
years age group decreased greatly during the decade, it remained more than
triple that of their white counterparts.

Table 6
Percent of Males Below Poverty Level by Race and Selected Age Cohorts:
1982 and 1992

| | 1982 | | 1992 | |
Age Cohort	African American	White	African American	White
18-24 Years	29.0	10.7	24.2 (-16.6%)	12.4 (+15.9%)
35-44 Years	16.2	8.0	18.4 (+13.6%)	6.9 (-13.8%)
Total Population	31.4	10.8	29.3 (-6.7%)	10.1 (-6.5%)

Source: Calculated by the National Urban League from U.S. Bureau of the Census, Current Population Reports, Series P60-144, *Characteristics of the Population Below the Poverty Level: 1982,* Table 1, and Series P60-185, *Poverty in the United States: 1992,* Table 1, Washington, DC, U.S. Government Printing Office, 1984 and 1992.

- In contrast to African-American females, "mature adult" African-American men saw an increase in their poverty rate between 1982 and 1992.

- Although there was a 6.7 percent decrease during the period among the total African-American male population, their 1992 poverty rate of 29.3 percent was almost three times the rate of white males (10.1 percent).

Table 7
Percent in Labor Force by Race and Selected Age Cohorts: 1980 and 1990

	1980		1990	
Age Cohort	African American*	White	African American	White
20-24 Years	65.7	77.1	68.8 (+4.7%)	77.9 (+1.0%)
35-44 Years	78.3	80.4	83.0 (+6.0%)	85.9 (+6.8%)
Total Population	59.8	63.7	63.1 (+5.5%)	66.4 (+4.2%)

*Figures for "black and other."

Source: Prepared by the National Urban League from U.S. Bureau of Labor Statistics, *Employment and Earnings,* Vol. 28, No. 4, April 1981, and Vol. 37, No. 4, (April 1990), Table A-4, Washington, DC, 1981 and 1990.

• The total African-American labor force participation rate (63.1percent) increased by 5.5 percent between 1980 and 1990 compared to an overall 4.2 percent increase for whites.

• Among the younger age cohorts, the percentage increase in participation rate during the 10-year period was considerably larger for African Americans (4.7 percent) than for whites (1.0 percent).

Table 8
Percent of Females in Labor Force by Race and Selected Age Cohorts:
1980 and 1990

| | 1980 | | 1990 | |
Age Cohort	African American*	White	African American	White
20-24 Years	56.5	68.5	63.2 (+11.9%)	71.7 (+4.7%)
35-44 Years	69.1	65.6	79.0 (+14.3%)	76.6 (+16.8%)
Total Population	52.0	51.0	58.2 (+11.9%)	57.1 (+12.0%)

*Figures for "black and other."

Source: Prepared by the National Urban League from U.S. Bureau of Labor Statistics, *Employment and Earnings,* Vol. 28, No. 4, April 1981, and Vol. 37, No. 4, April 1990, Table A-4, Washington, DC, 1985 and 1993.

- The total African-American female labor force participation rate increased by 11.9 percent between 1980 and 1990.

- Relative to their white counterparts, African-American females posted a particularly large percentage increase in participation.

Table 9
Percent of Males in Labor Force by Race and Selected Age Cohorts:
1980 and 1990

| | 1980 | | 1990 | |
| | African | | African | |
Age Cohort	American*	White	American	White
20-24 Years	77.0	86.0	75.5 (-1.9%)	84.5 (-1.7%)
35-44 Years	90.0	96.0	88.0 (-2.2%)	95.4 (-0.6%)
Total Population	69.4	77.7	69.2 (-0.3%)	76.5 (-1.5%)

*Figures for "black and other."

Source: Prepared by the National Urban League from U.S. Bureau of Labor Statistics, *Employment and Earnings,* Vol. 28, No. 4, April 1981, and Vol. 37, No. 4, April 1990, Table A-4, Washington, DC, 1985 and 1993.

• Between 1980 and 1990, the total African-American male labor force participation rate decreased only slightly, while larger declines occurred among the two age groups.

• The participation rate of African-American males remained well below that of their white counterparts during the period—both overall and within the two age groups.

Table 10
Unemployment Rate by Race and Selected Age Cohorts:
1983 and 1991

	1983		1991	
Age Cohort	African American	White	African American	White
20-24 Years	31.6	12.1	21.6 (-31.6%)	9.2 (-24.0%)
35-44 Years	12.4	6.3	8.6 (-30.6%)	4.7 (-25.4%)
Total Population	19.5	8.4	12.4 (-36.4%)	6.0 (-28.6%)

Source: Prepared by the National Urban League from U.S. Bureau of the Census, *Statistical Abstract of the United States: 1985* (105th edition), Table 658, and *Statistical Abstract of the United States: 1992* (112th edition), Table 622, Washington, DC, 1983 and 1992.

• Unemployment among the African-American civilian labor force declined during the period 1983 to 1991 by almost one-third for persons 20 to 24 and 35 to 44 years of age.

• In 1991, the unemployment rate for African-American 35- to 44-year-olds in 1991 was almost double that of their white counterparts; the rate for African-American 20- to 24-year-olds was almost two-and-one-half times that of whites in this age group.

Table 11
Female Unemployment Rate by Race and Selected Age Cohorts:
1983 and 1991

Age Cohort	1983 African American	1983 White	1991 African American	1991 White
20-24 Years	31.8	10.3	20.7 (-34.9%)	8.0 (-22.3%)
35-44 Years	11.4	6.2	7.6 (-33.3%)	4.3 (-30.6%)
Total Population	18.6	7.9	11.9 (-36.0%)	5.5 (-30.4%)

Source: Prepared by the National Urban League from U.S. Bureau of the Census, *Statistical Abstract of the United States: 1985* (105th edition), Table 658, and *Statistical Abstract of the United States: 1992* (112th edition), Table 622, Washington, DC, 1983 and 1992.

• The unemployment rates for African-American females are similar to the rates for the total African-American civilian labor force; both the young adult and the mature adult cohorts saw their rates decline by about one-third between 1983 and 1991.

• Again, the unemployment rate for African-American female 35- to 44-year-olds in 1991 was almost twice that of their white cohorts, while the rate for African-American 20- to 24-year-olds was almost two-and-one-half times the rate for white females this age.

Table 12
Male Unemployment Rate by Race and Selected Age Cohorts:
1983 and 1991

| | 1983 | | 1991 | |
Age Cohort	African American	White	African American	White
20-24 Years	31.4	13.8	22.4 (-28.7%)	10.2 (-26.1%)
35-44 Years	13.5	6.4	9.6 (-28.9%)	5.0 (-21.9%)
Total Population	20.3	8.8	12.9 (-36.5%)	6.4 (-27.3%)

Source: Prepared by the National Urban League from U.S. Bureau of the Census, *Statistical Abstract of the United States: 1985* (105th edition), Table 658, and *Statistical Abstract of the United States: 1992* (112th edition), Table 622, Washington, DC, 1983 and 1992.

• Mirroring the population as a whole, unemployment among African-American males ages 20 to 24 years and 35 to 44 years decreased sharply during the period 1983 to 1991.

• The 1991 unemployment rate for the younger adult African-American male cohorts was more than two times that for their white counterparts. In the "mature adults" category, the African-American rate was almost twice the rate of whites.

Table 13
Educational Attainment by Race and Selected Age Cohorts:
1982 and 1991

Age Cohort/ Education level	1982 African American	1982 White	1991 African American	1991 White
20-29 Years				
4 Years College or more	8.4	16.2	7.9 (-6.0%)	18.3 (+13.0%)
1-3 Years College	25.9	24.9	26.1 (+0.8%)	27.9 (+12.0%)
High School	44.7	44.6	46.4 (+3.8%)	39.4 (-11.7%)
Less than High School	21.0	14.3	19.6 (-6.7%)	14.4 (+0.7%)
35-44 Years				
4 Years College or more	10.0	22.9	15.2 (+52.0%)	28.4 (+24.0%)
1-3 Years College	13.0	17.4	22.3 (+71.5%)	22.9 (+31.6%)
High School	40.7	41.3	44.4 (+9.1%)	37.3 (-9.7%)
Less than High School	36.5	18.4	18.1 (-50.4%)	11.4 (-38.0%)
Total Population				
4 Years College or more	6.9	15.5	9.4 (+36.2%)	19.4 (+25.2%)
1-3 Years College	14.1	15.9	16.9 (+19.9%)	19.0 (+19.5%)
High School	32.3	37.9	36.5 (+13.0%)	37.6 (-0.8%)
Less than High School	46.7	30.7	37.2 (-20.3%)	24.0 (-21.8%)

Source: Calculated by the National Urban League from U.S. Bureau of the Census, Current Population Reports, Series P20-415, *Educational Attainment in the United States: March 1982-1985,* and P20-462, *Educational Attainment in the United States: March 1991 and 1990,* Washington, DC, U.S. Government Printing Office, 1987 and 1992, Table 1.

- Between 1982 and 1991, there were increases in the proportions of the total African-American population with four years of college or more (36.2 percent), one to three years of college (19.9 percent), and those who were high school graduates (13 percent).

- The proportion of African Americans 20 to 29 years of age completing four or more years of college decreased by 6 percent, while the proportion of their white cohorts **increased** by 13 percent.

- The proportion of African-American 35- to 44-year-olds completing college in 1991 was 52 percent larger than the proportion of this same age group completing college in 1982.

Table 14
Female Educational Attainment by Race and Selected Age Cohorts:
1982 and 1991

Age Cohort/ Education level	1982		1991	
	African American	White	African American	White
20-29 Years				
4 Years College or more	8.6	15.5	7.9 (-8.1%)	18.9 (+21.9%)
1-3 Years College	26.2	25.0	28.3 (+8.0%)	28.5 (+14.0%)
High School	44.5	45.6	43.5 (-2.2%)	39.1 (-14.3%)
Less than High School	20.7	13.9	20.3 (-1.9%)	13.5 (-2.9%)
35-44 Years				
4 Years College or more	9.4	17.8	17.0 (+80.9%)	26.0 (+46.1%)
1-3 Years College	13.8	17.0	21.9 (+59.0%)	23.3 (+37.1%)
High School	40.2	46.8	41.8 (+4.0%)	39.9 (-14.7%)
Less than High School	36.6	18.4	19.3 (-47.3%)	10.8 (-41.3%)
Total Population				
4 Years College or more	6.8	12.5	9.6 (+41.2%)	17.2 (+37.6%)
1-3 Years College	14.1	15.7	17.5 (+24.1%)	19.3 (+22.9%)
High School	32.7	41.2	36.4 (+11.3%)	40.0 (-2.9%)
Less than High School	46.4	30.6	36.5 (-21.3%)	23.5 (-23.2%)

Source: Calculated by the National Urban League from U.S. Bureau of the Census, Current Population Reports, Series P20-415, *Educational Attainment in the United States: March 1982-1985*, and P20-462, *Educational Attainment in the United States: March 1991 and 1990*, Washington, DC, U.S. Government Printing Office, 1987 and 1992, Table 1.

• Between 1982 and 1991, the proportion of African-American females completing four years of college or more increased by 41.2 percent, just over half that of their white cohorts.

• The proportion of African Americans ages 35 to 44 years who had completed college increased by 81 percent during the period: the proportion of this group who completed one to three years of college increased by 59 percent.

• The picture is much different for the "young adult" African Americans, who showed a decrease in the proportion of those with four years of college or more.

Table 15
Male Educational Attainment by Race and Selected Age Cohorts: 1982 and 1991

	1982		1991	
Age Cohort/ Education Level	African American	White	African American	White
20-29 Years				
4 Years College or more	8.0	16.9	7.9 (-1.3%)	17.7 (+4.7%)
1-3 Years College	25.7	24.8	23.5 (-8.6%)	27.2 (+9.7%)
High School	45.0	43.7	49.9 (+10.9%)	39.7 (-9.2%)
Less than High School	21.3	14.6	18.7 (-12.2%)	15.4 (+5.5%)
35-44 Years				
4 Years College or more	10.8	28.0	16.0 (+48.1%)	26.6 (-5.0%)
1-3 Years College	12.1	17.9	23.5 (+94.2%)	21.1 (+17.9%)
High School	41.2	35.6	41.5 (+0.7%)	39.7 (+11.5%)
Less than High School	35.9	18.5	19.0 (-47.1%)	12.6 (-31.9%)
Total Population				
4 Years College or more	7.0	18.8	9.1 (+30.0%)	21.8 (+16.0%)
1-3 Years College	14.2	16.2	16.1 (+13.4%)	18.7 (+15.4%)
High School	31.7	34.3	36.6 (+15.5%)	35.0 (+2.0%)
Less than High School	47.1	30.7	38.2 (-18.9%)	24.5 (-20.2%)

230

Source: Calculated by the National Urban League from U.S. Bureau of the Census, Current Population Reports, Series P20-415, *Educational Attainment in the United States: March 1982-1985,* and P20-462, *Educational Attainment in the United States: March 1991 and 1990,* Washington, DC, U.S. Government Printing Office, 1987 and 1992, Table 1.

• The proportion of African-American males completing four years of college or more from 1982 to 1991 increased by nearly one-third to 9.1 percent, representing just under one-half of the rate of their white cohorts. The proportion completing one to three years of college increased by 13.4 percent to 16.1 percent, which is just below the proportion for whites (18.7 percent). The proportion of high school graduates increased by 15.5 percent during the period.

• The proportion of African-American 35- to 44-year-olds who completed four years of college or more increased by 48.1 percent over the period, compared to a 5 percent decrease for whites in this age group.

• Again, the younger African-American cohorts showed a decrease in the proportion of those with four years of college or more and those who had one to three years of college.

Table 16
Percent of Female-Headed Families by Race and Selected Age Cohorts: 1982 and 1992

Age Cohort (Age of Family Head)	1982		1991	
	African American	White	African American	White
20-29 Years	49.8	13.3	60.4 (+21.3%)	18.1 (+36.1%)
35-44 Years	43.4	14.3	45.3 (+4.4%)	14.5 (+1.4%)
Total Population	40.6	12.4	46.4 (+14.3%)	13.5 (+8.9%)

Source: Calculated by the National Urban League from U.S. Bureau of the Census, Current Population Reports, Series P20-381, *Household and Family Characteristics: March 1982*, Table 3, and Steve W. Rawlings, *Household and Family Characteristics: March 1992* (Series P20-467), Table 3, Washington, DC, U.S. Government Printing Office, 1983 and 1993.

• Between 1982 and 1992, the proportion of female-headed families increased substantially, particularly in the younger age group. Although the rate of increase among the younger white cohort was greater, the incidence of female-headed families among this segment of the white population in 1992 remained well below the incidence among African Americans.

• Within the 35- to 44-year-old cohorts, there was only a slight increase in the proportion of female-headed families—for both African Americans and whites.

Table 17
Female Death Rate by Race and Selected Age Cohorts: 1980 and 1990.

| | 1980 | | 1990 | |
| | African | | African | |
Age Cohort	American	White	American	White
15-24 Years	71*	56	67	48
			(-5.6%)	(-14.3%)
35-44 Years	324	138	290	119
			(-10.5%)	(-13.8%)
Total Population	733	806	711	848
			(-3.0%)	(+5.2%)

*Per 100,000 population.

Source: U.S. Bureau of the Census, *Statistical Abstract of the United States: 1992* (112th edition), Washington, DC, 1992, Table 107.

- In general, the female death rate per 100,000 decreased during the 1980s. However, in the "young adult" cohort, the death rate for African Americans decreased by less than one-half of the decrease for whites.

- The death rate among "mature adult" African-American females showed a sharper decline than the rate for African-American "young adults."

Table 18
Male Death Rate by Race and Selected Age Cohorts:
1980 and 1990

| | 1980 | | 1990 | |
Age Cohort	African American	White	African American	White
15-24 Years	209*	167	259 (+23.9%)	141 (-15.6%)
35-44 Years	690	257	688 (-0.3%)	266 (+3.5%)
Total Population	1,034	983	942 (-8.9%)	937 (-4.7%)

*Per 100,000 population.

Source: U.S. Bureau of the Census, *Statistical Abstract of the United States: 1992* (112th edition), Washington, DC, 1992, Table 107.

- Between 1980 and 1990, the African-American male death rate per 100,000 population **increased** among 15- to 24-year-olds by 23.9 percent, while the corresponding white rate **decreased** by 15.6 percent.

- The African-American male death rate was 1.8 times that of their white counterparts for 15- to 24-year-olds, and 2.6 times that of white 35- to 44-year-olds.

Table 19
Female Death Rate for Homicide and Legal Intervention by Race and Selected Age Cohorts:
1980 and 1989

| | 1980 | | 1989 | |
Age Cohort	African American	White	African American	White
15-24 Years	18.4*	4.7	17.3 (-6.0%)	3.9 (-17.0%)
35-44 Years	17.7	4.1	14.7 (-16.9%)	3.3 (-19.5%)
Total Population	13.7	3.2	12.5 (-8.8%)	2.8 (-12.5%)

*Per 100,000 population.

Source: Alfred N. Garwood, ed., *Black Americans: A Statistical Sourcebook 1993*, Boulder, CO, Numbers and Concepts, 1993, Table 2.17.

- While the female death rate for homicide and legal intervention decreased between 1980 and 1989, particularly among 35- to 44-year-olds, African Americans in all three cohorts continued to die at more than four times the rate of whites.

- Although 15- to 24-year-old African-American females realized a 6 percent decrease in their homicide rate, the corresponding rate for whites fell nearly three times as fast.

Table 20
Male Death Rate for Homicide and Legal Intervention by Race and Selected Age Cohort:
1980 and 1989

Age Cohort	1980		1989	
	African American	White	African American	White
15-24 Years	84.3*	15.5	114.8 (+36.3%)	12.8 (-17.4%)
35-44 Years	110.3	15.5	78.6 (-28.7%)	10.5 (-32.3%)
Total Population	71.9	10.9	61.5 (-14.5%)	8.1 (-25.7%)

*Per 100,000 population.

Source: Alfred N. Garwood, ed., *Black Americans: A Statistical Sourcebook 1993*, Boulder, CO, Numbers and Concepts, 1993, Table 2.17.

• Between 1980 and 1989, the African-American male death rate for homicide and legal intervention increased by 36 percent within the 15- to 24-year-old cohorts. At the same time, the rate for white 15- to 24-year-olds decreased by 17.4 percent . The 1989 rate of 114.8 per 100,000 African-American males is almost 9 times the rate for the white 15- to 24-years cohort.

• Although 35- to 44-year-old African Americans saw their rate decrease, they were 7.5 times as likely to die from homicide and legal intervention as their white counterparts.

CONCLUSION
As evidenced from these "fast facts," African Americans continue to lag behind their white counterparts, despite making significant gains in many areas. According to some indicators, African Americans are doing only half as well as whites, a reality that is cause for continuing alarm. These conditions must be addressed with proactive measures to remedy them. The articles presented in this volume of *The State of Black America,* discuss some of these conditions more fully and make recommendations for positive necessary action.

Chronology of Events
1993[1]

Jan. 1: The nation celebrates the 130th anniversary of the Emancipation Proclamation, widely recognized as a monumental document that ended slavery in this country. The National Archives publicly displays all five pages of the fragile document for the first time since 1979.

Jan. 2: A lawsuit seeks to prevent Rep.-elect **Alcee Hastings** (D-FL) from taking his seat in Congress because of his impeachment when he was a federal judge, reports *The Associated Press*. Hastings is to be sworn in as a member of the U.S. House of Representatives on January 5.

Jan. 2: Capping a triumphant political comeback that began the day he left federal prison, former Washington, DC, Mayor **Marion Barry** is sworn in as a District Councilmember representing Southeast Washington's Ward 8—the District's poorest, reports *The Washington Post*.

Jan. 4: Three white men kidnap a black tourist from Brooklyn, NY, rob him, douse him with gasoline, and set him on fire in Varico, FL, reports *The Associated Press*. Police investigate whether the attack on **Christopher Wilson**, 31, is racially motivated.

Jan. 6: **Reggie Jackson**, garnering 93.6 percent of the ballots cast, is the only player named this year to the Baseball Hall of Fame, becoming the 29th player to make it to Cooperstown in his first year of eligibility, reports *The Associated Press*.

Jan. 6: The federal government releases its first national report on hate crimes, but both law enforcement officials and civil rights groups say it is virtually useless because many local governments did not cooperate, reports *The New York Times*. The greatest number of hate crimes in 1991 were committed against blacks, and the second-most likely victims were Jews, according to the report issued by the Federal Bureau of Investigation.

---

[1]This chronology is based on news reports. In some instances, the event may have occurred a day or so before the news item was reported.

Jan. 7: Jazz pioneer **John Birks "Dizzy" Gillespie**, who helped popularize jazz through a combination of humor and showmanship—with his trademark bulging cheeks, goatee, beret, and bent trumpet—dies in his sleep at age 75 in Englewood, NJ. He had been suffering from pancreatic cancer.

"Dizzy" Gillespie is credited with inventing the term "be-bop"; he was one of the most recognizable and beloved figures in American jazz, a genre he revolutionized in the 1940s as one of the fathers of the be-bop revolution.

At a memorial service attended by 8,000 to 10,000 people, an all-star cast leads testimonials for the jazzman, reports *The New York Times*.

Jan. 8: **Cecil Fielder** of the Detroit Tigers becomes the second-highest paid player in baseball. He agrees to a $36 million, five-year contract that includes a record $10 million signing bonus, reports *The Associated Press*.

Jan. 9: **George Joseph Ross**, 54, professor of music at the University of Maryland and founder of its jazz studies division, dies of a cerebral hemorrhage at his home in Richmond, VA, reports *The Washington Post*.

Jan. 12: The U.S. Supreme Court allows the Prince George's County, MD, school system to continue its policy of involuntarily transferring teachers from one school to another to satisfy racial quotas, reports *The Washington Post*.

Jan. 12: **Sidney Lowe** takes over as head coach of the Minnesota Timberwolves, doubling the number of minority coaches in the National Basketball Association, reports *The Washington Post*.

Jan. 13: **Phyllis A. Wallace**, 69, a labor economist at the Massachusetts Institute of Technology, dies at her home in Boston, reports *The New York Times*.

Jan. 14: Gov. **Steve Merrill** of New Hampshire signs an order creating a state holiday honoring the Rev. Dr. **Martin Luther King, Jr.** New Hampshire had been the last state without such a holiday, reports *The Associated Press*.

Jan. 14: The Rev. **Jesse Jackson** presents his 14-point agenda to baseball owners and calls on current players to join his campaign for the integration of front offices in baseball, reports *The Associated Press*.

238

Jan. 14:   Middleweight boxer **Marvin Hagler** will be inducted into the Boxing Hall of Fame in June, reports *USA Today*. Hagler, 39, turned pro at 18 and produced a record of 62-3-2 with 52 knockouts.

Jan. 15:   Whites get preferential treatment roughly six times as often as blacks and eight times as often as Latinos when they are job-hunting in the Washington area, but racial discrimination is often subtle and hard to pinpoint, says a report by the Fair Employment Council of Greater Washington, reports *The Washington Post*. The study paired similarly qualified black and white job applicants and Latino and white applicants and sent them to interview for the same jobs. It then compared the number of positive comments made to them and the number of times they were offered jobs or invited back for skills tests.

Jan. 15:   First Lady **Hillary Rodham Clinton** names **Margaret Williams**, 38, as her chief of staff, reports *The Washington Post*. Williams formerly worked for the Children's Defense Fund.

Jan. 15:   Dr. **Louis W. Sullivan** returns to Atlanta to become president of Morehouse School of Medicine, the position he held before becoming the nation's top public health official during the **Bush** administration, reports *The Associated Press*.

Jan. 17:   About 50 Ku Klux Klan members in Austin, TX, protest the **Martin Luther King, Jr.,** holiday and are met by about 5,000 opponents who throw eggs, beat drums, and shout them down, reports *The Associated Press*.

Jan. 18:   America's black middle class, which doubled in size a generation ago, is finding it hard to break out of government jobs and into the top ranks of the private sector, reports *The Washington Post*. Census figures document only a tiny African-American presence in prestigious jobs, most of them in the private sector. Blacks make up 10 percent of the nation's work force, but only 4 percent of doctors, 3 percent of lawyers and architects, and 2 percent of airline pilots.

Jan. 18:   President-elect **Clinton** honors the Rev. **Martin Luther King, Jr.,** as a great spiritual leader in America's pursuit of equality and freedom, reports *The Washington Post*. King was "the most eloquent voice for freedom and justice in my lifetime," Clinton tells more than 1,000 local officials and others at Howard University.

Jan. 19: **Reginald Lewis**, who ran America's largest black-owned business, dies of brain cancer at the age of 50 in Manhattan, NY. In 1987, he led a $985 million leveraged buyout of food giant Beatrice Co.'s international operations, which in 1991 posted sales of $1.5 billion. Lewis discouraged others viewing him as a symbol of black success. "To dwell on race, to see that as something that becomes part of my persona, is a mistake," he once said, according to *Black Enterprise*.

Jan. 20: **William Jefferson Clinton** is sworn in as the 42nd President of the United States, immediately following the swearing-in of his Vice President, former Tennessee Senator **Albert Gore, Jr.** One of the major highlights of the inaugural ceremony on Capitol Hill is the reading of the specially commissioned inaugural poem, "On the Pulse of Morning," by author/poet/Reynolds Professor at Wake Forest University **Maya Angelou**.

Jan. 21: The U.S. Senate confirms 15 **Clinton** appointees, including four blacks in the cabinet: Commerce Secretary **Ronald H. Brown**, Agriculture Secretary **Mike Espy**, Energy Secretary **Hazel O'Leary**, and Veterans Affairs Secretary **Jesse Brown**.

Jan. 24: **Thurgood Marshall**, the first black U.S. Supreme Court justice and a leading figure in the civil rights movement, dies of heart failure at age 84. *The New York Times* reports Justice Marshall, who retired from the high court in 1991, had been scheduled to administer the oath of office to Vice President **Al Gore**, but his failing health prevented him from doing so.

Thurgood Marshall was a figure of history well before he began his 24-year stint at the Supreme Court on Oct. 2, 1967. During more than 20 years as director-counsel of the NAACP Legal Defense and Educational Fund, he was the principal architect of the strategy of using the courts to provide what the political system would not: a definition of equality that assured black Americans the full rights of citizenship.

His greatest legal victory came in 1954 with the Supreme Court's decision in *Brown v. Board of Education*, which declared an end to the "separate but equal" system of racial segregation then in effect in the public schools of 21 states.

Jan. 25: U.S. District Court Judge **John G. Davis**, reversing a lower-court decision, rules prosecutors will not have to prove that white policemen had a racial motivation for beating black motorist **Rodney King** in Los Angeles, reports *The Associated Press*.

King was beaten March 3, 1991, after a car chase. An amateur cameraman videotaped the attack, and its national broadcast sparked an outcry over police brutality.

Jan. 27: The Federal Bureau of Investigation agrees to put its employment practices under a federal judge's supervision for five years, to promote six black agents, and to transfer an additional 57 blacks who contend they were victims of racial bias, reports *The Associated Press*. In settling the racial discrimination lawsuit, the agency also agrees to make 13 more black agents relief supervisors and to open training slots for 40 more black agents.

Jan. 27: Gospel legend **Thomas Andrew Dorsey**, 93, who wrote more than 1,000 songs, including "Take My Hand, Precious Lord," dies in his Chicago home, reports *The Washington Post*.

Jan. 27: **Bert Andrews**, a performing arts photographer whose pioneering work chronicled the history of black theater since the 1950s, dies in Manhattan at age 63, reports *The New York Times*.

Feb. 3 Major League Baseball's ruling executive council suspends Cincinnati Reds owner **Marge Schott** from day-to-day club operations for one year and fines her the maximum—$25,000—as punishment for her use of racially insensitive language. *The New York Times* reports Schott—the only woman who owns a Major League Baseball team—had called some of her players "dumb, lazy niggers," made references to "Jew bastards," and used the pejorative "Japs," among other remarks. Her language came to light a year ago in a deposition from a suit by a dismissed employee. The owners took action only after the threat of an opening-day boycott by civil rights activist **Jesse Jackson** and other black leaders.

Feb. 4: A Montgomery County, MD, judge sentences a white man, **John R. Ayers, Jr.,** of Rockville, MD, to 60 years in prison for assaulting two black women, twice the term called for under the state's sentencing guidelines, reports *The Washington Post*.

Feb. 6: A federal court decides that tax-supported colleges may continue to offer minority students scholarships based on race, reports *The New York Times*. A three-judge panel unanimously upholds a lower court's dismissal of a lawsuit by seven white students who contended that minority scholarships violated the 1964 Civil Rights Act.

Feb. 7:   **Arthur Ashe**, 49, the tennis legend and human rights activist, dies in New York 10 months after announcing he had contracted AIDS, apparently from a blood transfusion he received during heart bypass surgery, reports *The Washington Post*. A native of Richmond, VA, Ashe was a tennis prodigy who won U.S. junior indoor titles in 1960 and 1961. In 1973, he became the first black person to compete in an integrated sporting event in South Africa. The first black male to win the Wimbledon and U.S. Open singles' tournaments, Ashe was equally active off the courts, demonstrating for the elimination of apartheid in South Africa and for the rights of Haitians to be granted asylum in America. He was also a television sports commentator and author of several books, including the highly acclaimed *A Hard Road to Glory* and his last book—equally well-received—*Days of Grace*.

Feb. 7:   A Virginia judge grants a request by a dozen parents to delay integration of classes at an elementary school where pupils had been grouped by race for at least seven years, reports *The New York Times*. Judge **T.J. Markow** of Richmond Circuit Court says the school board had not held a required public hearing before ordering 74 of the 452 students at Bellevue Model Elementary School to move to new classes.

Feb. 8:   Struggling black farmers receive an average of $21,000 less per loan than white borrowers from a Farmers' Home Administration loan program that is intended to help save family farms, reports *The Associated Press*. The federal agency is a last resort for many farmers who cannot get loans elsewhere to buy land, livestock, seeds, and tractors.

Feb. 12:   The number of interracial couples in America has nearly doubled in the past 12 years, and now one out of every 20 marriages crosses the boundaries of race, reports *The Associated Press*.

Feb. 16:   **Coretta Scott King** defrosts the decades-old chilly relationship between her family and the Federal Bureau of Investigation by telling a predominantly black, standing-room only crowd at FBI headquarters: "The FBI of the 1990s has turned its back on the abuses of the Hoover era," reports *The Washington Post*. As FBI director—especially in the 1960s—**J. Edgar Hoover** was suspicious of **Martin Luther King, Jr.**, and kept close tabs on him, ordering secret surveillance and taping. Mrs. King also backed embattled director **William Sessions** for his affirmative action policies as he fights to keep his job despite a critical Justice Department report.

242

Feb. 21:   **Benjamin L. Hooks** makes his last report as executive director of the National Association for the Advancement of Colored People, but the topic dominating the meeting is news that the Rev. **Jesse Jackson** is one of a handful of finalists to replace Hooks, reports *The New York Times.*

Feb. 21:   Potomac Electric Power Co. agrees to pay $38.4 million and to change its personnel procedures in a settlement with black and female employees and job applicants who sued the Washington, DC-based utility for alleged discrimination, reports *The Washington Post.* As many as 20,000 blacks and women who worked for or applied to work at the utility in the past 10 years could qualify to receive awards, according to a summary of the proposed settlement.

Feb. 25:   A judge refuses to block the **Rodney King** federal beating trial over defense allegations that a black juror could be biased and a defendant's claims of attorney conflict, reports *The Associated Press.*

Feb. 25:   Lawyers for boxer and convicted rapist **Mike Tyson** ask an Indiana appeals court for a new trial, saying the former heavyweight boxing champion would have beaten the rape conviction if a judge had not denied the jury certain tools of evidence, reports *The Washington Post.*

Feb. 26:   The Justice Department's abrupt decision to seek a jury dismissal in the retrial of Rep. **Harold E. Ford** (D-TN) followed a campaign by Ford and his allies that included White House contacts and a meeting between Ford's lawyer and **Webster Hubbell**, the White House "point man" on the issue, reports *The Washington Post.* Ford was being tried on bank fraud and conspiracy charges.

Feb. 26:   Baltimore's **Kurt L. Schmoke**, serving his second term as mayor, announces he is considering a bid for the 1994 governor's race in Maryland, reports *The Baltimore Sun.*

Feb. 27:   At his Rainbow Commission for Fairness in Athletics meeting, **Jesse Jackson** reinforces an earlier message to the owners of Major League Baseball teams: If they do not come up with a plan to increase minority participation off the field by April 5, "We are prepared to take action," reports *The Washington Post.* Jackson says that action could include picketing and demonstrating at ballparks around the country.

Mar. 2:   **B. Doyle Mitchell**, chairman and president of the Industrial Bank of Washington, the nation's oldest minority-owned bank and one of the largest, dies at the Walter Reed Army Medical Center at age 78, reports *The Washington Post*.

Mar. 2:   **Walter McMillan** walks out of a Bay Minette, AL, courtroom a free man after prosecutors concede he spent six years awaiting execution on Alabama's death row because of perjured testimony and evidence withheld from his lawyers. Whether he was also convicted of shooting an 18-year-old white female store clerk because he is black is just one of several issues swirling around a case that has evoked broad questions of race and justice, reports *The New York Times*.

Mar. 3:   Ruling that a federal court improperly invalidated the redistricting of the Ohio legislature, the U.S. Supreme Court strengthens the power of states to shape voting districts with overwhelming majorities of black and other minority voters, reports *The New York Times*.

Mar. 3:   While doing research in the Amazon, Dr. **S. Allen Counter** says he discovered a monument to American slaves. Descendants of escaped slaves living in the jungle had erected shrines to ancestors taken forcibly in crowded ships to labor in the New World, reports *The Associated Press*. Counter, a Harvard physiologist, is the leader of an effort to commemorate that episode in history by carving a copy of a crowded slave ship out of granite in the nation's capital.

Mar. 3:   **Hillary Rodham Clinton** visits the Congressional Black and Hispanic Caucuses to express a willingness to increase minority group participation in the overhaul of health care underway, reports *The Washington Post*. "We have to understand the problems that all Americans face," Mrs. Clinton told reporters between the two sessions.

Mar. 3:   Opposite images of Florida's capital emerge in a Tallahassee courtroom: One depicts a powder keg ready to blow and the other a city set to host a racially recharged trial, reports *USA Today*. The apparent cause of the commotion is an upcoming retrial of Miami police officer **William Lozano**, suspended without pay when a multiracial Miami jury found the Hispanic officer guilty of manslaughter in the 1989 killing of two black men on a motorcycle. The deaths sparked several days of rioting in Miami.

244

The guilty verdict was later thrown out by a judge who said the jurors were unduly influenced by fear of more rioting if they had voted to acquit Lozano.

Mar. 8: **Billy Eckstine**, the influential band leader and suave bass-baritone balladeer dies at the age of 78 of complications from a stroke in Pittsburgh. Dubbed "Mr. B.," Eckstine was one of postwar America's most elegant and imitated singers, inspiring others such as **Joe Williams, Arthur Prysock**, and **Lou Rawls.** Among his hits: "Stormy Monday Blues" and "Everything I Have Is Yours." At his peak, he attracted larger audiences to New York's Paramount Theater than Frank Sinatra. "He had what nobody before him had," Newport Jazz Festival producer George Wein told *Newsweek.* "He oozed a certain quality—class."

Mar. 9: A federal judge rejects a constitutional challenge to voting privileges for Del. **Eleanor Holmes Norton** (D-DC) on the House floor, claiming the privilege she won in January is legal only because it is "symbolic" and "meaningless," reports *The Washington Post.* In a 57-page opinion, U.S. District Judge **Harold H. Greene** upholds House rules that give Norton and representatives of four U.S. territories limited voting rights on the House floor. Norton and House members challenge Greene's assessment, contending that Norton's enhanced status enables her to influence legislation on the House floor.

Mar. 9: **Rodney G. King** testifies in his federal civil rights trial that he led police on a high-speed car chase because he feared being returned to prison and that he tried to flee on foot after being stopped because he was afraid for his life. *The Washington Post* quotes from King's testimony the next day: "We're going to kill you, nigger, run," King said an officer shouted while King was on the ground. King rose to his feet, tried to run, and was fiercely struck with metal police batons.

Mar. 10: **B. Doyle Mitchell, Jr.**, 30, is named president of the Industrial Bank of Washington, the District's oldest black-owned financial institution. As president, he succeeds his father who died March 2, reports *The Washington Post.* Mitchell's grandfather founded the bank in 1934.

Mar. 10: State health officials, criticized for delays in the fight against AIDS among minorities, say they will distribute $3.9 million for prevention programs in black and Hispanic neighborhoods, re-

ports *The New York Times*. The financing will go to 24 organiza
tions dedicated to stopping the spread of AIDS among blacks an
Hispanics.

Mar. 12:   **Raymond L. Danner**, the embattled cofounder and largest share
holder of the Shoney's Inc., restaurant chain, is selling all hi
stock and leaving the corporation's board of directors following
$105 million settlement of a racial bias lawsuit, reports *Th
Washington Post*.

Mar. 13:   **Jesse Jackson** issues a 10-point recommendation for Major Leagu
Baseball and asks each team to have at least three minorit
members on its board of directors within two years, reports *Th
Washington Post*. Jackson asks each team to implement three- t
five-year affirmative action plans, hire at least 20 percent of thei
vendors from minority groups, consider at least two minoritie
for each executive and coaching opening, and appoint a full-tim
executive in charge of implementing minority guidelines.

Mar. 15:   Players from baseball's Negro League, barred for decades fron
the major leagues, are enjoying a revival of interest linked to th
boom in baseball memorabilia with their names appearing on T
shirts, trading cards, caps, and jackets reports *The New Yor
Times*. As their feats are revived, the former Negro Leaguers
about 200 of them, find themselves at the heart of a battle ove
how to best help and honor the men from the game's segregate
past. The fight is over who should control the marketing of Negr
League memorabilia and how the revenue should be used—fo
immediate help for old players in need or for the perpetuation o
the Negro League's history.

Mar. 18:   In the midst of a year-long FBI investigation of boxing promote
Don King, a federal grand jury in New York begins hearin
evidence of alleged criminal wrongdoing by King, reports *Th
New York Times*. The investigation, headed by the U.S. Attorney'
office in lower Manhattan, appears to center on the busines
practices of King, who has promoted fights for hundreds c
boxers, including former heavyweight champion **Mike Tyson**.

Mar. 18:   Civil rights leaders and relatives of prisoners who died by hang
ing in Missouri jails plead for a federal investigation, sayin
suspicion surrounds many of the deaths, reports *USA Toda*
Since 1987, 43 men and women were found dead by hanging i
local jails, and four prisoners wre found dead in state facilitie

246

About half the victims were black.

Mar. 21: The U.S. Army began spying on black Americans more than 75 years ago in a campaign that was centered on southern churches and covered three generations of **Martin Luther King**'s family, reports *The Commercial Appeal of Memphis*. The spying, which involved the Army's Green Berets, involved King's maternal grandfather, who was pastor of a Baptist church in Atlanta. It continued to include King's father and eventually the slain civil rights leader himself.

Mar. 24: Sgt. **Stacey C. Koon** takes the stand in his own defense at the **Rodney G. King** civil rights trial and testifies that he had tried to avoid using force in taking King into custody after a high-speed pursuit on March 3, 1991, reports *The Washington Post*. King was kicked and struck more than 50 times with metal police batons.

Mar. 25: **Wesley McD. Holder**, 95, a Democratic politician who helped break racial barriers to elective office as a senator, paving the way for Mayor **David N. Dinkins** and other black officials in New York City, dies at his home in Brooklyn, NY, reports *The New York Times*.

Mar. 25: Hundreds of protestors take to the streets in Fort Worth, TX, outraged when a 17-year-old white supremacist convicted in the murder of a black man is sentenced to probation, reports *The New York Times*. The sentence, imposed by Judge **Everett Young** of Tarrant County District Court, apparently resulted from a misunderstanding among the jurors, all of whom were white, as to the punishment they could recommend.

Mar. 25: For nonwhite people, it is becoming more difficult to find bone marrow donors, reports *The New York Times*. Of the 1,606 transplants arranged through the National Marrow Donor Program, only 28 involved black recipients. Only 3.6 percent of the people registered as donors in the Connecticut Marrow Donor Program are black.

Mar. 29: Representative **Harold E. Ford** (D-TN), Tennessee's first and only black Congressman, goes on trial for federal bank fraud charges, two years after a first jury deadlocks along racial lines. The case centers on what appears to be a charge that he accepted up to $1.2 million in personal payments under the guise of business loans, according to *The Washington Post.*

April 5: Twenty-five years after the assassination of **Martin Luther King, Jr.**, civil rights leaders remind a racially charged nation that Dr King dreamed of a land where children will not be judged by their skin color, reports *The Associated Press.* In the past year racial tensions erupted into violence in Los Angeles, Las Vegas, San Francisco, Seattle, Atlanta, and New York.

"It seems sometimes that we take two steps forward and three back," says **Elisa Graham**, a trustee at Ebenezer Baptist Church in Atlanta, where Dr. King was a co-pastor.

April 6: **Jesse Jackson** arrives for baseball's season opener in Baltimore, MD, to reinforce the National Rainbow Coalition's position that discrimination against minorities and women in baseball requires immediate attention, reports *The Richmond Times-Dispatch.*

April 6: The U.S. Supreme Court refuses to hear an appeal by a convicted federal judge, **Robert F. Collins** of New Orleans, raising the possibility that the U.S. House of Representatives will impeach a fourth judge in less than eight years, reports *The Washington Post.* Collins has been in prison since 1991, when he was convicted of taking a $100,000 bribe from a drug smuggler who wanted leniency.

April 6: A federal appeals court sides with the U.S. government in a dispute over a prosecution tactic that threatens to undo the fragile alliance among the four officers on trial in the beating of **Rodney G. King** in 1991, reports *The New York Times.* The ruling allows prosecutors to show jurors in the federal civil rights trial an edited version of videotaped testimony from the state trial a year ago in which one defendant described how another officer clubbed a defenseless King in the head.

April 7: The Green Bay Packers, a small-town symbol of pro football's past glory, steps into the big bucks, bid-for-best era when All-Pro defensive end **Reggie White** agrees to a four-year, $17 million contract, reports *USA Today.*

April 7: A senior enlisted man at Fort Richardson in Anchorage, Alaska, is demoted and fined for directing the mock lynching of a black soldier in his Army unit, reports *The Associated Press.* Master Sgt. **David Comley**, a 20-year Army veteran, pleaded guilty to willful dereliction of duty at a special court-martial in March after being accused of directing a mock hanging of Sgt. **Troy Scott**, 28, the only black in the 15-member unit.

April 8: The Rev. **Jesse Jackson**, citing a move by some NAACP board members to weaken the position of executive director, says he is no longer interested in heading the civil rights organization, reports *The Associated Press*. The withdrawal comes two days before the board votes on a successor to **Benjamin Hooks**, who is scheduled to retire at the end of the month.

April 8: A Superior Court judge in Los Angeles orders a three-month delay in the trial of three blacks accused of beating a white truck driver during the 1992 riots after the acquittal of police officers in the **Rodney King** beating trial, reports *The Associated Press*. The decision puts some distance between the **Reginald Denny** trial and the King trial scheduled to go to the jury any day.

April 8: **Marian Anderson**, the renowned contralto who touched the conscience of the nation with a 1939 concert at the Lincoln Memorial after having been refused permission to sing at Constitution Hall because she was black, dies in Portland, OR, a month after suffering a stroke. Her age was given as between 91 and 96, reports *The Washington Post*. Anderson's voice was described by the conductor **Arturo Toscanini** as "one that comes along only once in a century."

April 9: The city of Los Angeles is nervous as the second **Rodney King** beating trial nears an end, reports *The Associated Press*. However, determined to avoid a repeat of the riots that followed 1992 acquittals, the city has armored personnel carriers in place, police are packing rubber bullets and tear gas, merchants have stocked up on guns, and churches are preparing to remain open as long as necessary to patrol their neighborhoods.

April 10: The Rev. **Benjamin Chavis**, 45, is selected to succeed **Benjamin Hooks** as director of the NAACP, the nation's oldest civil rights group. Hooks will retire April 30, ending 16 years at the helm of the NAACP. Chavis, a civil rights crusader who spent four years in prison in the Wilmington 10 firebombing case before being freed by a federal appeals court, said he intends to computerize fully offices at the NAACP's Baltimore headquarters, build an endowment, increase lobbying efforts, and extend the organization to Hispanics, Indians, Asians, and American Indians, reports

The Washington Post.

April 11: A racially diverse jury is asked to ignore the city of Los Angeles' anxiety and reach an impartial judgment in the videotaped beating of black motorist **Rodney King** that shocked the world and that led to the deadly Los Angeles riots, reports *The Washington Post*. Urging jurors to put aside fears that riots will erupt again, defense attorney **Harland W. Braun** asks for the acquittal of the four Los Angeles police officers accused of violating King's civil rights.

April 15: An appeals court upholds a $12.5 million damage award against white supremacist **Tom Metzger** in the beating death of an Ethiopian man in 1988 in Salem, OR, reports *The Associated Press*. The state court of appeals refuses to consider all but one of the errors claimed by Metzger and his son, **John**, because they didn't properly raise them at their trial in 1990.

April 17: A federal judge convicts Los Angeles police officers **Stacey Koon** and **Laurence Powell** of violating the civil rights of black motorist **Rodney King** in a videotaped beating, bringing peace to Los Angeles where an earlier trial led to the nation's worst rioting in decades. Two other officers are acquitted, reports *The Washington Post*.

April 19: **Warmouth T. Gibbs, Sr.**, once described as "the greatest Aggie" of them all, dies at age 101, reports *The Greensboro (NC) Daily News*. In a career that spanned 40 years, Gibbs helped guide and shape NC A&T State University to a place of prominence among the nation's historically black universities. Gibbs arrived at A&T College in 1926 as a no-nonsense, Harvard-trained educator who had been one of the first black commissioned officers in World War I. As university president during the turbulent '60s, he was asked frequently about the A&T students who staged the Woolworth sit-ins, to which he coolly responded, "We teach our students *how* to think, not *what* to think."

April 20: The U.S. Supreme Court turns down a challenge to Michigan's program of setting aside 15 percent of highway-building contracts for companies owned by minorities or women, reports *The Associated Press*. The high court, without comment, refuses to hear arguments that the program discriminates against companies owned by white males.

April 21: In a case that could jeopardize 26 new black or Hispanic majority districts across the country, the U.S. Supreme Court is asked to overturn North Carolina's redistricting plan on grounds that it was intended to establish a racial quota of two black House members from North Carolina, reports *The Associated Press*. A ruling is expected by late summer.

April 26: Minorities with disabilities face more difficulties in society than do other Americans with disabilities, according to a federal study, reports *The Associated Press*. Disabled minorities "face double discrimination and double disadvantages in our society," says the National Council on Disabilities in a report to the president and to Congress.

April 27: **Jean S. Fugett, Jr.**, new head of the leading black-owned U.S. company and a former Super Bowl athlete, rebukes top pro sports teams for discouraging many recruits from finishing their education, reports *The Associated Press*. "Major sports have become a national disgrace," the chief executive oficer of TLC Beatrice International, Inc., tells the Society of American Business Editors and Writers.

April 29: **Lee P. Brown**, who headed police departments in New York, Houston, and Atlanta, is selected to head the Office of National Drug Control Policy. President **Bill Clinton**, in naming Brown, says he has "an extraordinary record of innovation in crime reduction and a sensitivity to the problems of real people," reports *The Washington Post*.

April 29: President **Bill Clinton** nominates University of Pennsylvania law professor **Lani Guinier** to be the chief of the Justice Department's civil rights division. *The New York Times* reports a firefight erupts when conservatives launch an attack against the lawyer's unconventional views on voting rights for minorities. *LIFE* magazine reports that a month later, in a move that angers African-American activists, a rattled Clinton withdraws the nomination, admitting he had never read Guinier's controversial writings.

May 7: Boston University can keep personal papers of the Rev. **Martin Luther King, Jr.**, despite his family's efforts to bring the documents back to the South, reports *USA Today*.

"Moral justice did not prevail," says **Coretta Scott King**, widow of the slain civil rights leader. "I have no doubt my husband wanted his papers returned to Atlanta, and no doubt that here is where they should reside."

May 7:   During the 1991 National Football League draft, **C. Lamont Smith** was the only African-American agent representing first-round picks, reports *USA Today*. Two years later, the number is seven times better. During April's draft, seven AfricanAmerican agents represented 10 of the 29 first-round picks. And of the players taken in the first two rounds, 36 percent (20 of 56) were represented by African Americans.

May 10:   After being shifted five times from one city to another, the racially charged retrial of a Miami police officer on charges of killing two young black men is scheduled to begin today in Orlando, FL, reports *The New York Times*. The case, which has preoccupied Florida for more than four years, has defied the efforts of Judge **W. Thomas Spencer** of Dade County Circuit Court to hold the trial where black people are most likely to be on the jury.

May 11:   **Julius Erving**, the gravity-defying "Dr. J.," who took the game above the rim with his dazzling dunks, is inducted into the Basketball Hall of Fame in Springfield, MA, reports *The Associated Press*. Erving called his induction "not the last tribute to a phenomenal career, but the beginning of a long road of added responsibilities."

May 12:   A federal judge rules that **Leonard Jeffries'** constitutional rights were violated when he was removed as chairman of City College's black studies department in New York after making an allegedly racist speech, reports *The Washington Post*. U.S. District Judge **Kenneth Conboy** instructs the jury to decide who specifically violated Jeffries' rights and to consider damages. Jeffries' lawsuit against City College seeks $25 million in damages and reinstatement as chairman.

May 15:   **Hakeem Olajuwon**, the centerpiece of the Houston Rockets' defense and the league leader in blocked shots for the third time in four years, is named NBA defensive player of the year, reports *The Associated Press*.

May 16:   Large U.S. businesses owned by blacks outperformed many companies last year, reports *Black Enterprise* magazine. Such businesses ranged from an Ohio food distributor to a Los Angeles hip-hop clothier.

May 25: As six black Secret Service officers file a federal civil rights lawsuit alleging that a Denny's restaurant in Annapolis, MD, discriminated against them, Denny's officials announce the firing of that restaurant's manager for not reporting the officers' complaint to corporate officials, reports *The Washington Post.*

May 28: Former Miami, FL, police officer **William Lozano**, who is Hispanic, is acquitted in Orlando, FL, on two manslaughter counts in the deaths of two black men in 1989. The victims were on a motorcycle being chased by a police car. Lozano shot and killed the driver, and the passenger was fatally injured in the subsequent crash of the cycle, according to *The Associated Press.* The acquittal resulted in only sporadic violence in Miami: five people were reported injured and more than 60 were arrested.

May 30: Virginia Governor **L. Douglas Wilder**'s plan to build a national memorial to African-American history could fulfill a pledge made more than 60 years ago by popular black evangelist **Lightfoot Soloman Michaux**, reports *The Richmond Times-Dispatch.* In the course of building one of the first religious broadcasting empires and establishing the Gospel Spreading Church of God, Elder Michaux bought a 1,000-acre farm in 1936 on a site near Jamestown, where he believed the first slaves landed in the New World. Wilder, during a recent speech in Africa, pledged that he would lead a private effort to build a national memorial to slavery in Jamestown.

June 1: **Sun Ra**, the influential pianist and orchestra leader noted for his intergalactic treks into jazz and avant-garde music and regarded as the Salvador Dali of jazz, dies at age 79 in Birmingham, AL, reports *The Associated Press.* In a career spanning 60 years, he gained wide notice in the jazz world for encompassing everything from bop and gospel to blues and electronic sounds.

June 3: President **Clinton**, acknowledging that he will anger the civil rights community, yanks his nomination of University of Pennsylvania law professor **Lani Guinier** to be chief enforcer of the nation's civil rights laws. *USA Today* reports that, after meeting with Guinier for more than an hour in the Oval Office, Clinton says he found it "difficult to defend" ideas she expressed in articles. Guinier expresses frustration at not being able to defend herself before the Senate, *The New York Times* reports.

June 4: Two of the nation's foremost civil rights leaders find themselves on opposite sides of a racial discrimination dispute involving the Denny's restaurant chain, reports *USA Today*. NAACP executive director **Benjamin Chavis** says his organization is establishing a "mutual working relationship" with TW Services, Denny's parent company, that will increase minority involvement. However, **Jesse Jackson** plans to join an upcoming protest march at a Denny's in Annapolis, MD.

June 6: A racially biased system of home lending exists in the Washington area, with local banks and savings and loans providing mortgages to white neighborhoods twice the rate they do to comparable black ones, reports *The Washington Post*. The newspaper's computer-assisted study, which analyzed more than 130,000 deeds of homes sold in 1985 and 1991, showed that race, not income or housing characteristics, was the decisive factor in determining where local banks and thrifts made home loans in the Washington area.

June 7: Rep. **Kweisi Mfume** (D-MD), chairman of the Congressional Black Caucus, says that dropping **Lani Guinier**'s nomination as chief civil rights enforcer will make it harder for President **Clinton** to get black support, reports *The Associated Press*. Mfume, on NBC's "Meet the Press," says that he's bothered by the "back-and-forth, up-and-down, in-and-out motion of this administration and of this president."

June 7: A federal appeals court in New Orleans hears arguments in an 18-year-old school desegregation case that some say could kill historically black colleges, reports *USA Today*. At issue: Judge **Charles Schwartz**'s finding that Louisiana operates a segregated system of higher education and must merge its 17 public colleges and universities under one board. The case is considered the most important desegregation case since *Brown v. The Board of Education*.

June 8: About 120 protesters march for three hours outside the White House to demonstrate their anger over President **Clinton**'s withdrawal of his nomination of **Lani Guinier** to be his civil rights chief, reports *The Washington Post*. The **Congressional Black Caucus**, meanwhile, arranges for a meeting with Clinton to discuss ways their fractured relationship can be mended after Caucus members unleashed stinging criticism following his withdrawal of Guinier's nomination.

June 8: Accused of using reverse discrimination to diversify the municipal work force, the **David Dinkins** administration in New York agrees to give raises and higher ranks to about 75 supervisors at the Human Resources Administration who contended that they were passed over for advancement because they were white, reports *The New York Times*. However, the administration acknowledged no wrongdoing in settling a lawsuit by the Social Service Employees Union, which charged that top officials systematically manipulated city rules to promote black and Hispanic supervisors who did not perform as well as whites on civil service tests.

June 9: **Arthur Alexander** of Cleveland, OH, whose music was influenced by blues, gospel, and country music, dies of a heart attack at age 53, reports *The Associated Press*.

June 9: Lawmakers on Capitol Hill and in the District government call for an investigation into the racially biased practices of area banks and thrifts, following a series of articles in *The Washington Post*, the newspaper reports.

June 10: The **Congressional Black Caucus** rejects President **Clinton**'s request for a White House meeting, signaling the displeasure of its 39 Democratic members over Clinton's withdrawal of **Lani Guinier**'s nomination for the Justice Department and the direction of budget compromises with the Senate, reports *The Washington Post*. The Caucus also threatens to defeat Clinton's budget package if his compromises with the Senate include retreats on Medicare, the earned income-tax credit, child hunger programs, and summer jobs for youths.

June 10: In what he calls a "gut-wrenching, but regrettably necessary decision," Atlanta Mayor **Maynard Jackson** says that he will not seek reelection to a fourth term, reports *The New York Times*. The announcement means that for the first time in two decades, the city's politics will open up to new faces and names that may not necessarily be tied to the city's pivotal role in civil rights history.

June 11: The Port Authority of New York and New Jersey resumes its program of earmarking a large share of its purchasing budget for businesses owned by minorities or women, reports *The New York Times*. The budget includes nearly a billion dollars a year in contracts for construction, equipment, and services.

June 11: **Scott Barrie**, an American designer known for sexy matte jersey dresses in the 1960s and 1970s, dies at the Alessandria Hospital in Alessandria, Italy, outside Milan, reports *The New York Times*. He was 52.

June 15: **Nathanael Pollard, Jr.**, a mathematician, is named to lead the 4,800-student campus at Bowie State University in Prince George's County, MD, reports *The Washington Post*. Pollard, 53, an Alabama native, has more than 20 years' experience in higher education administration, including acting president at Virginia State University.

June 15: The **Johnson Products Company**, whose portfolio of grooming and cosmetic products for minority consumers has made it one of the nation's largest black-owned businesses, will be acquired in a stock swap with the IVAX Corporation, reports *The New York Times*. The deal could range in value from $61 million to $73 million, depending on share prices of the two firms prior to the closing.

June 17: University of Oklahoma regents vote to establish a law professorship in the name of **Anita Hill**, despite protests that the law professor lied when she accused **Clarence Thomas** of sexual harassment in 1991 when he was a nominee to the U.S. Supreme Court, reports *The Associated Press*.

June 17: **Maurice T. Turner, Jr.,** who opened doors for himself in the segregated Washington, DC, police department and then, as a commander and eventually chief, opened doors to thousands of other black officers, dies at age 57 in the nation's capital, reports *The Washington Post*. Turner spent 32 years on the job before turning in his gun and badge July 26, 1989.

June 17: Lawyers representing black Secret Service officers who sued Denny's restaurants for race discrimination say they have learned of at least 10 other incidents in five states in which Denny's black customers, including a federal judge, say they received prejudicial treatment, reports *The Washington Post*.

June 18:   Dr. **Doxey A. Wilkerson,** an education expert who was a leader in union civil rights and civic causes, dies at a Norwalk, CT, hospital at age 68, reports *The New York Times.* Dr. Wilkerson, who specialized in early childhood development, served as chairman of Yeshiva University's Education Department of Curriculum and Instruction from 1963-73. He also taught at Virginia State College, Howard University, and Bishop College; he was also the faculty and curriculum director of the Jefferson School of Social Change.

June 19:   **James Benton Parsons,** 81, the first black appointed as a federal district court judge, dies in Chicago, reports *The Washington Post.* Parsons was appointed in 1961 by President **John F. Kennedy**.

June 20:   Basketball superstar **Michael Jordan** is voted championship series Most Valuable Player as his Chicago Bulls win their third consecutive National Basketball Association title, defeating the Phoenix Suns, four games to two. In Chicago, fans go on a rampage that results in nearly 700 arrests, reports *The Chicago Sun-Times.*

June 23:   After dominating Detroit politics and government for two decades, **Coleman A. Young**, the first black mayor of the nation's eighth-largest city, says he will not seek reelection in the fall, reports *The New York Times.* Young, 75, becomes the latest political retiree among a group of blacks whose election and longevity as big-city mayors brought a new era of black urban enfranchisement beginning in the 1960s.

June 23:   The owner of the Denny's restaurant chain, accused of racial discrimination against black customers, hires a black executive to oversee its employees. Flagstar, which also owns Hardees and Quincy's restaurants, hires **Norman Hill** of Memphis for the newly created job of vice president of human resources, reports *The Associated Press.* Flagstar also recently changed its name from TW Services.

June 24:   **Archie Williams**, 78, a 1936 Olympic Gold Medal winner in the 400-meter race, dies in Fairfax, CA, reports *Emerge* magazine.

June 24:   The National Planning Commission in Washington, DC, approves designs for monuments honoring blacks who fought as Union soldiers in the Civil War and Korean War veterans. The Civil War memorial, the first of its kind, will be built near Howard University, reports *Emerge* magazine.

June 25: Governor **L. Douglas Wilder** of Virginia announces he will oppose Sen. **Charles S. Robb** (D-VA) for the Democratic Senate nomination in 1994, reports *The New York Times*.

June 26: **James "Son" Thomas**, a singer and guitarist who played traditional Mississippi Delta blues spiced with humor and irony, dies at age 66 in Greenville, MS, reports *The Associated Press*.

June 26: Baseball Hall of Famer **Roy Campanella**, often hailed as the heart and soul of the Brooklyn Dodgers, dies in California at the age of 71, reports *The Richmond Times-Dispatch*. Campanella came to the National League at the time **Branch Rickey** was tearing down the color barrier in baseball. **Jackie Robinson** blazed the trail, but Campanella carried a heavier burden, according to most sports writers and historians: As the first Major League black catcher who called the shots, he bore the brunt of the bigotry, and the racial taunts lingered. Campanella was the recipient of three Most Valuable Player Awards.

June 27: Tennis pro **Zina Garrison-Jackson** defeats top seed **Mary Jo Fernandez** 6-0, 6-1 in the Wimbledon quarterfinal matches, reports *The New York Times*.

June 28: The U.S. Supreme Court rules 5-to-4 it may be unconstitutional for states to carve out new district lines for the sole purpose of creating districts where a majority of voters are nonwhite. The shape of the North Carolina district in question was "bizarre," *The New York Times* reports the high court as saying, "resembling the most egregious racial gerrymanders of the past," and the state must demonstrate a "compelling interest" for such design over one with compact and contiguous districts. The ruling jeopardizes more than two dozen "majority-minority" congressional districts, created after the 1990 Census, which sent 13 blacks and six Hispanics to Congress.

June 30: Thirty-one people are indicted in New York on charges that they ran eight groups that, under the guise of obtaining construction jobs for black and Hispanic workers, violently extorted thousands of dollars from building contractors, reports *The New York Times*. The indictments add another chapter to the contentious history of minority hiring in the construction industry.

July 1: Mayor **Tom Bradley**, a Texas sharecropper's son who transformed Los Angeles into a modern city but lost his luster in the fires of the 1992 riots, steps down after 20 years of dominating the political landscape in Southern California, reports *The Washington Post.*

"He was the right man at the right time," says **Richard Riordan**, his successor. "He brought this city together and moved it forward. I think he'll be remembered kindly." Bradley, 75, was one of the first black mayors of a major U.S. city.

July 1: The NAACP signs a $1 billion "fair share" financial agreement with Denny's restaurants that will increase black employment and management opportunities, reports *The Washington Post.* **Jerry Richardson**, chairman of Flagstar Corp., pledged a minority recruitment and training program to add 325 management positions by the year 2000; he also vowed to create 53 black-owned franchises by 1997.

July 9: Lawyers for six black Secret Service officers say they have filed in federal court more than 50 new allegations of bias against Denny's restaurants in a dozen states, reports *The Washington Post.*

July 9: Blacks who quit smoking are more likely than whites or Hispanics to start again, health authorities report as they launch a campaign to persuade blacks to kick the cigarette habit, reports *The Washington Post.* "We want to get the message to as many in the African-American community as possible . . . that this addiction to tobacco use can be overcome," says **Robert Robinson** of the federal government's Office on Smoking and Health.

July 9: The U.S. Department of Education said the Richmond (VA) school system violated federal civil rights laws last year when it grouped white students in the same classrooms within two largely black elementary schools in a practice known as "clustering," reports *The New York Times.* The department, which released its findings to the school board after a four-month investigation, said the district had already corrected the problem by discontinuing the practice after some parents complained.

July 12: As Major League Baseball basks in the glow from its 64th All-Star Game, the issue of equal opportunity in employment and advancement for minorities in the so-called national pastime still lurks in the shadows, reports *The Washington Post*. Despite what some feel are deceiving appearances on the playing field, the starting line-ups for the American and National Leagues July 13 at Oriole Park at Baltimore's Camden Yards (MD) will feature nine black or Hispanic players (not including pitchers).

July 12: **Mario Bauza**, an instrumentalist and band leader who helped change the sound of American music, dies at his home in Manhattan, NY, at age 82, reports *The New York Times*.

July 13: The U.S. Supreme Court's North Carolina redistricting decision on June 28 once again forces to the surface the conflict between the goal of a color-blind society and the practical realities of a political system—in the South and elsewhere—with a history of discrimination and racial voting, reports *The Washington Post*. Rep. **John Lewis** (D-GA) acknowledges that his solution is to come down on both sides of the debate: "On one side our goal (civil rights movement) was to create a truly interracial democracy. . . . We must move beyond race." But on the other side, Lewis added, "We are not there yet."

July 13: Vice President **Al Gore** spoke at the annual meeting of the NAACP as part of an effort to improve the Clinton administration's strained relations with blacks, reports *The New York Times*. But the group's chairman, **William Gibson**, criticized President **Clinton**'s withdrawal of the nomination of University of Pennsylvania law professor **Lani Guinier** as the nation's top civil rights officer at the Justice Department.

July 14: **Lani Guinier**, whose nomination to be assistant attorney general for civil rights was withdrawn by President **Clinton,** lashes out at the U.S. Supreme Court for creating what she calls a new constitutional right for whites, reports *The Washington Post*. In a speech before the NAACP's annual convention, Guinier criticizes the high court's decision that white voters in a North Carolina case could challenge the constitutionality of a strangely drawn redistricting plan that appeared to separate voters by race.

Guinier also says that President Clinton's abandonment of her was "an unfortunate metaphor for the way race and racism are viewed in this society. We are being defined, we are being characterized, are being misrepresented by other people . . . who are not sympathetic to issues of equality and real democracy."

July 15: **Ronald Ray Howard**, 19, is sentenced to death in Austin, TX, after jurors reject his claim that anti-police rap music persuaded him to pull the trigger and kill Trooper **Bill Davidson**, reports *The Washington Post*.

July 15: U.S. Postmaster General **Marvin T. Runyon**'s affirmative action plans for the government's largest civilian agency continues to draw fire, reports *The Washington Post*. Several members of the board of governors express concern about the lack of power that Runyon has given his new department of diversity development. Their comments, echoing complaints by lawmakers and the NAACP, follow those of departmental vice president **Veronica O. Collazo**, who describes her 80-member staff as "consultants."

July 16: A U.S. Senate committee postpones confirmation hearings for U.S. Surgeon General nominee **Joycelyn Elders** after questions arise regarding her finances, reports *The Washington Post*. The White House is prepared to fight over the outspoken Arkansas health official.

July 16: Federal authorities say they have arrested eight white supremacists who were preparing to blow up one of the largest black churches in Los Angeles and to kill **Rodney G. King** in an effort to incite a spasm of racial violence around the country, reports *The New York Times*.

July 16: The New Orleans City Council votes to banish from city streets a gray granite obelisk commemorating an 1874 uprising of angry whites against Louisiana's biracial Reconstruction government, reports *The New York Times*. In recent years the monument has been used as a rallying point by **David Duke** and the Ku Klux Klan, making it a symbol of white supremacy and an embarrassment to the city.

July 21: A chain of leadership failures by New York Mayor **David N. Dinkins**, top City Hall advisers, and the city's leading police commanders caused the August 1991 disturbances in Crown Heights to escalate unabated into a four-day "riot" in which Hasidic Jews were singled out by bands of black youths, according to a report commissioned by Gov. **Mario M. Cuomo** and overseen by **Richard H. Girgenti**, New York's director of criminal justice, reports *The New York Times*.

July 22: Warning that suburbs are becoming a "new frontier in discrimination," the Southern Christian Leadership Conference says it will hold its annual convention this year in Rockville, MD, and launch a 30th anniversary "March on Washington" via the subways of Metro's Red Line, reports *The Washington Post*. **James C. Moore**, president of the Montgomery County (MD) SCLC chapter, says a suburban site is appropriate because of increasing incidents of crime and racial intolerance in areas surrounding large cities.

July 22: **Roscoe Robinson, Jr.,** 64, the first African American to become a four-star general in the U.S. Army, dies in Washington, DC, reports *The Washington Post*.

July 23: The U.S. Senate's only black member, **Carol Moseley-Braun** (D-IL), grabs the chamber's attention with impassioned tears and shouts, stopping Sen. **Jesse Helms** (R-NC) in his tracks as he defends his amendment to renew the United Daughters of the Confederacy's patent on the Confederate flag insignia. *The Washington Post* reports that, with many Senators unaware of what they were voting for, Helms won a test vote of 52 to 48. Then Moseley-Braun took the floor in outrage at the defense of a symbol of slavery.

"On this issue, there can be no consensus. It is an outrage. It is an insult. It is absolutely unacceptable to me and to millions of Americans, black or white, that we would put the imprimatur of the United States Senate on a symbol of this kind of idea." As word of the debate spreads, more and more Senators come to the floor, taking her side. The Senate, convinced the flag was an insult, kills the Helms' amendment, 75 to 25.

July 24: White news managers and black journalists have widely differing perceptions about racial bias in the promotion and advancement of minorities in the nation's newsrooms, according to a survey conducted by the National Association of Black Journalists and reported in *The Washington Post*.

The survey, released during the NABJ's convention in Houston, said African-American reporters and editors face "gross underrepresentation in management (and) chronic problems of promotion and retention," with "few black journalists in plum assignments," reports *The Washington Post*.

July 24: Civil rights leaders demand a federal investigation after newspaper reports say that police in an affluent suburban area of Houston, TX, arrest far more minorities than whites for routine traffic offenses, reports *The Associated Press.*

July 28:   **Reggie Lewis**, leading scorer and captain of the Boston Celtics last season, dies after collapsing for the second time while playing basketball, reports *The Baltimore Sun.* Lewis, 27, reportedly stopped breathing while shooting baskets with an unidentified person at the Celtics' practice facility at Brandeis University at Waltham, MA.

July 29:   Dr. **Dale W. Lick**, a finalist for the presidency of Michigan State University, withdraws after a campus uproar over a remark he made in 1989 that some black athletes are naturally superior to white athletes, reports *The Associated Press.*

July 29:   The **Congressional Black Caucus** sharply restricts the participation of its only Republican member, Rep. **Gary Franks** (R-CT), following his criticism of the Voting Rights Act, reports *The Washington Post.* The motion, passed without dissent among a majority of the Caucus's 40 members, allows Franks to attend weekly luncheon meetings for only the first half-hour, when members typically eat and talk informally. The rest of the meetings are deemed a caucus of black Democratic lawmakers.

July 29:   Jury selection in the racially charged trial of two men accused of attempted murder in the televised beating of truck driver **Reginald O. Denny** begins in Los Angeles, reports *The Washington Post.* Denny, who is white, was dragged from his cement truck and beaten as news helicopters hovered overhead at the corner of Florence and Normandie avenues. Charged in the beating are **Damian Williams**, 20, and **Henry Watson**, 28, who are black.

July 30:   President **Clinton** nominates DC Superior Court Judge **Eric H. Holder** as U.S. Attorney for the District of Columbia, the first time a black lawyer is named to that post, reports *The Washington Post.*

Holder, if confirmed by the U.S. Senate, will assume the largest federal prosecutor's office in the nation and walk into several raging controversies, including the federal investigation of House Ways and Means Committee Chairman **Dan Rostenkowski** (D-IL) in the House Post Office scandal. Holder is confirmed following the congressional summer recess.

Aug. 1:   The National Urban League opens its annual conference in Washington, DC, with the theme "Developing 21st Century African-American Communities." Guest speakers include **Marian Wright Edelman**, Dr. **Cornel West**, Dr. **Alvin Poussaint,** and U.S. Commerce Secretary **Ronald H. Brown**.

        The Washington Post reports League President and Chief Executive Officer **John E. Jacob** urged African Americans to "get mad; get involved; get organized . . . in order to create 21st century African-American communities that are socially just, economically competitive . . . and capable of leading the nation and the world . . . to new standards of prosperity and accomplishment. . . . Our single most important task," Jacob continued, is "our own self-development. We must create 21st century communities that nurture 21st century citizens."

Aug. 2:   The early successes of African-American women in Congress are among the topics of conversation at the biennial convention of the National Political Congress of Black Women in Washington, DC, reports *The Washington Post.* Discussions include the heated debate over federal funding of abortions; Sen. **Carol Moseley-Braun**'s (D-IL) passionate assault on a proposal by Sen. **Jesse Helms** (R-NC) to renew a design patent for the insignia of the United Daughters of the Confederacy which depicted the original flag of the Confederacy; and an amendment to the House-approved flood relief package authorizing $100 weekly stipends to unemployed young adults while they receive job training.

Aug. 3:   Black Democratic Illinois Attorney General **Roland Burris** celebrates his 56th birthday by announcing he will run for Governor in 1994, reports *FOCUS* newsletter. Burris held press conferences in 12 cities during a two-day swing through the state to launch his campaign. For Burris, attempting to unseat an incumbent Republican governor in a state that is 78 percent white and 15 percent black will be a challenge.

Aug. 3:   The body of **James Jordan**, father of basketball superstar **Michael Jordan**, is found floating in Gump Swamp Creek near Bennettsville, SC, *The New York Times* reports. Police later charge two North Carolina men in the murder, which they say began as a robbery at a highway rest stop, *LIFE* magazine reports.

Aug. 3:   Howard University files a post-trial motion in Washington, DC, Superior Court requesting a new trial in the **Sanya Tyler** sex discrimination case, reports *The Washington Post*. On June 24, a six-person Superior Court jury awarded Tyler, Howard's basketball coach, $2.4 million after finding that the school violated the DC Human Rights Act by discriminating and retaliating against Tyler once she filed suit. The jury determined that the university violated Title IX statutes barring sex discrimination at schools and colleges. Tyler claimed in her lawsuit that she had inadequate office space and locker room facilities, no full-time assistant coach or secretary, and a salary about half that of **Butch Beard**, the men's basketball coach.

Aug. 4:   Federal judge **John Davies** sentences two police officers to 2½ years in prison for violating the civil rights of **Rodney G. King**, saying that he was being lenient because King had provoked their violence and that the officers had already suffered from widespread vilification and from having to face repeated judicial proceedings, reports *The New York Times*. The two men, Sgt. **Stacey Koon** and Officer **Laurence Powell**, were ordered to begin serving their sentences September 27. Although many in the black community in Los Angeles objected to the relatively lenient sentences, the city remains calm.

Aug. 4:   The **NAACP** accuses the Hughes Aircraft Company of violating federal guidelines that require government contractors to diversify their work forces and management, reports *The New York Times*. Officials of the civil rights group say they will present evidence at a news conference in Washington, DC, that Hughes, which employs 55,000 people, has only two black vice presidents and that blacks are grossly underrepresented in its work force.

Aug. 5:   A federal judge reinstates Dr. **Leonard Jeffries** as chairman of the black studies department at City College in New York, ruling that while Dr. Jeffries had made "hateful, poisonous and reprehensible statements" and had behaved in a "thuggish" way, his removal had violated his constitutional rights, reports *The New York Times*. Dr. Jeffries gained notoriety for espousing a view that white people are "ice people" who are cruel and aggressive.

Aug. 5:   The **Congressional Black Caucus** agrees to let its lone Republican, Rep. **Gary Franks** (R-CT), fully participate in the organization's decisions, reports *The Washington Post*. Rep. **Kweisi Mfume** (D-MD), caucus chairman, tells a news conference that the 40-member organization voted to reverse the frequent exclusion of Franks and to include him in all deliberations.

Aug. 5: In Chicago, a Detroit investment group controlled and operated by African Americans, purchases **Indecorp, Inc.,** one of the nation's largest black-owned holding companies, with more than $265 million in assets. Lead investor **William Johnson** calls the move a milestone in his vision of creating the first black-owned multibank holding company covering several years, reports *Emerge* magazine.

Aug. 7: An Indianapolis State Appeals Court upholds **Mike Tyson**'s rape conviction and six-year sentence in a 2-1 ruling that rejected several defense arguments, reports *The Associated Press.*

Aug. 8: The National Medical Association says health maintenance organizations do a poor job of hiring minority doctors and administrators, reports *The Associated Press.* Minority patients often are better served by physicians of the same ethnic background, says Dr. **Leonard Lawrence**, president of the 16,000-member NMA, the largest black physicians group.

Aug. 10: For the first time in its 150-year history, The Citadel chooses a black student as its highest-ranking cadet when **Norman P. Doucet** becomes the regimental commander of the corps of cadets in Charleston, SC, reports *The Associated Press.*

Aug. 11: Former and current employees of the National Institutes of Health say their supervisors retaliated against them—using verbal abuse, ostracism, and occasionally demotion—after they complained of discrimination because of race, sex, or physical disabilities, reports *The Washington Post.*

Aug. 14: Federal, state, and local officials begin a search for the murderer of **James Jordan**, the father of Chicago Bulls basketball superstar **Michael Jordan**, reports *The Washington Post.* The senior Jordan's body, with a gunshot wound to the chest, was found in a South Carolina creek. Jordan, 57, had been missing since July 22.

Aug. 16: **Michael Jordan** and his family say goodbye to his slain father at a private funeral service in Teachey, NC. **James Jordan** was shot to death in late July by robbers when he pulled his car off a highway to rest, reports *The Washington Post.* A tearful Michael Jordan addresses about 200 mourners and speaks about what he

266

and others learned from his father. Arrested for Jordan's murder are **Daniel Andre Green** and **Larry Martin Demery**, both 18.

Aug. 17: **Robert C. Maynard**, 56, a former editor and publisher of *The Oakland Tribune* and the first black person to own a daily general-circulation newspaper in the United States, dies of prostate cancer at his home in Oakland, reports *The Washington Post*. A high school dropout from Brooklyn, NY, Maynard's career took him to the highest councils of American journalism, and his influence extended far beyond the San Francisco Bay area that his newspaper served. His credentials included six years on the *York (PA) Gazette & Daily*; a Nieman Fellowship at Harvard University; and a decade at *The Washington Post*. During his tenure at the *Tribune*, the paper won a Pulitzer Prize for its photographic coverage of the Loma Prieta earthquake, which devastated parts of the San Francisco Bay area.

Aug. 21: **Delano E. Lewis**, long-time president of Chesapeake & Potomac Co. of Washington, announces he is leaving to head National Public Radio, reports *The Washington Post*, becoming the first black to hold the prestigious post.

Aug. 22: While **Michael Jackson** is in Bangkok on a world concert tour, California police search his Neverland estate for evidence in a child-sex abuse case centered on the entertainer, *LIFE* magazine reports.

Aug. 23: Almost 30 years after they fought and died, a monument for the U.S. Colored Troops who served in the Civil War is erected at Petersburg National Battlefield in Petersburg, VA, reports *The Richmond Times-Dispatch*. Park Service officials say it is the first monument to black soldiers at the national park and joins a growing public recognition of black participation in the Civil War. A monument depicting the 180,000 black Union soldiers was recently commissioned by the District of Columbia.

Aug. 24: **Citibank** sharply curtailed home mortgage lending to black and Hispanic borrowers in the New York metropolitan region in 1992, while loans to white applicants rose substantially, reports *The Associated Press*. The bank says the wide disparity was an unintentional side effect of a restructuring of its troubled mortgage lending business.

Aug. 24: **J. B. Fuqua**, an Atlanta industrialist who graduated from a segre-

267

gated Virginia high school, says he will donate $10 million to try to erase one of the enduring reminders of the commonwealth's massive resistance to integration, reports *The Washington Post*.

Aug. 24: Two former Detroit police officers, **Larry Nevers**, 53, and **Walter Budzyn**, 47, are convicted of murdering **Malice Green** last November outside a crack house, reports *The Associated Press*. A third policeman was acquitted of assault; the two convicted officers were allowed to go free until their October 12 sentencing.

Aug. 24: **David Satcher**, president of Meharry Medical College, is named director of the federal Centers for Disease Control and Prevention, reports *The Associated Press*. He will be the first black ever to hold the prestigious post.

Aug. 25: Representatives of pop star **Michael Jackson**—accused of sexually abusing a child— strike back, saying the singer is the victim of a plot to extort $20 million from him, reports *The New York Times*.

Aug. 26: In Vidor, TX, two black men, who were the first to integrate the all-white town 100 miles east of Houston, leave after six months of bomb threats, harassment, and rejected job applications, reports *The Associated Press*. **John DecQuir** and **Bill Simpson** moved to Vidor after a federal court ordered that the town's public housing project be desegregated. Vidor has not been integrated in at least 70 years.

Aug. 26: Leaders of the 30th Anniversary March on Washington will not meet with President **Clinton** as they envisioned because the meeting was not officially requested until a few days before the march, and the White House pleaded short notice, reports *The Washington Post*.

Aug. 26: The Southern Christian Leadership Conference opens its four-day convention in Rockville, MD, with calls for marches on behalf of DC statehood, justice for minorities, and a reconfiguration of the Rockville Metro station, which some say has blocked in a historically black neighborhood, reports *The Washington Post*.

Aug. 27: Pop music superstar **Michael Jackson**, citing a doctor's orders, postpones a concert in Thailand for the second night in a row, while in Los Angeles, police quietly continue their investigation into child sexual abuse allegations against the singer, reports *The Washington Post.*

Aug. 27: Civil rights leader **Jesse Jackson** and DC Mayor **Sharon Pratt Kelly** are arrested on Capitol Hill while protesting on behalf of statehood for the District of Columbia, reports *The Associated Press.* The protest is part of a series of weekly demonstrations by activists who support turning the city into the state of New Columbia.

Aug. 27: Blacks win control of the Selma, AL, City Council in the city where a bloody clash between civil rights marchers and the police three decades ago galvanized the nation and spurred passage of the Voting Rights Act in 1965, reports *The New York Times.* Blacks constitute 58 percent of the city's 24,000 residents, but it took a court-ordered redistricting plan for blacks to win five of the nine seats in recent elections.

Aug. 29: Tens of thousands of people of all ages and races gather at the Lincoln Memorial to commemorate the 30th anniversary of the March on Washington, to measure a dream, and to walk the same mile that **Martin Luther King, Jr.**, walked in 1963, reports *The Washington Post.*

Aug. 29: A federal court denies bail to two police officers convicted in the beating of **Rodney G. King**, confirming that they must begin their prison sentences in four weeks, reports *The Washington Post.*

Sept. 1: **Jones Morgan**, one of the last "Buffalo Soldiers," dies at age 110 in Richmond, VA, reports *The Richmond Times-Dispatch.* Buffalo Soldiers were the U.S. Army's only black regiment that helped settle the West and helped fight during the Spanish-American War.

Sept. 3: In West Palm Beach, FL, white laborers **Mark Kohut** and **Charles Rourk** are convicted of all charges in the New Year's Day burning of a black tourist, **Christopher Wilson** of Brooklyn, NY, who said they taunted him with racial slurs, doused him with gasoline, and set him on fire, reports *The Washington Post.* A teenager testifying against Kohut and Rourk said they had been drinking and "were acting like it was a big game."

Sept. 3: **William Simpson**, the last black to move out of the all-white public housing complex in Vidor, near Beaumont, TX, is slain by a gunman who tried to rob him, reports *The Washington Post*. Simpson moved out of Vidor because he feared for his life.

Sept. 7: Dr. **Joycelyn Elders**, a former Arkansas health director who is controversial because of her outspoken support of abortion rights and contraceptives for teenagers, is confirmed as U.S. Surgeon General by the U.S. Senate on a vote of 65-34, reports *Knight-Ridder Newspapers*.

Sept. 13: **Colston A. Lewis**, the former senior member of the U.S. Equal Employment Opportunity Commission and a civil rights leader, dies at age 81 in Richmond, VA, reports *The Richmond Times-Dispatch*. Lewis was appointed to the commission in February 1970 by President **Nixon** and served until 1977, when the **Ford** administration left office.

Sept. 15: A study by researchers at the University of Alabama, Stanford University, and Valparaiso University says that African Americans suffer disproportionately from kidney failure but wait twice as long as whites for transplants because federal rules require closely matched donor organs, reports *The Washington Post*.

Sept. 15: Officials at the University of Pennsylvania try to end an embarrassing episode involving the school's handling of racial tensions and free speech on campus by dismissing disciplinary proceedings against nine black students, reports *The New York Times*. The students had confiscated 14,000 copies of the student newspaper as a protest against the newspaper's policy and a conservative columnist's writings.

Sept. 16: **Florence Small Gaynor**, the first black woman to head a major teaching hospital in the United States, dies in Newark, at age 72, reports *The New York Times*. A registered nurse by training, she rose through the ranks of administration at several large NY hospitals at a time when few women or blacks were in such positions. In 1971, she was chosen from a field of 20 candidates—the rest of them male—to be executive director of Sydenham Hospital in Harlem, making her the first black woman ever to head one of the city's municipal hospitals. Eighteen months later, she went to Martland Hospital in Newark, a 600-bed teaching hospital, now part of the University of Medicine and Dentistry of New Jersey.

Sept. 17: Minnesota Twins all-star **Dave Winfield** becomes the 19th player in baseball history to get 3,000 career hits, reports *USA Today*. The hit, before 14,600 fans at Metropolitan Stadium in Minneapolis, was a hard single to left field in the ninth inning against **Dennis Eckersley** of the Oakland Athletics.

Sept. 17: **AT&T**, the nation's largest long-distance telephone company, apologizes for a cartoon printed in an employee magazine that company officials characterized as a "racist illustration," reports *The Washington Post*. The drawing shows people on various continents making telephone calls; the caller in Africa is depicted as a gorilla.

Sept. 20: **Kimberly Clarice Aiken** of South Carolina is crowned Miss America. The black 18-year-old says she plans to focus attention on homelessness during her reign, reports *The New York Times*.

Sept. 20: Lured by black consumers' $282 billion annual income, marketers are taking a closer look at black shoppers, reports *USA Today*. According to studies, black consumers value prestigious brand names more highly than general-market consumers and are more willing to dig into their pocketbooks for those brands. Black consumers also pay more attention to advertising; they are less likely to cut back on spending during an economic pinch; and, while many consumers regard shopping as a time-gobbling chore, black consumers still enjoy it.

Sept. 29: Texas lawyer **Anthony Griffin**, who is black, says he hates the Ku Klux Klan, but First Amendment laws led him to represent Klansman **Michael Lowe** in his fight to protect the Klan's membership rolls, reports *The Associated Press*. Lowe also claims that he and his associates did not intimidate and scare away black residents seeking to live in the all-white town of Vidor.

Sept. 29: **Makaza Kumanyika**, a civil rights leader in New York City in the 1960s whose name then was **Jerbert Callender**, dies at his home in East Orange, NJ, at age 60. Kumanyika helped lead civil rights protests as chairman of the Bronx chapter of the Congress of Racial Equality, beginning in 1963 with demonstrations against the White Castle hamburger chain, which the group asserted had discriminatory hiring practices, reports *The New York Times*.

Sept. 29: President **Clinton** says he "stands by" Commerce Secretary **Ronald H. Brown** and accepts his assurance that he did nothing wrong in meetings with a Vietnamese businessman whose dealings with Brown are being probed by a federal grand jury, reports *The Washington Post*.

Sept. 29: Almost 1,000 poor black and Hispanic families will be offered apartments in predominantly white middle-class areas of Westchester County, NY, under a settlement of a lawsuit, reports *The New York Times*.

Sept. 30: **William P. Grayson,** former executive vice president of Johnson Publishing Company and associate publisher of *Ebony* and *Jet* magazines, dies in Los Angeles at age 79, reports *Jet* magazine.

Sept. 30: Gen. **Colin Luther Powell,** chairman of the Joint Chiefs of Staff, retires after 35 years of military service, reports *The Washington Post*. Powell was the first black and youngest person to hold the position. The recipient of two Presidential Medals of Freedom, he will be paid an estimated $6 million to write his autobiography and will charge $60,000 for speaking engagements.

Sept. 30: **John E. Jacob,** National Urban League President and Chief Executive Officer, announces his retirement. During his 12-year tenure at the helm, the civil rights organization set up a $10 million development fund and expanded its education, career development, and job training programs, reports *The New York Times*.

Oct. 3: **Rubin "Hurricane" Carter,** a former middleweight contender who became a national symbol of a criminal-justice system gone badly astray, makes an impassioned plea to enlarge a planned federal review of state court convictions retained, reports *The New York Times*. Carter, 57, spent nearly 20 years in a New Jersey prison for a triple murder. He was ultimately freed by a federal judge who ruled that state prosecutors and police violated his constitutional rights.

Oct. 5: **Barbara Ross-Lee,** 51, becomes the first black woman ever to head a U.S. medical school as dean of Ohio University's College of Osteopathic Medicine in Athens, OH, reports *USA Today*. Ross-Lee is also the sister of entertainer **Diana Ross**.

Oct. 6: **Michael Jordan,** acclaimed by many as the greatest basketball player ever, announces his retirement. After leading North Carolina to the NCAA championships in 1982, Jordan had starred for nine years with the Chicago Bulls of the NBA. In a gymnasium filled with family, friends, teammates, hundreds of reporters, and officials from every walk of professional basketball, Jordan—who led his team to an unprecedented three NBA championships—told the crowd, "I've always stressed that when I lost the sense of motivation and having something to prove, it would be time to move away. . . . This is the perfect time for me to walk away," reports *The Washington Post*. He said his retirement was not based on the murder of his father, to whom he was greatly devoted, during the summer.

Oct. 7:   **Toni Morrison**, Princeton University Distinguished Professor and Pulitzer prize winning-author of *Beloved, Song of Solomon, Jazz,* and three other lyrically narrated novels of black American life, wins the 1993 Nobel Prize for Literature. *The New York Times* quotes the Nobel Committee of the Swedish Academy in Stockholm as saying that Morrison's fiction has "epic power," that she "gives life to an essential aspect of American reality" in novels "characterized by visionary force and poetic import." This year's award is worth $825,000, to which Morrison—the eighth woman and the first black to receive the prestigious prize—reacted: "I am outrageously happy! . . . Winning as an American is very special—but winning as a black American is a knockout. Most importantly, my mother is alive to share this delight with me."

Oct. 8:   Point guard and all-American **Anfernee Hardaway** of Memphis State agrees to a multiyear contract worth $65 million with the Orlando Magic basketball team, reports *The New York Times*. The contract is the second highest in professional team sports behind the 12-year, $84 million deal signed Oct. 5 by **Larry Johnson** and The Charlotte Hornets.

Oct. 8:   A week after a black minister suggested that **Rudolph Giuliani** was supported by some "fascist" elements, the Republican-Liberal mayoral candidate makes his most impassioned counterattack of the campaign, painting a picture of a year-long, well-orchestrated effort by supporters of New York Mayor **David Dinkins** to depict him as a dangerous right-wing fanatic surrounded by supporters of the Ku Klux Klan, reports *The New York Times*.

Oct. 8:   Appearing onstage in blackface while making a series of racial and sexual jokes, actor **Ted Danson** offends members of a celebrity-filled audience at a New York City Friar's Club roast honoring his actress girlfriend, **Whoopi Goldberg**. Five weeks later, according to *LIFE* magazine, Danson and Goldberg will announce they are no longer seeing each other. Meanwhile, tabloids report that Goldberg is dating her orthodontist.

Oct. 9: The National Basketball Association officially concludes its investigation of **Michael Jordan** and his high-stakes gambling, deciding that the former Chicago Bulls star violated no legal rules, reports *The Washington Post*.

Oct. 15: For their effort in dismantling apartheid in South Africa, African National Congress President **Nelson Mandela** and South Africa's President, **F.W. de Klerk**, are awarded the Nobel Peace Prize. A month later, they will join other pro-democracy negotiators, *LIFE* magazine reports, in signing a new interim constitution that grants black and white South Africans equal rights for the first time in more than 300 years.

Oct. 15: New York Mayor **David Dinkins**, standing beside First Lady **Hillary Rodham Clinton** two weeks after President **Bill Clinton** said some New Yorkers were reluctant to back Dinkins because of his race, appeals to voters to "support me not because of my color but because of the content of my heart," reports *The New York Times*.

Oct. 18: A Los Angeles jury acquits two black men, **Damian Williams** and **Henry Watson**, of the most severe charges against them in the beating of white truck driver **Reginald Denny** and seven other people in last year's rioting, reports *The New York Times*.

Oct. 20: After a first-ever meeting that both sides hope will have "historic" consequences, the **Black Coaches Association** and the **Congressional Black Caucus** announce the formation of a partnership to investigate issues or grievances against the National Collegiate Athletic Association and to fight jointly what one participant termed nothing less than "the battle to win the lives of our children," reports *The Washington Post*.

Nov. 2: After elections across the nation, black mayors no longer control leading cities that they have led before, such as New York, Philadelphia, Chicago, and Los Angeles, reports *The Associated Press*. Detroit remains among those with black chief executives, however, with Democrat **Dennis Archer** succeeding 20-year incumbent **Coleman Young**.

274

In New York, on the other hand, after one of the most racially polarized mayoral elections in the city's history, **Rudolph Giuliani** unseats **David Dinkins** by a margin of 51 percent to 48 percent.

Nov. 9: U.S. Deputy Secretary of State **Clifton Wharton** resigns, apparently at the behest of the **Clinton** administration, becoming the first high-ranking official to leave the president's embattled foreign policy team, reports *The Washington Post*. Wharton, 67, one of the top blacks in the Clinton administration, said it had become clear he was being subjected to classic Washington politics through "sustained anonymous leaks to the media."

Nov. 9: **Sidney Poitier** and **Harry Belafonte** are named the 1993 recipients of the Thurgood Marshall Lifetime Achievement Award, honoring their "long-standing commitment to civil rights and excellence in the portrayal of minorities in the film and entertainment industry," reports *USA Today*.

Nov. 10: Professor **Cornel West**, a leading scholar of African-American studies and religion and a best-selling author, announces he will move from Princeton University to Harvard University next fall, reports *The New York Times*. West is author of the best-seller, *Race Matters*, in which he argues the major obstacle to harmonious race relations in the United States is nihilism—the sense of worthlessness that he sees as growing among blacks.

Nov. 10: **Ed Rollins**, the campaign manager for GOP gubernatorial candidate **Christine Todd Whitman** in New Jersey, says the campaign paid nearly half a million dollars to black ministers who agreed not to rally their flock to vote for incumbent Democratic Gov. **Jim Florio**, thus ensuring Whitman's victory, reports *The New York Times*.

In the meantime, black ministers across the state express shock and anger over Rollins's assertions that they had accepted what he called "walking around money" from the campaign to remain politically neutral before the election, *The New York Times* continues.

Nov. 11: **James Yates**, who went from the cotton fields of Mississippi to the battlefields of the Spanish Civil War and New York's civil rights struggles, dies in Manhattan at age 87, reports *The New York Times*. Yates chronicled his journey in *Mississippi to Madrid: Memoir of a Black American in the Abraham Lincoln Brigade*.

Nov. 11:   New Jersey Gov.-elect **Christine Todd Whitman** says her cam
             paign manager, **Ed Rollins**, was "off the wall" when he boasted
             that the campaign paid to suppress black voter turnout, but Demo
             crats from President **Clinton** on down denounce the controversial
             tactics, reports *The Washington Post*. Rollins previously said a
             much as $500,000 was channeled to black ministers and precinct
             workers in a calculated effort to keep the black vote to a mini
             mum.

Nov. 12:   The U.S. Justice Department will investigate whether alleged
             payments by the campaign of New Jersey Gov.-elect **Christine
             Todd Whitman** to suppress black voter turnout would violate
             federal law, reports *The Associated Press*. The department's civil
             rights division and the public integrity section of its criminal
             division will study if the alleged payments described, then de
             nied, by campaign manager, **Ed Rollins**, would break federal
             law, says spokesman **Carl Stern**. Rollins declares a week later
             that he was "just trying to get a rival's goat" when he bragged on
             the alleged vote suppression scheme, *LIFE* magazine reports
             Says one Democratic attorney: "I am not going to drop our
             investigation based on this bizarre explanation."

Nov. 23:   Del. **Eleanor Holmes Norton** (D-DC), buoyed by the results of
             the first congressional vote on District statehood, says she be
             lieves that the city will now have an easier time winning approval
             of steps that would fall short of statehood but greatly enhance
             home rule, reports *The Washington Post*. Norton says the House
             vote, which ended in a lopsided defeat for the city, has encour
             aged her to push for the District to have the right to manage its
             budget and pass laws with less congressional oversight.

Nov. 24:   A group of current and former employees accuse **GEICO Corp**
             of systematically screening out blacks who seek car and
             homeowners' insurance from the large, Chevy Chase, MD-based
             company, reports *The Washington Post*.

Nov. 24:   Atlanta City Councilman **Bill Campbell** trounces former Fulton
             County Commissioner **Michael Lomax** in Atlanta's mayoral run
             off after a campaign dominated by a bribery scandal, reports *The
             Associated Press*. With 175 of 177 precincts reporting, Campbell
             had 46,438 votes, or 73 percent, to Lomax's 17,301 votes, or 27
             percent.

Nov. 24: Blues guitarist **Albert Collins**, 61, dies of lung cancer at his Las Vegas home, reports *The Associated Press*. Known as the "master of the Telecaster"—after the electric guitar from which he coaxed bitingly percussive licks delivered with a distinctively pure tone, Collins was one of the world's best-known and respected bluesmen who greatly influenced rock 'n' roll; among his disciples: the late **Jimi Hendrix**. He won a 1986 Grammy for his album "Showdown." Among his biggest hits was "Get Your Business Straight," released in 1972. *Musician Magazine* called him "the most powerful blues guitarist in the world."

Nov. 25: **Claudia McNeil**, an actress known for her performances on stage and in screen productions of "A Raisin in the Sun," dies of complications from diabetes in the Actors Fund Nursing Home in Englewood, NJ, at age 77, reports *The New York Times*. McNeil won praise for her heroic performance as the matriarch in a black family on the South Side of Chicago, with critics declaring that she imbued the simple character with nobility and spirit.

Nov. 26: No bribery charges will be filed against former Los Angeles Mayor **Tom Bradley** over allegations that a developer bought his help for a housing project, reports *The Associated Press*. There was insufficient evidence to file charges against him, the Los Angeles County district attorney's office explained.

Nov. 29: **William J. Trent, Jr.**, the executive director of the United Negro College Fund for 20 years after its inception in 1944, dies in Greensboro, NC, reports *The New York Times*. In his years as the executive director of the fund, Trent oversaw the raising of about $78 million, which he said had helped to make "strong citadels of learning, carriers of the American dream, seedbeds of social evolution and revolution."

Nov. 30: A New Jersey school district with no high school is turned down by the U.S. Supreme Court in its bid to end its alliance with a predominantly black high school and to let its students go to another nearby school where most of the students are white, reports *The New York Times*. The court, without comment, rejects the argument by the Englewood Cliffs Board of Education that the state violated its students' constitutional rights by requiring the continued partnership with Dwight Morrow High School in Englewood.

Dec. 1: The New York State Democratic Party accuses Republicans c conducting a campaign to intimidate minority voters in the may oral election that unseated incumbent **David Dinkins**, report *The New York Times*. Party Chairman **Al Gordon** said at least 7 incidents have been reported by Democratic pollwatchers, addin that the information would be forwarded to the Justice Depart ment, which is reviewing complaints of fraud in the race.

Dec. 2: **Pearl Stewart**, 43, editor of the *Oakland Tribune*, resigns on year after becoming the first black woman to edit a major U.S daily newspaper, reports *Reuters News Service*. Stewart says sh is resigning December 14 because of differences with **Davi Burgin**, who was reappointed as editor-in-chief of the *Tribune* parent company.

Dec. 4: Virginia Gov.-elect **George Allen** selects **Kay Coles James**, prominent antiabortion spokeswoman, for his top health adviso reports *The Washington Post*. The move immediately draws criti cism from abortion-rights leaders. James, a member of the Fairfa County (VA) School Board, will become secretary of health an human resources, a post that oversees many of Virginia's birth control programs. She is also a former public affairs director fc the National Right to Life Committee.

Dec. 7: Following a closed-door meeting with New York Gov. **Mari Cuomo**, a group of black state legislators issues a plea for radical redistribution of state resources to fight "a culture c violence" among youths that they say have turned cities into w: zones, reports *The New York Times*. The lawmakers will prese to Cuomo a detailed "Marshall Plan," proposing using feder: anti-crime money earmarked for prison construction instead fc youth counseling, job programs, and school-based health clinic

Assemblyman **Roger Green**, a Brooklyn Democrat, say "We've had a 200 percent increase in prison construction in th last 10 years, and no one here would say our streets have becom safer."

Dec. 7: Washington, DC, Mayor **Sharon Pratt Kelly** announces plans t reduce violent crime by targeting more city services and prc grams in two public housing complexes, reports *The Washingto Post*. Facing reelection in nine months, Kelly promises to deliv to the housing complexes and surrounding neighborhoods moi social services, including prenatal care and recreational progran

278

such as nighttime basketball.

Dec. 8: **Damian Williams**, the 20-year-old black assailant of white truck driver **Reginald Denny**, is given the maximum 10-year sentence for his role in the beating during the Los Angeles riots last year. *TIME* magazine reports the judge based the maximum penalty in part on Williams' lack of remorse. With good behavior, Williams could be out in less than four years.

Dec. 8: A 29-cent **Buffalo Soldiers** stamp, recalling the black cavalry that served on the Western frontier, is scheduled for release in April, reports *The New York Times*.

Dec. 9: U.S. Surgeon General **Joycelyn Elders** says that legalization of drugs could lead to a significant decrease in crime and should be studied, reports *The Washington Post*. The Clinton administration immediately repudiates Elders' comments and notes the Surgeon General is "not speaking for the administration. The president's position is . . . against legalizing drugs, and it will not happen on his watch," said White House spokeswoman **Dee Dee Myers**.

Dec. 12: **Charlie Ward** of Florida State University is named winner of the Heisman Trophy, reports *The Richmond Times-Dispatch*. He is the first player from Florida State and the first from the Atlantic Coast Conference to win the Heisman. Of the 59 winners, Ward is the 48th senior and 20th quarterback selected. He may also be the first Heisman winner to play in the National Basketball Association. Soon after FSU's football season ends, Ward will join the Seminoles' basketball team.

Dec. 12: Scotland Yard reopens the investigation of the death of rock guitarist **Jimi Hendrix** 23 years after he dies from an apparent drug overdose, reports *The Associated Press*. In the original inquest, a pathologist concluded that Hendrix choked to death after drinking and taking an overdose of barbiturates.

Dec. 12: A federal appeals court rejects a desegregation order from Louisiana's colleges and universities in a dispute that began 24 years ago, reports *The New York Times*. The decision sends the case back to Judge **Charles Schwartz** of U.S. District Court, who ruled last year that the state's fragmented governing-board system perpetuated segregation.

279

Dec. 13: U.S. Supreme Court Associate Justice **Thurgood Marshall** i posthumously awarded the Medal of Freedom, the nation's highes civilian honor, reports *TIME* magazine. President **Bill Clinto** presented the prestigious honor to suffragist **Marjory Stonema** **Douglas**, retired Associate Justice **William Brennan**, ex-appeal court judge **John Minor Wisdom**, and the late civil rights attorney activist **Joseph Rauh**.

Dec. 14: Despite three decades of costly and difficult efforts to integrat public schools, a Harvard University study finds the number o black and Hispanic students attending schools that are "predomi nantly minority" is rising, reports *The New York Times*. The ris is attributed to higher birth rates and immigration rather tha white flight to the suburbs.

Dec. 14: **Shawmut National**, without admitting it discriminated, agrees t pay at least $960,000 to settle federal charges that its mortgag unit discriminated against black and Hispanic applicants, report *USA Today*. The deal among Shawmut Mortgage, the Justic Department, and the Federal Trade Commission was approved b a federal judge in Connecticut and announced by U.S. Attorne General **Janet Reno**.

Dec. 15: In recognition of his efforts during the 1991 Gulf War, U.S Army General (Ret.) **Colin L. Powell**, 56, the former Chairma of the Joint Chiefs of Staff, receives an honorary knighthoo from Queen **Elizabeth** at Buckingham Palace. He was the sec ond U.S. citizen to be knighted in 1993, according to *The Associ ated Press*; former President **George Bush** was so honored i November. Because Powell is not British, he is not allowed to b addressed as "Sir Colin."

Dec. 15: Tenor saxophonist **Carter Jefferson** dies in Poland while on tou at age 49, reports *The Washington Post*. Jefferson, a Washingto DC, native, was a fixture on the international jazz scene for 2 years.

Dec. 15: President **Clinton** appoints former Rep. **Barbara Jordan** (E TX) to head the U.S. Commission on Immigration Reform, re ports *The Associated Press*.

Dec. 16: **Moses Gunn**, 64, an actor whose career of more than thre decades included roles ranging from Othello to Booker T. Wash ington, dies at his home in Guilford, CT. Once hailed by critic as one of the country's finest actors, Gunn continued to work until his final illness (complications of asthma) by playing provocative roles on stage and screen. Gunn, a cofounder of the Negro Ensemble Co., received an NAACP Image Award for his portrayal of Booker T. Washington in the 1981 movie "Ragtime," and an Emmy nomination for his role in the 1977 television miniseries "Roots."

Dec. 17: Final arguments in a school desegregation lawsuit involving Hartford, CT, and its suburbs are suspended when the trial judge questions whether a new state law promoting regional integration plans effectively barred him from issuing an order of his own, reports *The New York Times*. The lawsuit, *Sheff v. O'Neill*, requires every town and city in Connecticut to take part in discussions on drafting regional school integration plans. But it sets no goals and provides no penalties for towns that refuse to cooperate, and thus is far weaker than a court order.

Dec. 18: Black women's groups, led by Dr. **C. DeLores Tucker**, National Chair of the National Political Congress of Black Women, launch a nationwide crusade to persuade the music industry to clean up violent "gangsta rap" lyrics that they say demean and threaten women, reports the *Associated Press*.

Dec. 19: Nation of Islam Minister **Louis Farrakhan** denies charges of racism and anti-Semitism during a fiery speech in New York's Jacob Javits Center, reports *The New York Times*. He defends megastar entertainer **Michael Jackson**, who has been accused of sexually molesting a child and calls on black entertainers to present positive images. Farrakhan addressed more than 20,000 people in his first appearance in a major New York venue since 1985.

Dec. 21: The NAACP enters the **Michael Jackson** fray, saying the entertainer had been victimized by the news media, reports *The Associated Press*.

"Our members are deeply concerned that the media in this country see fit to give hour after hour to negative allegations rather than report the good that is being attempted in the African-American community," says **Shannon F. Reeves**, West Coast region director for the National Association for the Advancement of Colored People. Jackson is accused in a lawsuit of molesting a 13-year-old boy. He has denied wrongdoing, and his representatives say the allegations stem from a foiled $20 million extortion attempt by the boy's father. No criminal charges have been filed; authorities are investigating.

Dec. 24: Two black men, **Charles Gill**, 35, of Chesterfield County, VA, and **Percy Ray Pridgen**, 69, of Washington, DC, equally split a $90 million Powerball® jackpot lottery, reports *The Washington Post*. Powerball® is played in a dozen states, including Delaware, Idaho, Indiana, Iowa, Kansas, and Kentucky, as well as in the District of Columbia.

Dec. 25: A Christmas Day fire guts the four-story Grand View, NY, country home of Nobel laureate **Toni Morrison**, but a portion of her original manuscripts and other papers in the basement study are not badly damaged, reports *The New York Times*. "The house was almost totally destroyed, but indications are that the major parts of the manuscripts and other materials in the basement were not severely damaged," says **Howard Dodson**, chief of the Schomburg Center for Research in Black Culture, a unit of the New York Public Library. Morrison was not home at the time, but her 28-year-old son, **Slade Kevin**, told firefighters the blaze might have started when an ember from the fireplace made contact with a sofa.

INDEX OF AUTHORS AND
ARTICLES

In 1987, the National Urban League began publishing *The State of Black America* in a new, smaller, typeset format. By so doing, it became easier to catalog and archive the various essays by author and article name.

The 1994 edition of *The State of Black America* is the second to contain an index of the authors and articles published since the 1987 conversion. The authors are alphabetically listed first in this section; their contributions are listed chronologically, beginning with the most recent. The articles are listed in the second half, alphabetically by title, irrespective of year of publication.

Reprints of the articles catalogued herein are available from AG Publishing, Inc., 75 Varick Street, New York, NY 10013; 212/274-9600.

Index of Authors

THE STATE OF BLACK AMERICA: 1987-1994

Coleman, Dr. Henry A., *The State of Black America 1992*, "Interagency and Intergovernmental Coordination: New Demands for Domestic Policy Initiatives," pp. 249-263.

Comer, Dr. James P. (with Drs. Muriel Hamilton-Lee and Norris M. Haynes), *The State of Black America 1990*, "School Power: A Model for Improving Black Student Achievement," pp. 225-238.

Darity, Jr., Dr. William A. (with Dr. Samuel L. Myers, Jr.), *The State of Black America 1992*, "Racial Earnings Inequality into the 21st Century," pp. 119-139.

Dilworth, Dr. Mary E., *The State of Black America 1994*, "Historically Black Colleges and Universities: Taking Care of Home," pp. 127-151.

Edelin, Dr. Ramona, *The State of Black America 1990*, "Toward an African-American Agenda: An Inward Look," pp. 173-183.

Edelman, Marian Wright, *The State of Black America 1989*, "Black Children in America," pp. 63-76.

Edwards, Dr. Harry, *The State of Black America 1994*, "Playoffs and Payoffs: The African-American Athlete as an Institutional Resource," pp. 83-112.

Fair, T. Willard, *The State of Black America 1993*, "Coordinated Community Empowerment: Experiences of the Urban League of Greater Miami," pp. 217-233.

Glasgow, Dr. Douglas D., *The State of Black America 1987*, "The Black Underclass in Perspective," pp. 129-144.

Gray, Sandra T., *The State of Black America 1992*, "Public-Private Partnerships: Prospects for America . . . Promise for African Americans," pp. 231-247.

Hamilton, Dr. Charles V., *The State of Black America 1993*, "Promoting Priorities: African-American Political Influence in the 1990s," pp. 59-69; *The State of Black America 1989*, "On Parity and Political Empowerment," pp. 111-120.

Hamilton-Lee, Dr. Muriel (with Drs. James P. Comer and Norris M. Haynes), *The State of Black America 1990*, "School Power: A Model for Improving Black Student Achievement," pp. 225-238.

Hare, Dr. Bruce R., *The State of Black America 1988*, "Black Youth at Risk," pp. 81-93.

Haynes, Dr. Norris M. (with Drs. James P. Comer and Muriel Hamilton-Lee), *The State of Black America 1990*, "School Power: A Model for Improving Black Student Achievement," pp. 225-238.

Henderson, Geraldine R. (with Dr. Marcus Alexis), *The State of Black America 1994*, "The Economic Base of African-American Communities: A Study of Consumption Patterns," pp. 51-82.

286

Henderson, Dr. Lenneal J., *The State of Black America 1994,* "African Americans in the Urban Milieu: Conditions, Trends, and Development Needs," pp. 11-29; *The State of Black America 1993,* "Empowerment through Enterprise: African-American Business Development," pp. 91-108; *The State of Black America 1992,* "Public Investment for Public Good: Needs, Benefits, and Financing Options," pp. 213-229; *The State of Black America 1991,* "Budgets, Taxes, and Politics: Options for the African-American Community," pp. 77-93; *The State of Black America 1990,* "Budget and Tax Strategy: Implications for Blacks," pp. 53-71; *The State of Black America 1987,* "Blacks, Budgets, and Taxes: Assessing the Impact of Budget Deficit Reduction and Tax Reform on Blacks," pp. 75-95.

Hill, Dr. Robert B., *The State of Black America 1992,* "Urban Redevelopment: Developing Effective Targeting Strategies," pp. 197-211; *The State of Black America 1989,* "Critical Issues for Black Families by the Year 2000," pp. 41-61.

Holden, Jr., Dr. Matthew, *The State of Black America 1990,* "The Rewards of Daring and the Ambiguity of Power: Perspectives on the Wilder Election of 1989," pp. 109-120.

Howard, Dr. Jeff P., *The State of Black America 1993,* "The Third Movement: Developing Black Children for the 21st Century," pp. 11-34.

Jones, Dr. Dionne J. (with Greg Harrison of the Research Department), *The State of Black America 1994,* "Fast Facts: Comparative Views of African-American Status and Progress," pp. 213-236.

Jones, Dr. Shirley J., *The State of Black America 1994,* "Silent Suffering: The Plight of Rural Black America," pp. 171-188.

Kornblum, Dr. William (with Dr. Terry Williams), *The State of Black America 1991,* "A Portrait of Youth: Coming of Age in Harlem Public Housing," pp. 187-207.

Leffall, Jr., Dr. LaSalle D., *The State of Black America 1990,* "Health Status of Black Americans," pp. 121-142.

Lincoln, Dr. C. Eric, *The State of Black America 1989,* "Knowing the Black Church: What It Is and Why," pp. 137-149.

McAlpine, Robert, *The State of Black America 1991,* "Toward a Development of a National Drug Control Strategy," pp. 233-241.

McBay, Dr. Shirley M., *The State of Black America 1992,* "The Condition of African-American Education: Changes and Challenges," pp. 141-156.

McHenry, The Honorable Donald F., *The State of Black America 1991,* "A Changing World Order: Implications for Black America," pp. 155-163.

McKenzie, Dr. Floretta Dukes, *The State of Black America 1991,* "Education Strategies for the '90s," pp. 95-111.

McMurray, Georgia L., *The State of Black America 1990*, "Those of Broader Vision: An African-American Perspective on Teenage Pregnancy and Parenting," pp. 195-211.

Malveaux, Dr. Julianne M., *The State of Black America 1992*, "The Parity Imperative: Civil Rights, Economic Justice, and the New American Dilemma," pp. 281-303.

Massey, Dr. Walter E., *The State of Black America 1992*, "Science, Technology, and Human Resources: Preparing for the 21st Century," pp. 157-169.

Mendez, Jr., Dr. Garry A., *The State of Black America 1988*, "Crime Is Not a Part of Our Black Heritage: A Theoretical Essay," pp. 211-215.

Miller, Jr., Dr. Warren F., *The State of Black America 1991*, "Developing Untapped Talent: A National Call for African-American Technologists," pp. 111-127.

Murray, Sylvester, *The State of Black America 1992*, "Clear and Present Danger: The Decay of America's Physical Infrastructure," pp. 171-182.

Myers, Jr., Dr. Samuel L. (with Dr. William A. Darity, Jr.), *The State of Black America 1992*, "Racial Earnings Inequality into the 21st Century," pp. 119-139.

National Urban League Research Staff, *The State of Black America 1992*, "African Americans in Profile: Selected Demographic, Social, and Economic Data," pp. 309-325.

Nobles, Dr. Wade W., *The State of Black America 1989*, "Drugs in the African-American Community: A Clear and Present Danger," pp. 161-181.

Pemberton, Dr. Gayle, *The State of Black America 1991*, "It's the Thing That Counts, Or Reflections on the Legacy of W.E.B. Du Bois," pp. 129-143.

Persons, Dr. Georgia A., *The State of Black America 1987*, "Blacks in State and Local Government: Progress and Constraints," pp. 167-192.

Pinderhughes, Dr. Dianne M., *The State of Black America 1992*, "Power and Progress: African-American Politics in the New Era of Diversity," pp. 265-280; *The State of Black America 1991*, "The Case of African Americans in the Persian Gulf: The Intersection of American Foreign and Military Policy with Domestic Employment Policy in the United States," pp. 165-186; *The State of Black America 1988*, "Civil Rights and the Future of the American Presidency," pp. 39-60.

Primm, Dr. Beny J., *The State of Black America 1987*, "Drug Use: Special Implications for Black America," pp. 145-158; and "AIDS: A Special Report," pp. 159-166.

Richardson, W. Franklyn, *The State of Black America 1994*, "Mission to Mandate: Self-Development Through the Black Church," pp. 113-126.

Robinson, Dr. Eugene S., *The State of Black America 1990*, "Television Advertising and Its Impact on Black America," pp. 157-171.

Robinson, Dr. Sharon P., *The State of Black America 1987*, "Taking Charge: An Approach to Making the Educational Problems of Blacks Comprehensible and Manageable," pp. 37-47.

Schexnider, Dr. Alvin J., *The State of Black America 1988*, "Blacks in the Military: The Victory and the Challenge," pp. 115-128.

Solomon, Dr. Barbara Bryant, *The State of Black America 1987*, "Social Welfare Reform," pp. 113-127.

Sudarkasa, Dr. Niara, *The State of Black America 1988*, "Black Enrollment in Higher Education: The Unfulfilled Promise of Equality," pp. 7-22.

Swinton, Dr. David H., *The State of Black America 1993*, "The Economic Status of African Americans During the Reagan-Bush Era: Withered Opportunities, Limited Outcomes, and Uncertain Outlook," pp. 135-200; *The State of Black America 1992*, "The Economic Status of African Americans: Limited Ownership and Persistent Inequality," pp. 61-117; *The State of Black America 1991*, "The Economic Status of African Americans: 'Permanent' Poverty and Inequality," pp. 25-75; *The State of Black America 1990*, "Economic Status of Black Americans During the 1980s: A Decade of Limited Progress," pp. 25-52; *The State of Black America 1989*, "Economic Status of Black Americans," pp. 9-39; *The State of Black America 1988*, "Economic Status of Blacks 1987," pp. 129-152; and *The State of Black America 1987*, "Economic Status of Blacks 1986," pp. 49-73.

Thomas, Jr., Dr. R. Roosevelt, *The State of Black America 1991*, "Managing Employee Diversity: An Assessment," pp. 145-154.

Tidwell, Dr. Billy J., *The State of Black America 1993*, "African Americans and the 21st Century Labor Market: Improving the Fit," pp. 35-57, and with Monica B. Kuumba, Dr. Dionne J. Jones, and Dr. Betty C. Watson, "Fast Facts: African Americans in the 1990s," pp. 243-265; *The State of Black America 1992*, "Serving the National Interest: A Marshall Plan for America," pp. 11-30; *The State of Black America 1991*, "Economic Costs of American Racism," pp. 219-232; *The State of Black America 1990*, "The Unemployment Experience of African Americans: Some Important Correlates and Consequences," pp. 213-223; *The State of Black America 1988*, "Black Wealth: Facts *and* Fiction," pp. 193-210; *The State of Black America 1987*, "A Profile of the Black Unemployed," pp. 223-237.

Wallace-Benjamin, Dr. Joan, *The State of Black America 1994*, "Organizing African-American Self Development: The Role of Community-Based Organizations," pp. 189-205.

Walters, Dr. Ron, *The State of Black America 1994*, "Serving the People: African-American Leadership and the Challenge of Empowerment," pp. 153-170.

Watson, Dr. Bernard C., *The State of Black America 1992*, "The Demographic Revolution: Diversity in 21st Century America," pp. 31-59; *The State of Black America 1988*, "Tomorrow's Teachers: Who Will They Be, What Will They Know?," pp. 23-37.

Webb, Dr. Michael B., *The State of Black America 1993*, "Programs for Progress and Empowerment: The Urban League's National Education Initiative," pp. 203-216.

Williams, Dr. Terry M. (with Dr. William Kornblum), *The State of Black America 1991*, "A Portrait of Youth: Coming of Age in Harlem Public Housing," pp. 187-207.

Willie, Dr. Charles V., *The State of Black America 1988*, "The Black Family: Striving Toward Freedom," pp. 71-80; *The State of Black America 1987*, "The Future of School Desegregation," pp. 37-47.

Wilson, Dr. Reginald, *The State of Black America 1989*, "Black Higher Education: Crisis and Promise," pp. 121-135.

Wirschem, David, *The State of Black America 1991*, "Community Mobilization for Education in Rochester, New York: A Case Study," pp. 243-248.

Index of Articles

THE STATE OF BLACK AMERICA: 1987-1994

"The Case of African Americans in the Persian Gulf: The Intersection of American Foreign and Military Policy with Domestic Employment Policy in the United States," Dianne M. Pinderhughes, **1991**, pp. 165-186.

"A Changing World Order: Implications for Black America," Donald F. McHenry, **1991**, pp. 155-163.

"Civil Rights and the Future of the American Presidency," Dianne M. Pinderhughes, **1988**, pp. 39-60.

"Clear and Present Danger: The Decay of America's Physical Infrastructure," Sylvester Murray, **1992**, pp. 171-182.

"Community Mobilization for Education in Rochester, New York: A Case Study," David Wirschem, **1991**, pp. 243-248.

"The Condition of African-American Education: Changes and Challenges," Shirley M. McBay, **1992**, pp. 141-156.

"Coordinated Community Empowerment: Experiences of the Urban League of Greater Miami," T. Willard Fair, **1993**, pp. 217-233.

"Crime in the Black Community," Lee P. Brown, **1988**, pp. 95-113.

"Crime Is Not a Part of Our Black Heritage: A Theoretical Essay," Garry A. Mendez, **1988**, pp. 211-215.

"Critical Issues for Black Families by the Year 2000," Robert B. Hill, **1989**, pp. 41-61.

"Critical Perspectives on the Psychology of Race," Price M. Cobbs, **1988**, pp. 61-70.

"The Demographic Revolution: Diversity in 21st Century America," Bernard C. Watson, **1992**, pp. 31-59.

"Developing Untapped Talent: A National Call for African-American Technologists," Warren F. Miller, Jr., **1991**, pp. 111-127.

"Dollars for Deeds: Some Prospects and Prescriptions for African-American Financial Institutions," William D. Bradford, **1994**, pp. 31-50.

"Drugs in the African-American Community: A Clear and Present Danger," Wade W. Nobles, **1989**, pp. 161-181.

"Drug Use: Special Implications for Black America," Beny J. Primm, **1987**, pp. 145-158.

"The Economic Base of African-American Communities: A Study of Consumption Patterns," Marcus Alexis and Geraldine R. Henderson, **1994**, pp. 51-82.

"Economic Costs of American Racism," Billy J. Tidwell, **1991**, pp. 219-232.

"The Economic Status of African Americans During the Reagan-Bush Era: Withered Opportunities, Limited Outcomes, and Uncertain Outlook," David H. Swinton, **1993**, pp. 135-200.

"The Economic Status of African Americans: Limited Ownership and Persistent Inequality," David H. Swinton, **1992**, pp. 61-117.

"The Economic Status of African Americans: 'Permanent' Poverty and Inequality," David H. Swinton, **1991**, pp. 25-75.

"Economic Status of Black Americans," David H. Swinton, **1989**, pp. 9-39.

"Economic Status of Black Americans During the 1980s: A Decade of Limited Progress," David H. Swinton, **1990**, pp. 25-52.

"Economic Status of Blacks 1987," David H. Swinton, **1988**, pp. 129-152.

"Economic Status of Blacks 1986," David H. Swinton, **1987**, pp. 49-73.

"Education Strategies for the '90s," Floretta Dukes McKenzie, **1991**, pp. 95-111.

"The Elusive Quest for Racial Justice: The Chronicle of the Constitutional Contradiction," Derrick Bell, **1991**, pp. 9-23.

"Empowerment through Enterprise: African-American Business Development," Lenneal J. Henderson, **1993**, pp. 91-108.

"Fast Facts: African Americans in the 1990s," Billy J. Tidwell (with Monica B. Kuumba, Dionne J. Jones, and Betty C. Watson), **1993**, pp. 243-265.

"Fast Facts: Comparative Views of African-American Status and Progress," Dionne J. Jones (with Greg Harrison of the Research Department), **1994,** pp. 213-236.

"The Future of School Desegregation," Charles V. Willie, **1987**, pp. 37-47.

"Health Status of Black Americans," LaSalle D. Leffall, Jr., **1990**, pp. 121-142.

"Historically Black Colleges and Universities: Taking Care of Home," Mary E. Dilworth, **1994**, pp. 127-151.

"Housing Opportunity: A Dream Deferred," Phillip Clay, **1990**, pp. 73-84.

"Interagency and Intergovernmental Coordination: New Demands for Domestic Policy Initiatives," Henry A. Coleman, **1992**, pp. 249-263.

"It's the Thing That Counts, Or Reflections on the Legacy of W.E.B. Du Bois," Gayle Pemberton, **1991**, pp. 129-143.

"Knowing the Black Church: What It Is and Why," C. Eric Lincoln, **1989**, pp. 137-149.

"The Law and Black Americans: Retreat from Civil Rights," Julius L. Chambers, **1987**, pp. 15-30.

"Managing Employee Diversity: An Assessment," R. Roosevelt Thomas, Jr., **1991**, pp. 145-154.

"Mission to Mandate: Self-Development Through the Black Church," W. Franklyn Richardson, **1994**, pp. 113-126.

"Money Matters: Lending Discrimination in African-American Communities," William D. Bradford, **1993**, pp. 109-134.

"On Parity and Political Empowerment," Charles V. Hamilton, **1989**, pp. 111-120.

"Organizing African-American Self-Development: The Role of Community-Based Organizations," Joan Wallace-Benjamin, **1994**, pp. 189-205.

"The Parity Imperative: Civil Rights, Economic Justice, and the New American Dilemma," Julianne M. Malveaux, **1992**, pp. 281-303.

"Playoffs and Payoffs: The African-American Athlete as an Institutional Resource," Harry Edwards, **1994**, pp. 83-112.

"A Portrait of Youth: Coming of Age in Harlem Public Housing," William Kornblum and Terry Williams, **1991**, pp. 187-207.

"Power and Progress: African-American Politics in the New Era of Diversity," Dianne M. Pinderhughes, **1992**, pp. 265-280.

"Preventing Black Homicide," Carl C. Bell, **1990**, pp. 143-155.

"A Profile of the Black Unemployed," Billy J. Tidwell, **1987**, pp. 223-237.

"Programs for Progress and Empowerment: The Urban League's National Education Initiative," Michael B. Webb, **1993**, pp. 203-216.

"Promoting Priorities: African-American Political Influence in the 1990s," Charles V. Hamilton, **1993**, pp. 59-69.

"Public Investment for Public Good: Needs, Benefits, and Financing Options," Lenneal J. Henderson, **1992**, pp. 213-229.

"Public-Private Partnerships: Prospects for America . . . Promise for African Americans," Sandra T. Gray, **1992**, pp. 231-247.

"Racial Earnings Inequality into the 21st Century," William A. Darity, Jr., and Samuel L. Myers, Jr., **1992**, pp. 119-139.

"The Rewards of Daring and the Ambiguity of Power: Perspectives on the Wilder Election of 1989," Matthew Holden, Jr., **1990**, pp. 109-120.

"School Power: A Model for Improving Black Student Achievement," James P. Comer, Muriel Hamilton-Lee, and Norris M. Haynes, **1990**, pp. 225-238.

"Science, Technology, and Human Resources: Preparing for the 21st Century," Walter E. Massey, **1992**, pp. 157-169.

"Serving the National Interest: A Marshall Plan for America," Billy J. Tidwell, **1992**, pp. 11-30.

"Serving the People: African-American Leadership and the Challenge of Empowerment," Ron Walters, **1994**, pp. 153-170.

"Silent Suffering: The Plight of Rural Black America," Shirley J. Jones, **1994**, pp. 171-188.

"Social Welfare Reform," Barbara Bryant, **1987**, pp. 113-127.

"Taking Charge: An Approach to Making the Educational Problems of Blacks Comprehensible and Manageable," Sharon P. Robinson, **1987**, pp. 37-47.

"Television Advertising and Its Impact on Black America," Eugene S. Robinson, **1990**, pp. 157-171.

"The Third Movement: Developing Black Children for the 21st Century," Jeff P. Howard, **1993**, pp. 11-34.

"Those of Broader Vision: An African-American Perspective on Teenage Pregnancy and Parenting," Georgia L. McMurray, **1990**, pp. 195-211.

"To Make Wrong Right: The Necessary and Proper Aspirations of Fair Housing," John O. Calmore, **1989**, pp. 77-109.

"Tomorrow's Teachers: Who Will They Be, What Will They Know?," Bernard C. Watson, **1988**, pp. 23-37.

"Toward an African-American Agenda: An Inward Look," Ramona Edelin, **1990**, pp. 173-183.

"Toward a Development of a National Drug Control Strategy," Robert McAlpine, **1991**, pp. 233-241.

"Toward Economic Self-Sufficiency: Independence Without Poverty," Lynn C. Burbridge, **1993,** pp. 71-90.

"Understanding African-American Family Diversity," Andrew Billingsley, **1990**, pp. 85-108.

"The Unemployment Experience of African Americans: Some Important Correlates and Consequences," Billy J. Tidwell, **1990**, pp. 213-223.

"Urban Infrastructure: Social, Environmental, and Health Risks to African Americans," Robert D. Bullard, **1992**, pp. 183-196.

"Urban Redevelopment: Developing Effective Targeting Strategies," Robert B. Hill, **1992**, pp. 197-211.

"Valuing Diversity: The Myth and the Challenge," Price M. Cobbs, **1989**, pp. 151-159.

ACKNOWLEDGMENTS

The editor expresses appreciation to the authors in this l9th edition of *The State of Black America*. Their commitment and professionalism were apparent throughout.

Once again, associate editor, Paulette Robinson, was indispensable to producing the publication. Her high quality standards are well represented. Likewise, the efforts of assistant editors Johnnie Griffin and Michele Long Pittman were characteristically deliberate and proficient. Bonnie Stanley, too, deserves praise for her exhausting work on the "Chronology of Events 1993."

The encouragement and guidance of John E. Jacob, President and Chief Executive Officer, and Frank Lomax III, Executive Vice President, facilitated the cooperative endeavor among National Urban League staff. The Public Relations and Communications Department, led by Richard W. Keough, responded forthrightly to the demands. Communications staffers Ernie Johnston, Jr.; B. Maxwell Stamper; Farida Syed; Faith V. Williams; and Denise Wright were more than equal to the tasks before them. Recognition is due, also, to Daniel S. Davis and Betty Ford in the Office of the President.

Robert McAlpine and members of the Policy and Government Relations Department—Suzanne Bergeron, Lisa Bland-Malone, and Robin Doroshow—were dedicated and thoughtful in their work on the "Recommendations" section of the book. Dionne Jones and volunteer intern Greg Harrison of the Research Department are acknowledged for producing the "Appendix." Other staff in the Washington Operations office—Gwendolyn Duke, Arnold Hall, and Thea Sanders—provided valuable administrative assistance, while Kathleen Daley and Deborah Searcy Holiday deserve special recognition for coordinating much of the work.

Finally, Ronald and Mitchell Koff, in the fine tradition of their late father, Zale, are to be credited for the productive performance of Astoria Graphics and its staff.

Order Blank

National Urban League Publications
500 East 62nd Street
New York, NY 10021

	Per Copy	# of Copies	Total
The State of Black America 1994	$24.95	_____	_____

Recent Volumes in series:

	Per Copy	# of Copies	Total
The State of Black America 1993	$24.95	_____	_____
The State of Black America 1992	$24.95	_____	_____
The State of Black America 1991	$19.95	_____	_____
The State of Black America 1990	$19.00	_____	_____
The State of Black America 1989	$19.00	_____	_____
The State of Black America 1988	$18.00	_____	_____
The State of Black America 1987	$18.00	_____	_____

Postage and handling:
Individual volumes—

	$ 2.00/book rate	_____	_____
	$ 3.00/first class	_____	_____

Total amount enclosed $ _____

"Music—That Lordly Power"

The limited-edition, numbered lithograph of "Music—That Lordly Power" is signed by the internationally acclaimed photographer, Gordon Parks. "Music—That Lordly Power " is the seventh in the "Great Artists" series on African Americans commissioned for the National Urban League by the House of Seagram; proceeds benefit League programs.

The unframed lithograph, measuring 19-1/4"x13", costs $1,000, which includes postage and handling.

For more information or to order, contact:

National Urban League, Inc.
Office of Development
500 East 62nd Street
New York, NY 10021

Please make check or money order payable to:
National Urban League, Inc.

Notes

Notes

Notes

Notes

Notes